STAR WARS®

Darkness

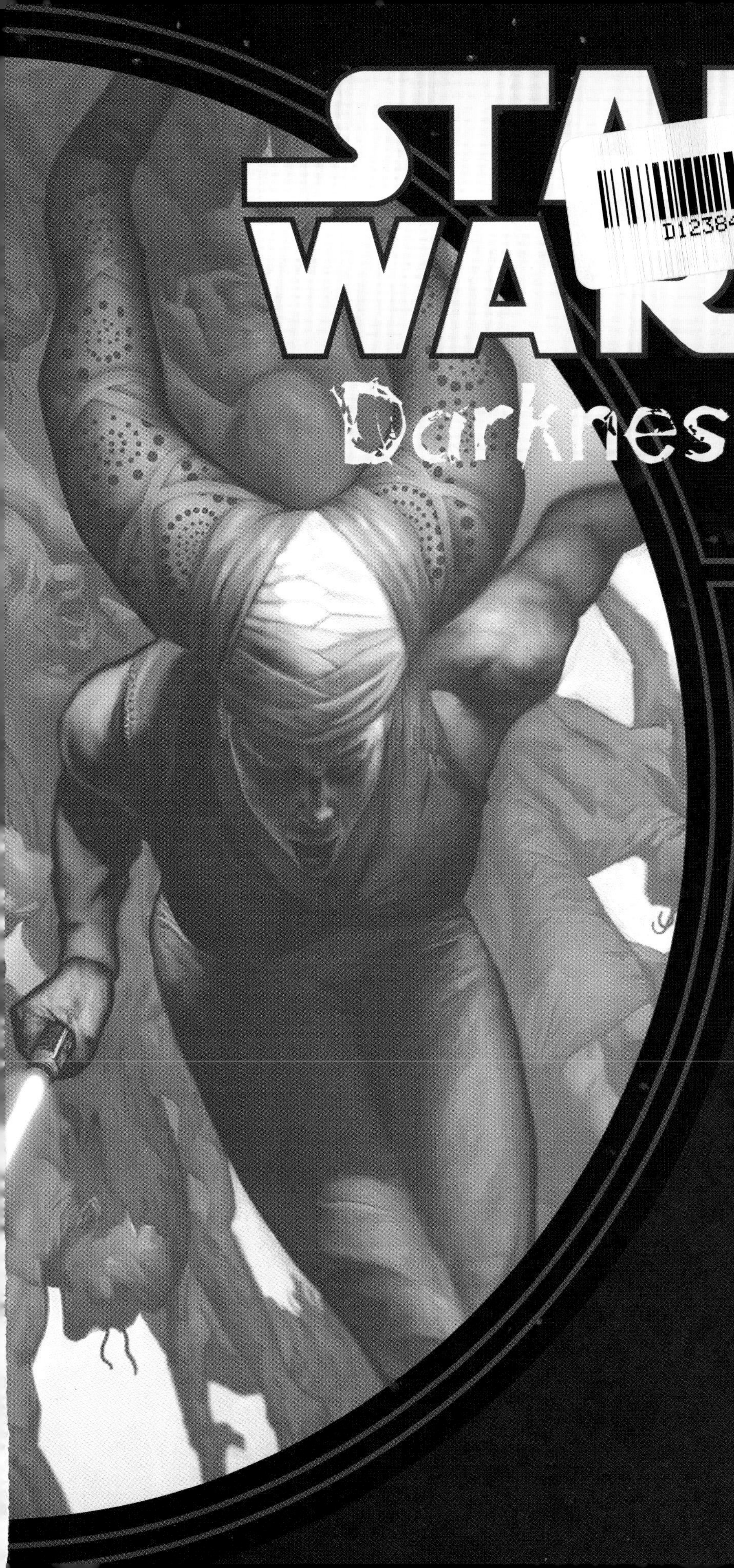

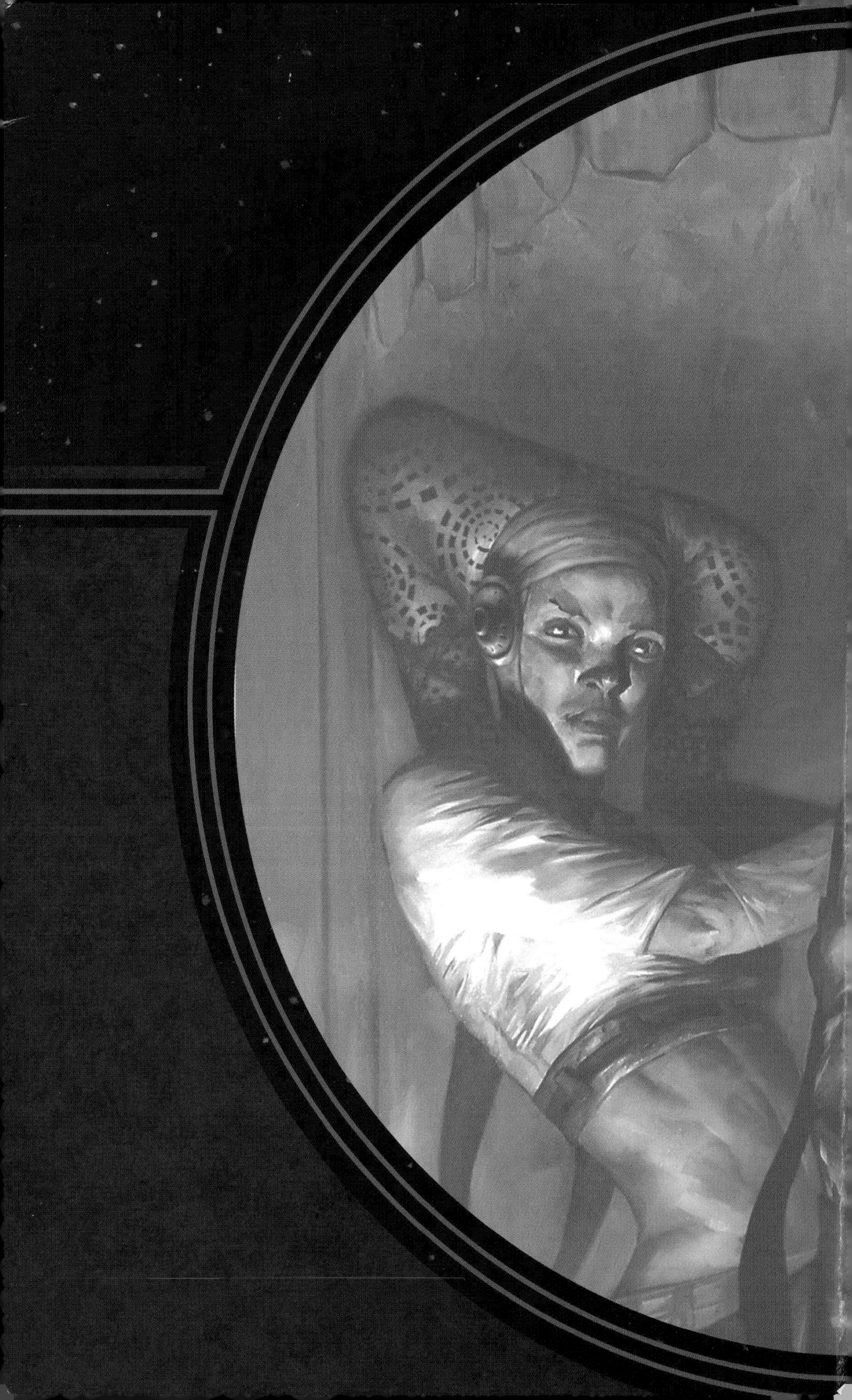

STAR WARS®

Darkness

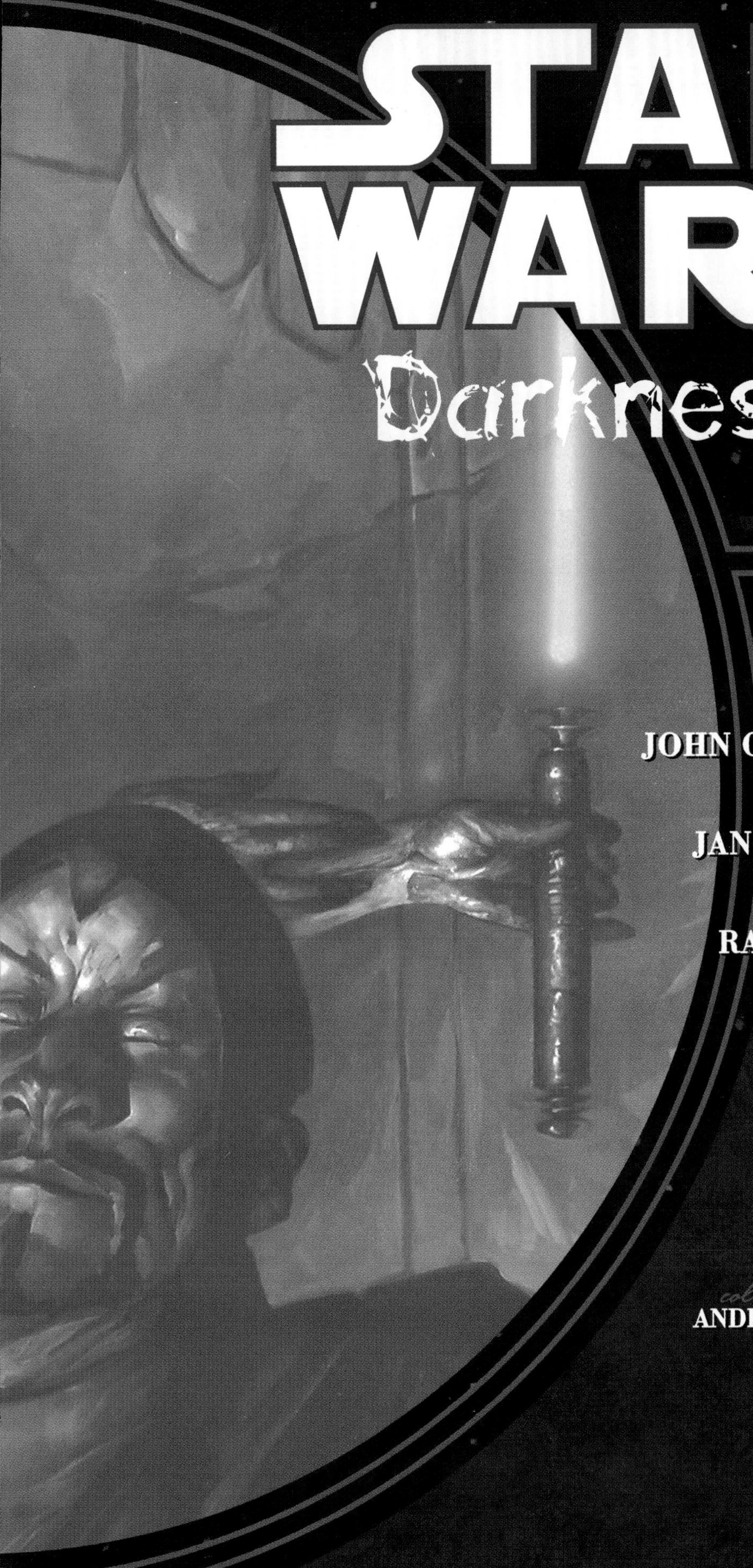

script
JOHN OSTRANDER

pencils
JAN DUURSEMA

inks
RAY KRYSSING

colors
DAVE McCAIG

letters
STEVE DUTRO

collection cover artist
ANDREW ROBINSON

DARK HORSE COMICS®

publisher
MIKE RICHARDSON

editor
DAVE LAND

assistant editor
PHILIP SIMON

collection designer
LANI SCHREIBSTEIN

art director
MARK COX

Special thanks to CHRIS CERASI
and LUCY AUTREY WILSON at Lucas Licensing

STAR WARS®: DARKNESS

This book collects issues 32 through 35 of the Dark Horse comic-
book series *Star Wars*®

Published by
Dark Horse Comics, Inc.
10956 SE Main Street
Milwaukie, OR 97222

www.darkhorse.com

Comic Shop Locator Service: (888) 266-4226

First edition: August 2002
ISBN: 1-56971-659-5

10 9 8 7 6 5 4 3 2 1

PRINTED IN CHINA

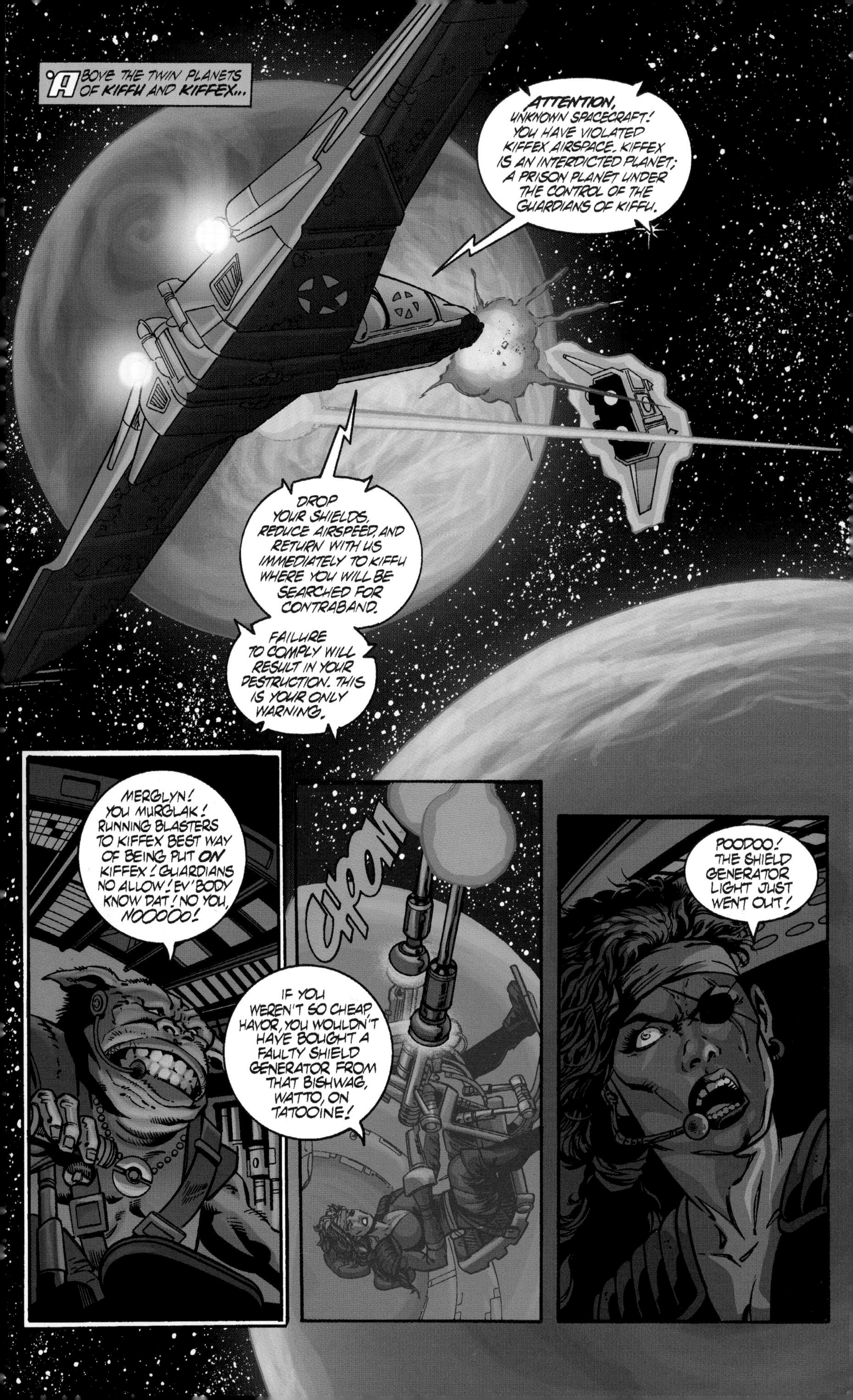
Above the twin planets of Kiffu and Kiffex...
ATTENTION, UNKNOWN SPACECRAFT! YOU HAVE VIOLATED KIFFEX AIRSPACE. KIFFEX IS AN INTERDICTED PLANET; A PRISON PLANET UNDER THE CONTROL OF THE GUARDIANS OF KIFFU.
DROP YOUR SHIELDS, REDUCE AIRSPEED, AND RETURN WITH US IMMEDIATELY TO KIFFU WHERE YOU WILL BE SEARCHED FOR CONTRABAND.
FAILURE TO COMPLY WILL RESULT IN YOUR DESTRUCTION. THIS IS YOUR ONLY WARNING.
MERGLYN! YOU MURGLAK! RUNNING BLASTERS TO KIFFEX BEST WAY OF BEING PUT ON KIFFEX! GUARDIANS NO ALLOW! EV'BODY KNOW DAT! NO YOU, NOOOOO!
CHOOM
IF YOU WEREN'T SO CHEAP, HAVOR, YOU WOULDN'T HAVE BOUGHT A FAULTY SHIELD GENERATOR FROM THAT BISHWAG, WATTO, ON TATOOINE!
POODOO! THE SHIELD GENERATOR LIGHT JUST WENT OUT!

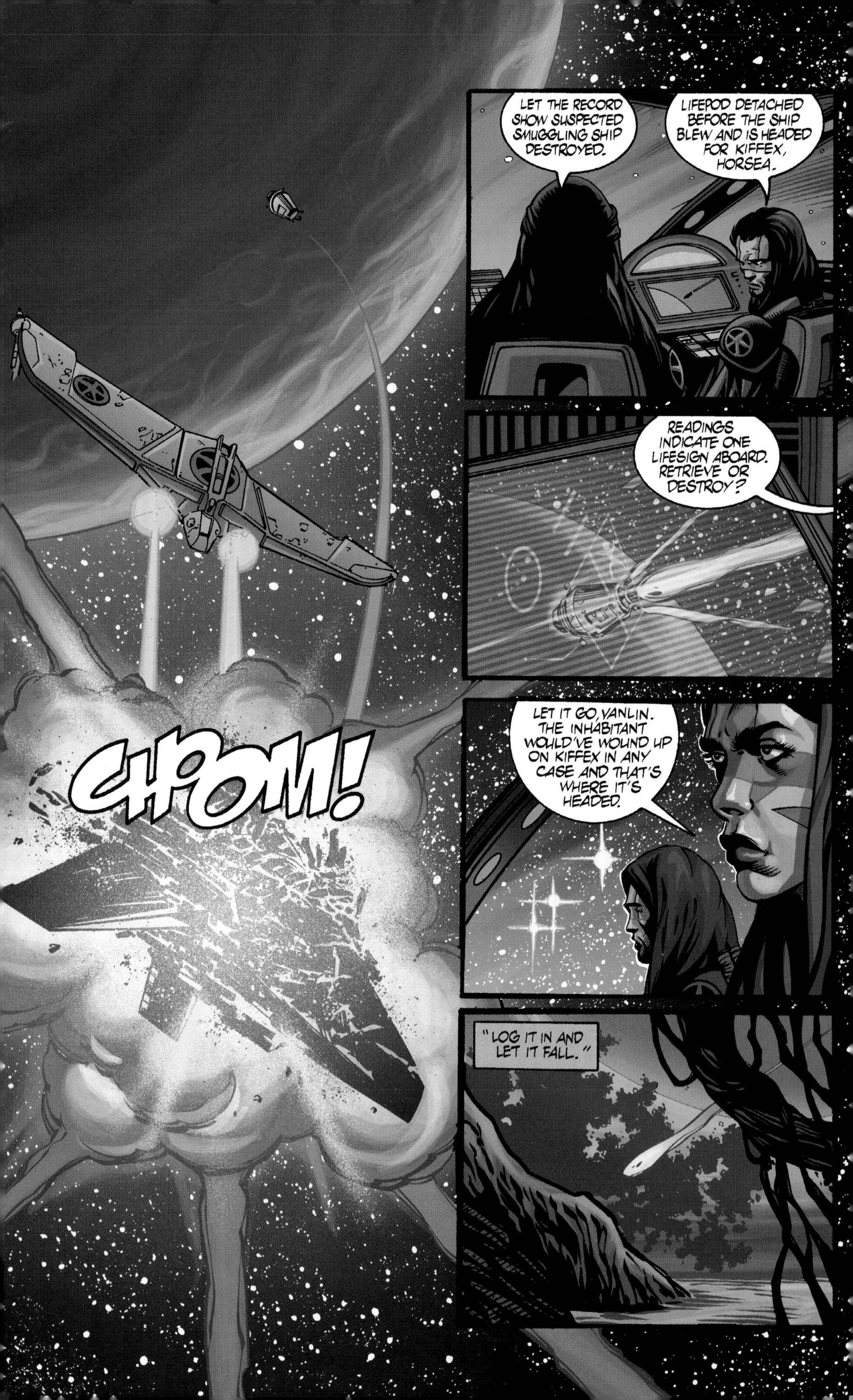
CHOOM!
LET THE RECORD SHOW SUSPECTED SMUGGLING SHIP DESTROYED.
LIFEPOD DETACHED BEFORE THE SHIP BLEW AND IS HEADED FOR KIFFEX, HORSEA.
READINGS INDICATE ONE LIFESIGN ABOARD. RETRIEVE OR DESTROY?
LET IT GO, YANLIN. THE INHABITANT WOULD'VE WOUND UP ON KIFFEX IN ANY CASE AND THAT'S WHERE IT'S HEADED.
"LOG IT IN AND LET IT FALL."

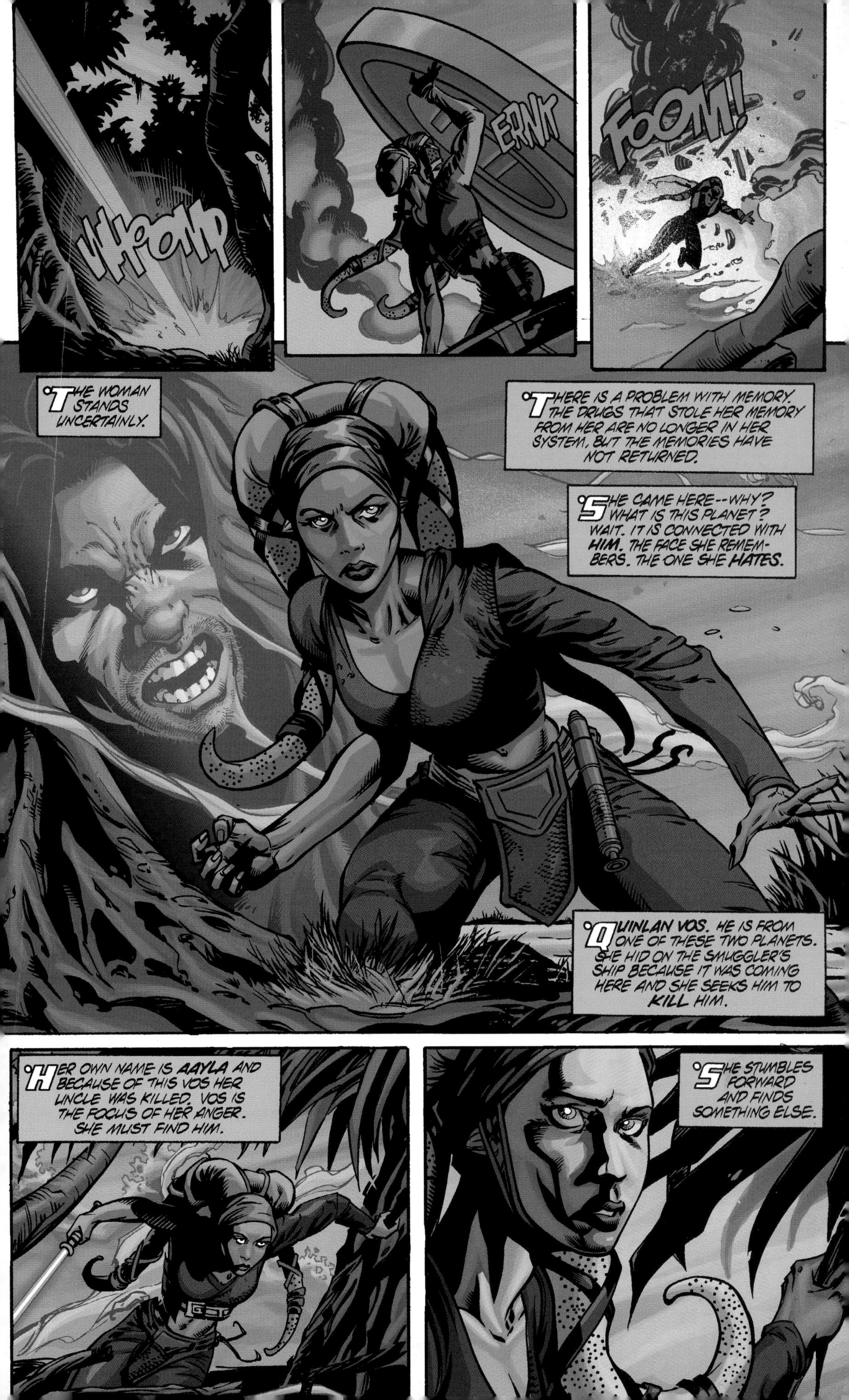
WHOOMP
ERNK
FOOM!!
THE WOMAN STANDS UNCERTAINLY.
THERE IS A PROBLEM WITH MEMORY. THE DRUGS THAT STOLE HER MEMORY FROM HER ARE NO LONGER IN HER SYSTEM, BUT THE MEMORIES HAVE NOT RETURNED.
SHE CAME HERE--WHY? WHAT IS THIS PLANET? WAIT. IT IS CONNECTED WITH HIM. THE FACE SHE REMEMBERS. THE ONE SHE HATES.
QUINLAN VOS. HE IS FROM ONE OF THESE TWO PLANETS. SHE HID ON THE SMUGGLER'S SHIP BECAUSE IT WAS COMING HERE AND SHE SEEKS HIM TO KILL HIM.
HER OWN NAME IS AAYLA AND BECAUSE OF THIS VOS HER UNCLE WAS KILLED. VOS IS THE FOCUS OF HER ANGER. SHE MUST FIND HIM.
SHE STUMBLES FORWARD AND FINDS SOMETHING ELSE.

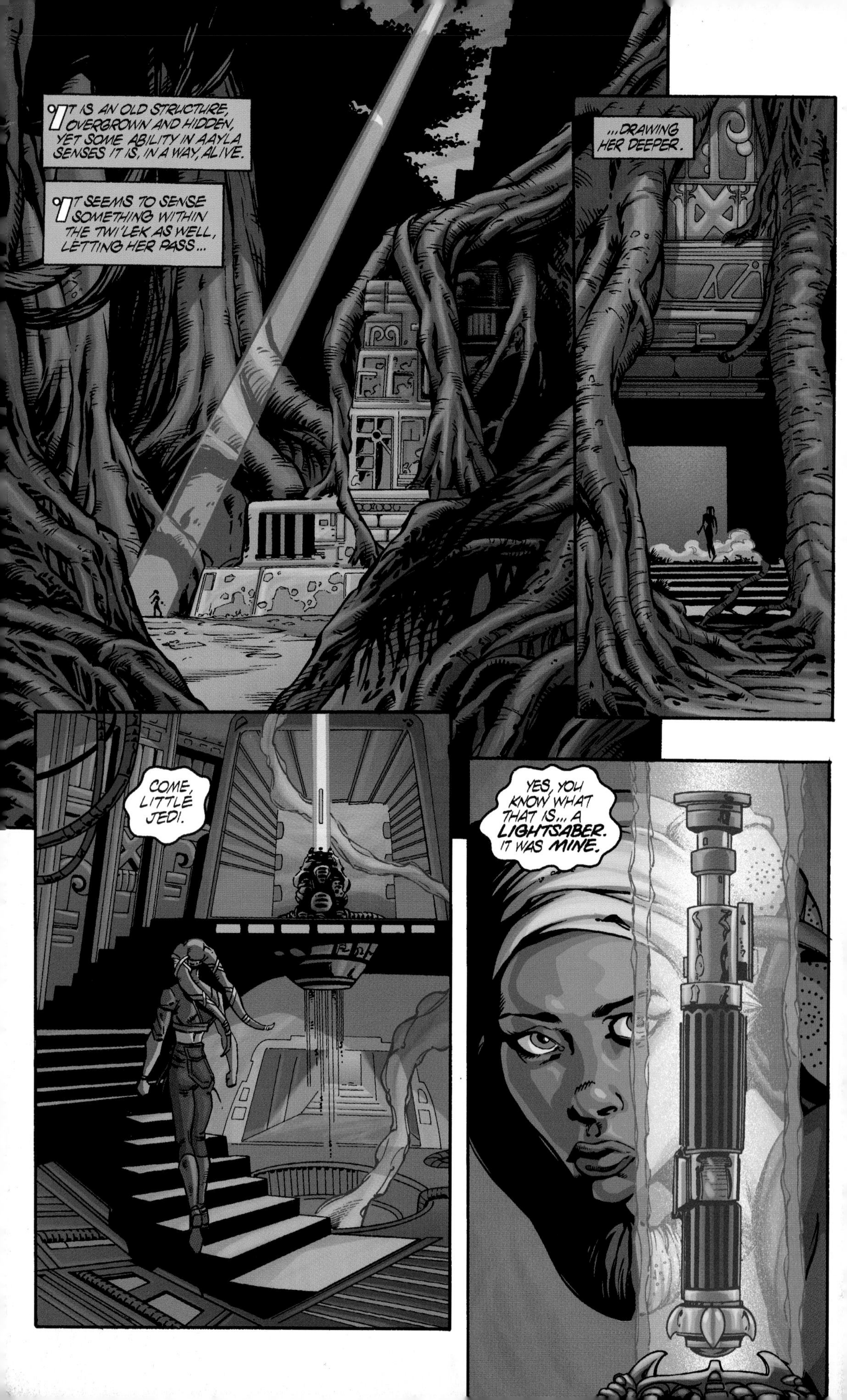
IT IS AN OLD STRUCTURE, OVERGROWN AND HIDDEN, YET SOME ABILITY IN AAYLA SENSES IT IS, IN A WAY, ALIVE.
IT SEEMS TO SENSE SOMETHING WITHIN THE TWI'LEK AS WELL, LETTING HER PASS...
...DRAWING HER DEEPER.
COME, LITTLE JEDI.
YES, YOU KNOW WHAT THAT IS... A LIGHTSABER. IT WAS MINE.

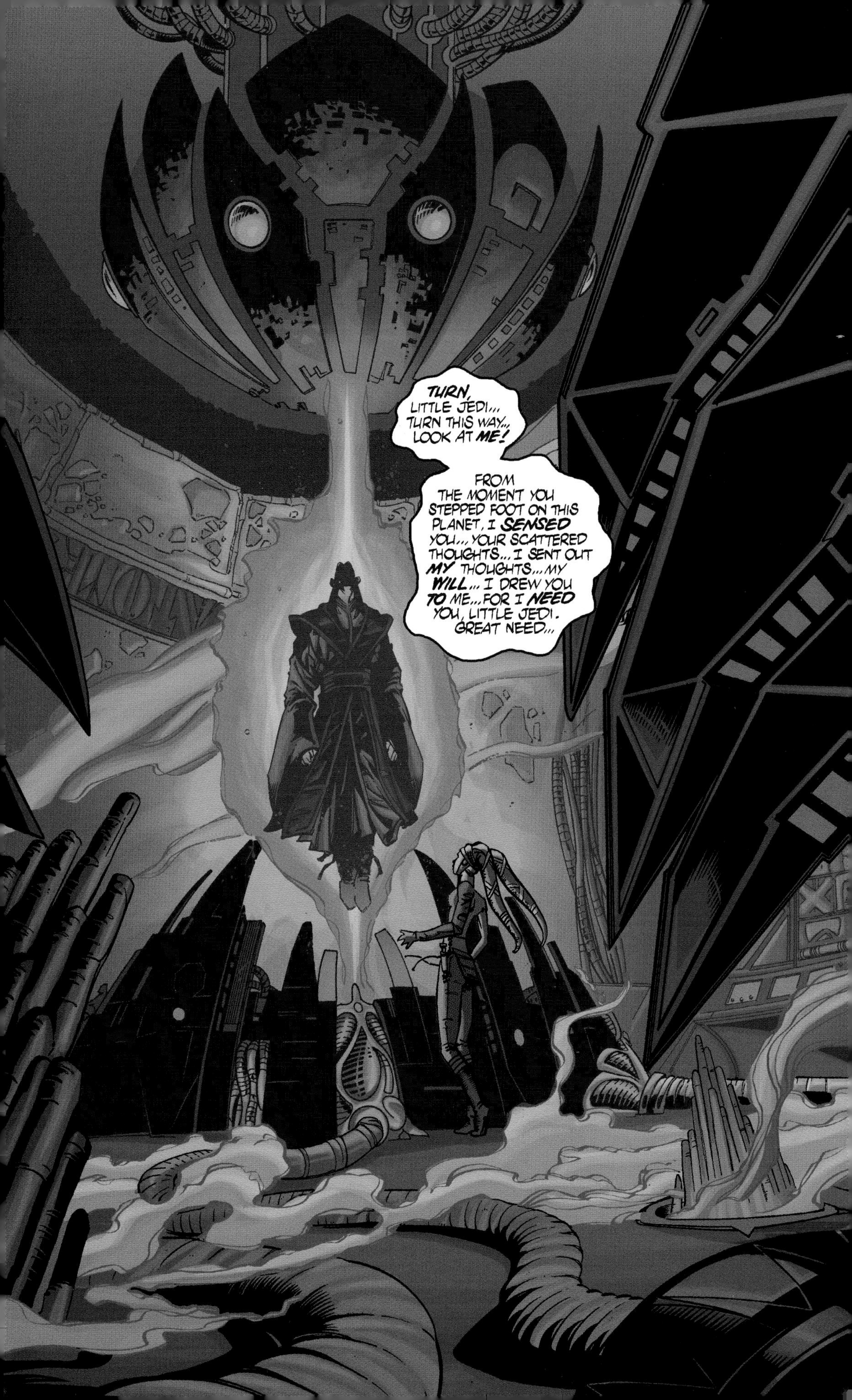
TURN, LITTLE JEDI... TURN THIS WAY... LOOK AT ME!
FROM THE MOMENT YOU STEPPED FOOT ON THIS PLANET, I SENSED YOU... YOUR SCATTERED THOUGHTS... I SENT OUT MY THOUGHTS... MY WILL... I DREW YOU TO ME... FOR I NEED YOU, LITTLE JEDI. GREAT NEED...

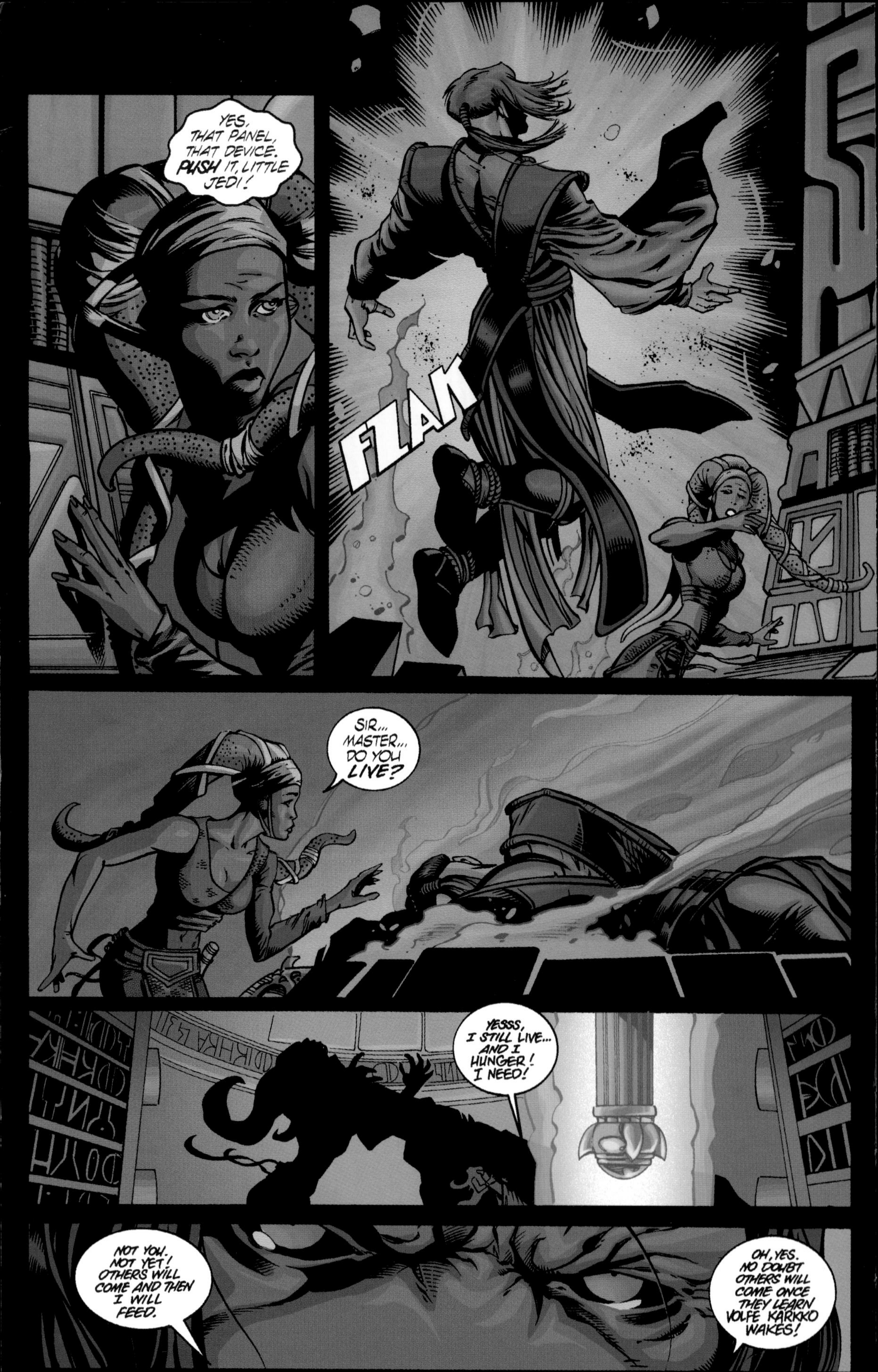
YES, THAT PANEL, THAT DEVICE. PUSH IT, LITTLE JEDI!
FZAK
SIR... MASTER... DO YOU LIVE?
YESSS, I STILL LIVE... AND I HUNGER! I NEED!
NOT YOU. NOT YET! OTHERS WILL COME AND THEN I WILL FEED.
OH, YES. NO DOUBT OTHERS WILL COME ONCE THEY LEARN VOLFE KARKKO WAKES!

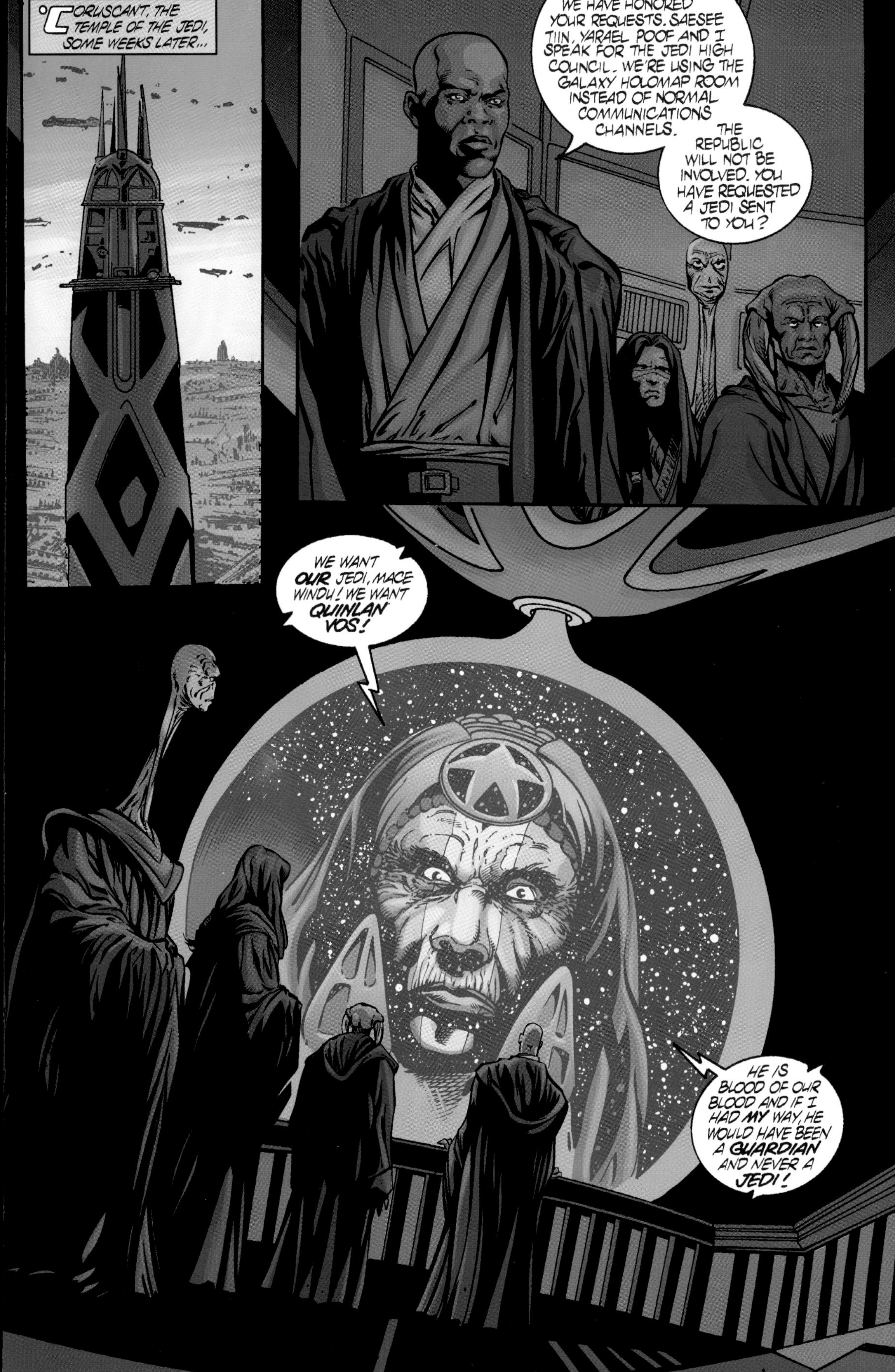
CORUSCANT, THE TEMPLE OF THE JEDI, SOME WEEKS LATER...
WE HAVE HONORED YOUR REQUESTS. SAESEE TIIN, YARAEL POOF AND I SPEAK FOR THE JEDI HIGH COUNCIL. WE'RE USING THE GALAXY HOLOMAP ROOM INSTEAD OF NORMAL COMMUNICATIONS CHANNELS.
THE REPUBLIC WILL NOT BE INVOLVED. YOU HAVE REQUESTED A JEDI SENT TO YOU?
WE WANT OUR JEDI, MACE WINDU! WE WANT QUINLAN VOS!
HE IS BLOOD OF OUR BLOOD AND IF I HAD MY WAY, HE WOULD HAVE BEEN A GUARDIAN AND NEVER A JEDI!

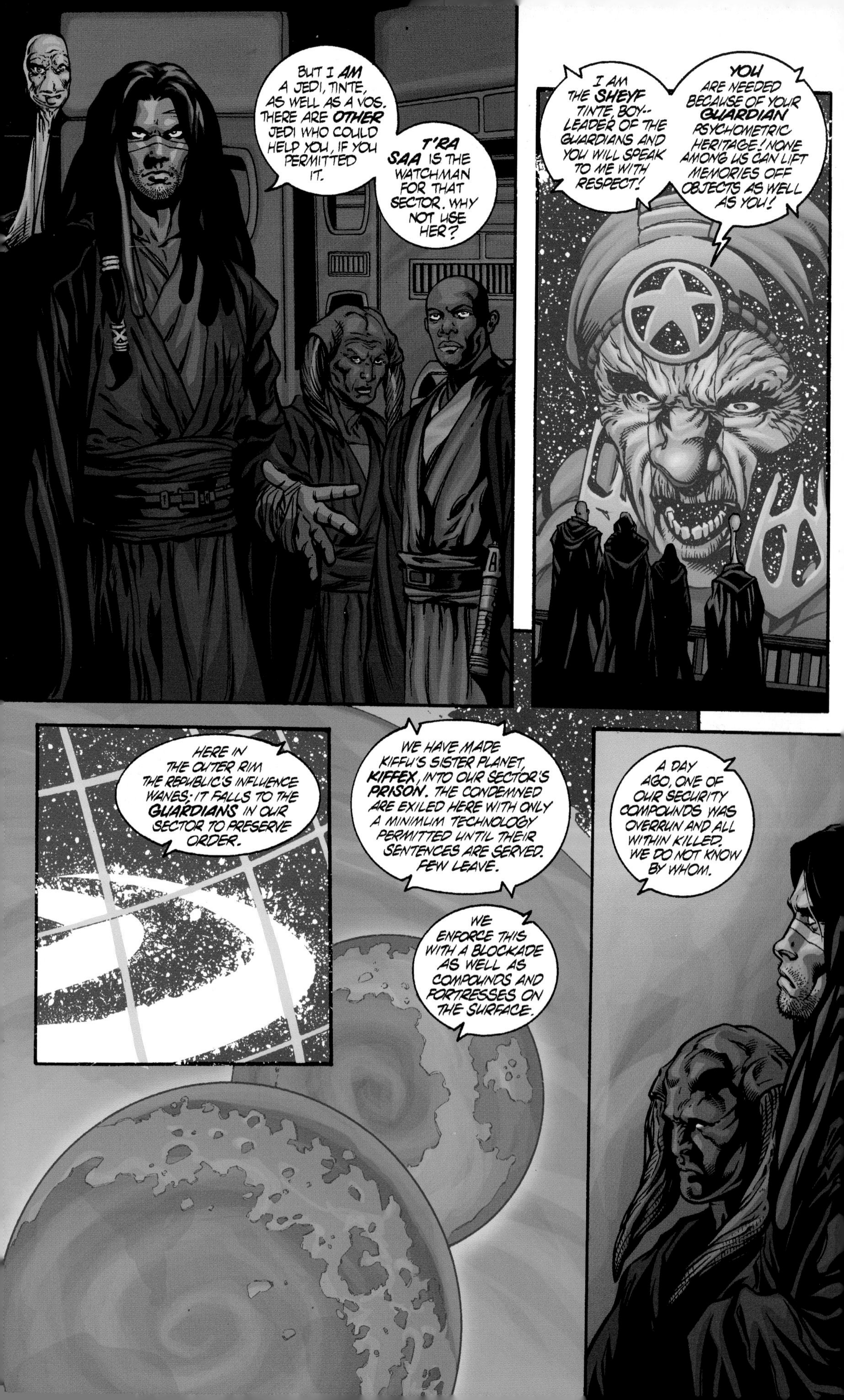

BUT I AM A JEDI, TINTE, AS WELL AS A VOS. THERE ARE OTHER JEDI WHO COULD HELP YOU, IF YOU PERMITTED IT.
T'RA SAA IS THE WATCHMAN FOR THAT SECTOR. WHY NOT USE HER?
I AM THE SHEYF TINTE, BOY-- LEADER OF THE GUARDIANS AND YOU WILL SPEAK TO ME WITH RESPECT!
YOU ARE NEEDED BECAUSE OF YOUR GUARDIAN PSYCHOMETRIC HERITAGE! NONE AMONG US CAN LIFT MEMORIES OFF OBJECTS AS WELL AS YOU!
HERE IN THE OUTER RIM THE REPUBLIC'S INFLUENCE WANES; IT FALLS TO THE GUARDIANS IN OUR SECTOR TO PRESERVE ORDER.
WE HAVE MADE KIFFU'S SISTER PLANET, KIFFEX, INTO OUR SECTOR'S PRISON. THE CONDEMNED ARE EXILED HERE WITH ONLY A MINIMUM TECHNOLOGY PERMITTED UNTIL THEIR SENTENCES ARE SERVED. FEW LEAVE.
WE ENFORCE THIS WITH A BLOCKADE AS WELL AS COMPOUNDS AND FORTRESSES ON THE SURFACE.
A DAY AGO, ONE OF OUR SECURITY COMPOUNDS WAS OVERRUN AND ALL WITHIN KILLED. WE DO NOT KNOW BY WHOM.

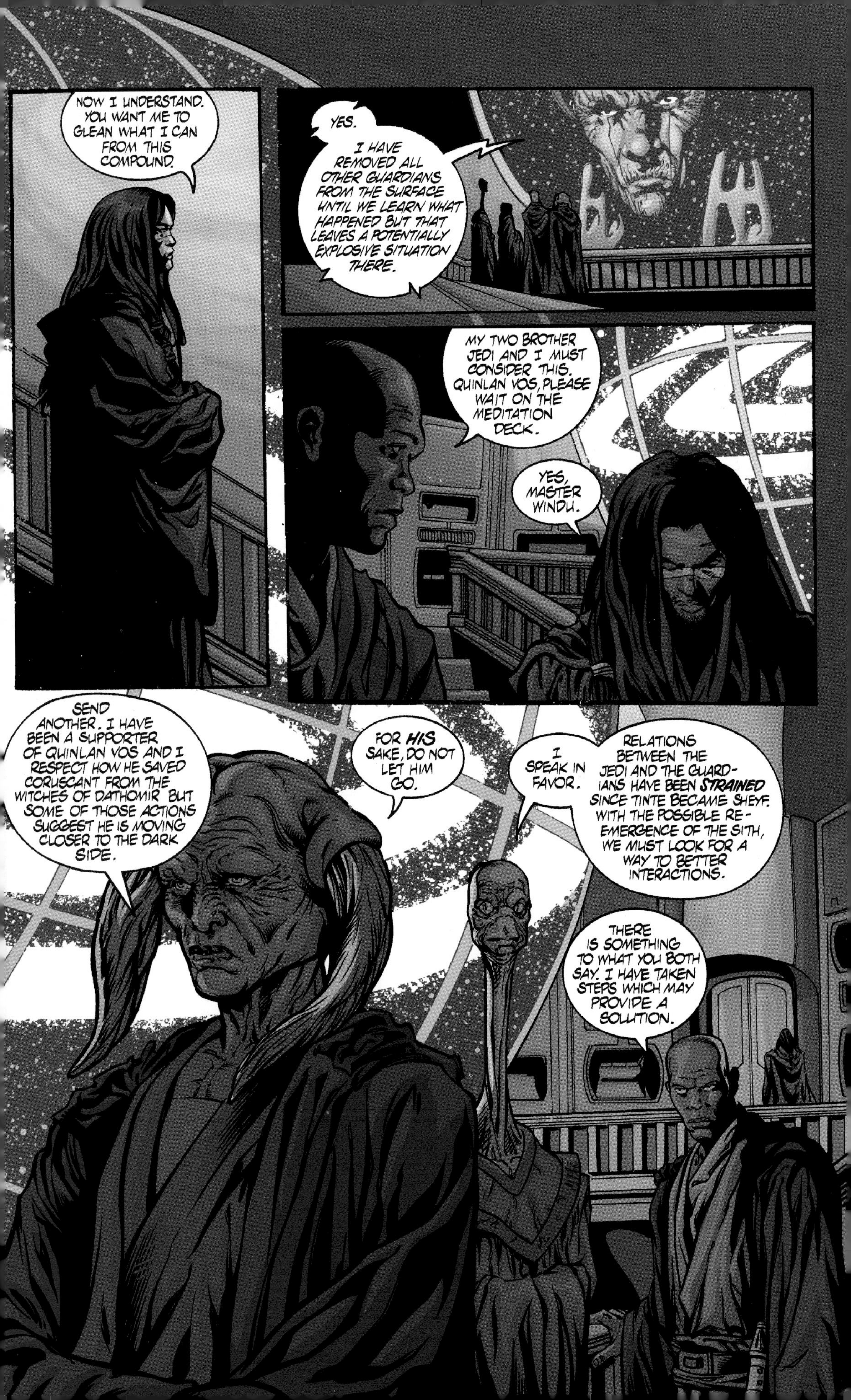
NOW I UNDERSTAND. YOU WANT ME TO GLEAN WHAT I CAN FROM THIS COMPOUND.
YES.
I HAVE REMOVED ALL OTHER GUARDIANS FROM THE SURFACE UNTIL WE LEARN WHAT HAPPENED BUT THAT LEAVES A POTENTIALLY EXPLOSIVE SITUATION THERE.
MY TWO BROTHER JEDI AND I MUST CONSIDER THIS. QUINLAN VOS, PLEASE WAIT ON THE MEDITATION DECK.
YES, MASTER WINDU.
SEND ANOTHER. I HAVE BEEN A SUPPORTER OF QUINLAN VOS AND I RESPECT HOW HE SAVED CORUSCANT FROM THE WITCHES OF DATHOMIR BUT SOME OF THOSE ACTIONS SUGGEST HE IS MOVING CLOSER TO THE DARK SIDE.
FOR HIS SAKE, DO NOT LET HIM GO.
I SPEAK IN FAVOR.
RELATIONS BETWEEN THE JEDI AND THE GUARDIANS HAVE BEEN STRAINED SINCE TINTE BECAME SHEYF. WITH THE POSSIBLE RE-EMERGENCE OF THE SITH, WE MUST LOOK FOR A WAY TO BETTER INTERACTIONS.
THERE IS SOMETHING TO WHAT YOU BOTH SAY. I HAVE TAKEN STEPS WHICH MAY PROVIDE A SOLUTION.

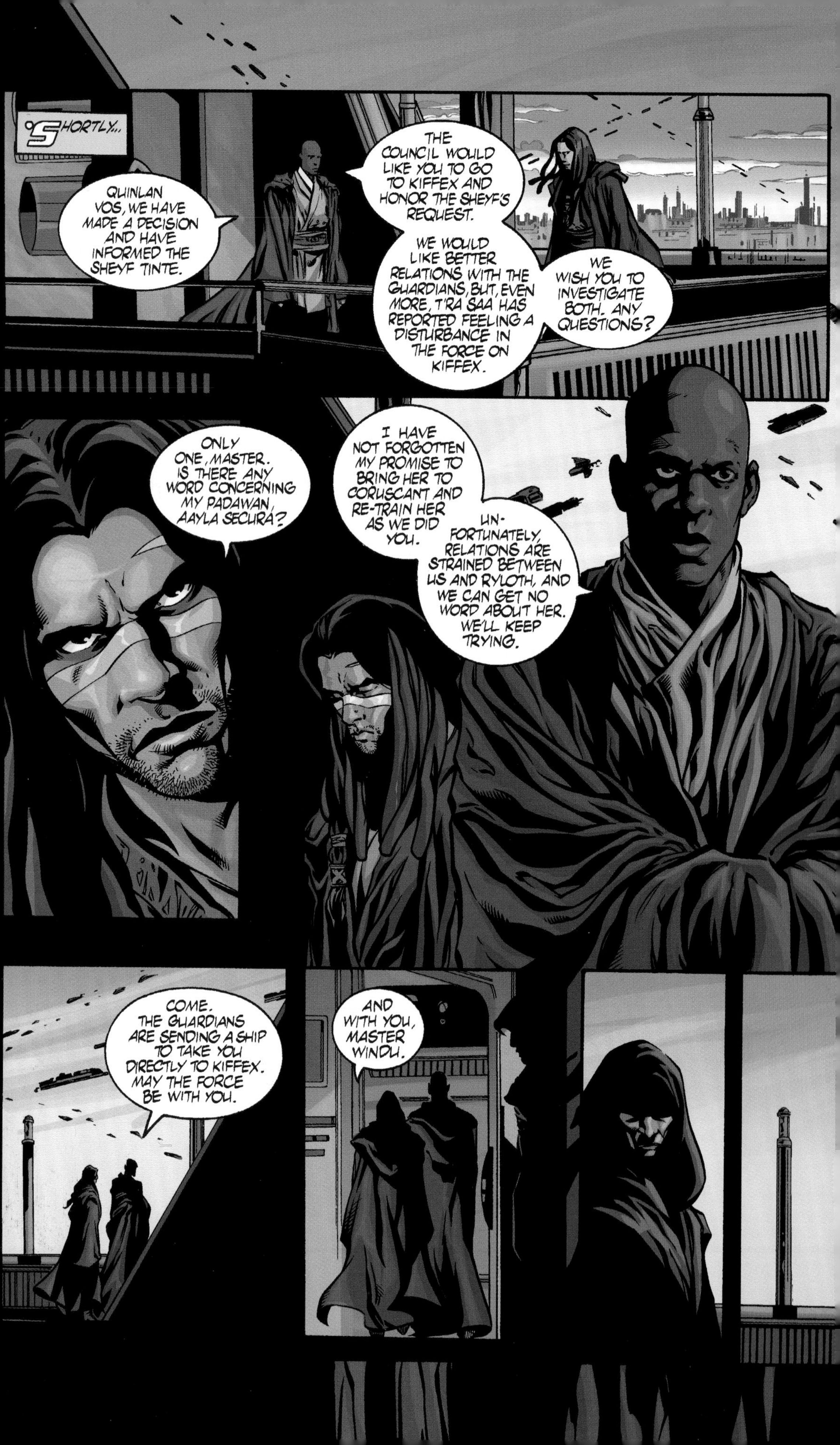
SHORTLY...
QUINLAN VOS, WE HAVE MADE A DECISION AND HAVE INFORMED THE SHEYF TINTE.
THE COUNCIL WOULD LIKE YOU TO GO TO KIFFEX AND HONOR THE SHEYF'S REQUEST.
WE WOULD LIKE BETTER RELATIONS WITH THE GUARDIANS, BUT, EVEN MORE, T'RA SAA HAS REPORTED FEELING A DISTURBANCE IN THE FORCE ON KIFFEX.
WE WISH YOU TO INVESTIGATE BOTH. ANY QUESTIONS?
ONLY ONE, MASTER. IS THERE ANY WORD CONCERNING MY PADAWAN, AAYLA SECURA?
I HAVE NOT FORGOTTEN MY PROMISE TO BRING HER TO CORUSCANT AND RE-TRAIN HER AS WE DID YOU.
UN-FORTUNATELY, RELATIONS ARE STRAINED BETWEEN US AND RYLOTH, AND WE CAN GET NO WORD ABOUT HER. WE'LL KEEP TRYING.
COME. THE GUARDIANS ARE SENDING A SHIP TO TAKE YOU DIRECTLY TO KIFFEX. MAY THE FORCE BE WITH YOU.
AND WITH YOU, MASTER WINDU.

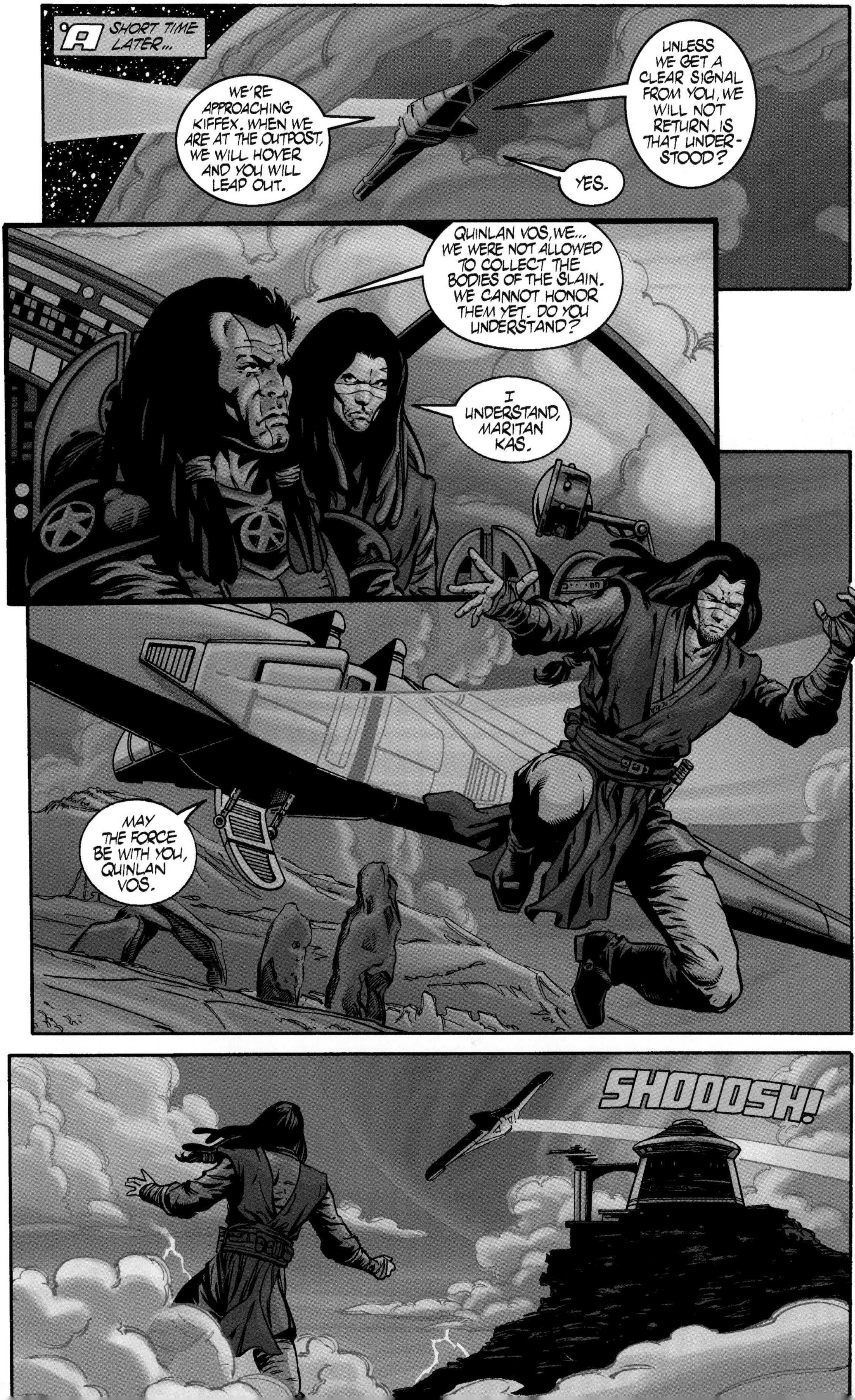
A SHORT TIME LATER...
WE'RE APPROACHING KIFFEX. WHEN WE ARE AT THE OUTPOST, WE WILL HOVER AND YOU WILL LEAP OUT.
UNLESS WE GET A CLEAR SIGNAL FROM YOU, WE WILL NOT RETURN. IS THAT UNDERSTOOD?
YES.
QUINLAN VOS, WE... WE WERE NOT ALLOWED TO COLLECT THE BODIES OF THE SLAIN. WE CANNOT HONOR THEM YET. DO YOU UNDERSTAND?
I UNDERSTAND, MARITAN KAS.
MAY THE FORCE BE WITH YOU, QUINLAN VOS.
SHOOOSH!

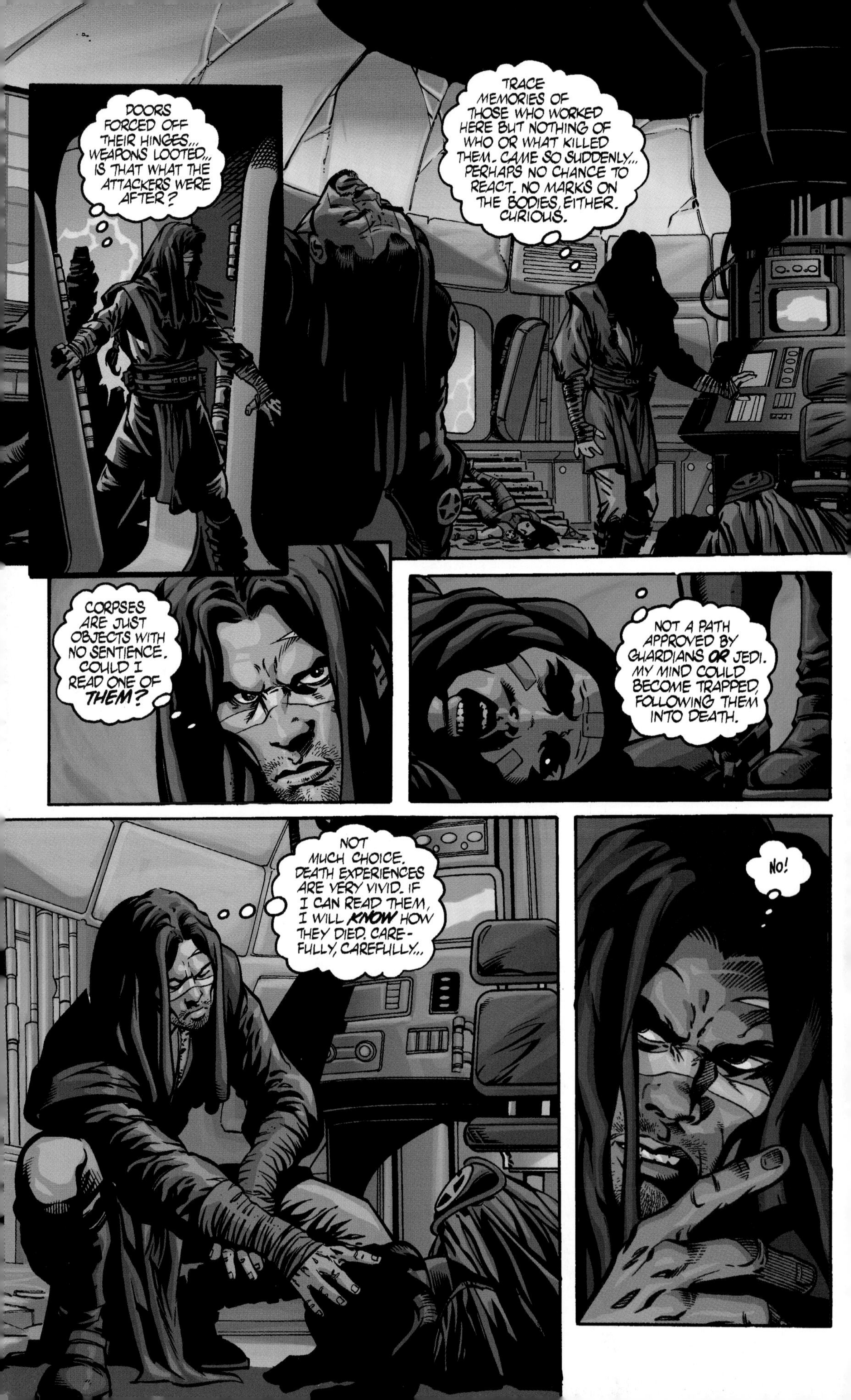
DOORS FORCED OFF THEIR HINGES... WEAPONS LOOTED... IS THAT WHAT THE ATTACKERS WERE AFTER?
TRACE MEMORIES OF THOSE WHO WORKED HERE BUT NOTHING OF WHO OR WHAT KILLED THEM. CAME SO SUDDENLY... PERHAPS NO CHANCE TO REACT. NO MARKS ON THE BODIES, EITHER. CURIOUS.
CORPSES ARE JUST OBJECTS WITH NO SENTIENCE. COULD I READ ONE OF *THEM*?
NOT A PATH APPROVED BY GUARDIANS *OR* JEDI. MY MIND COULD BECOME TRAPPED, FOLLOWING THEM INTO DEATH.
NOT MUCH CHOICE. DEATH EXPERIENCES ARE VERY VIVID. IF I CAN READ THEM, I WILL *KNOW* HOW THEY DIED. CARE-FULLY, CAREFULLY...
NO!

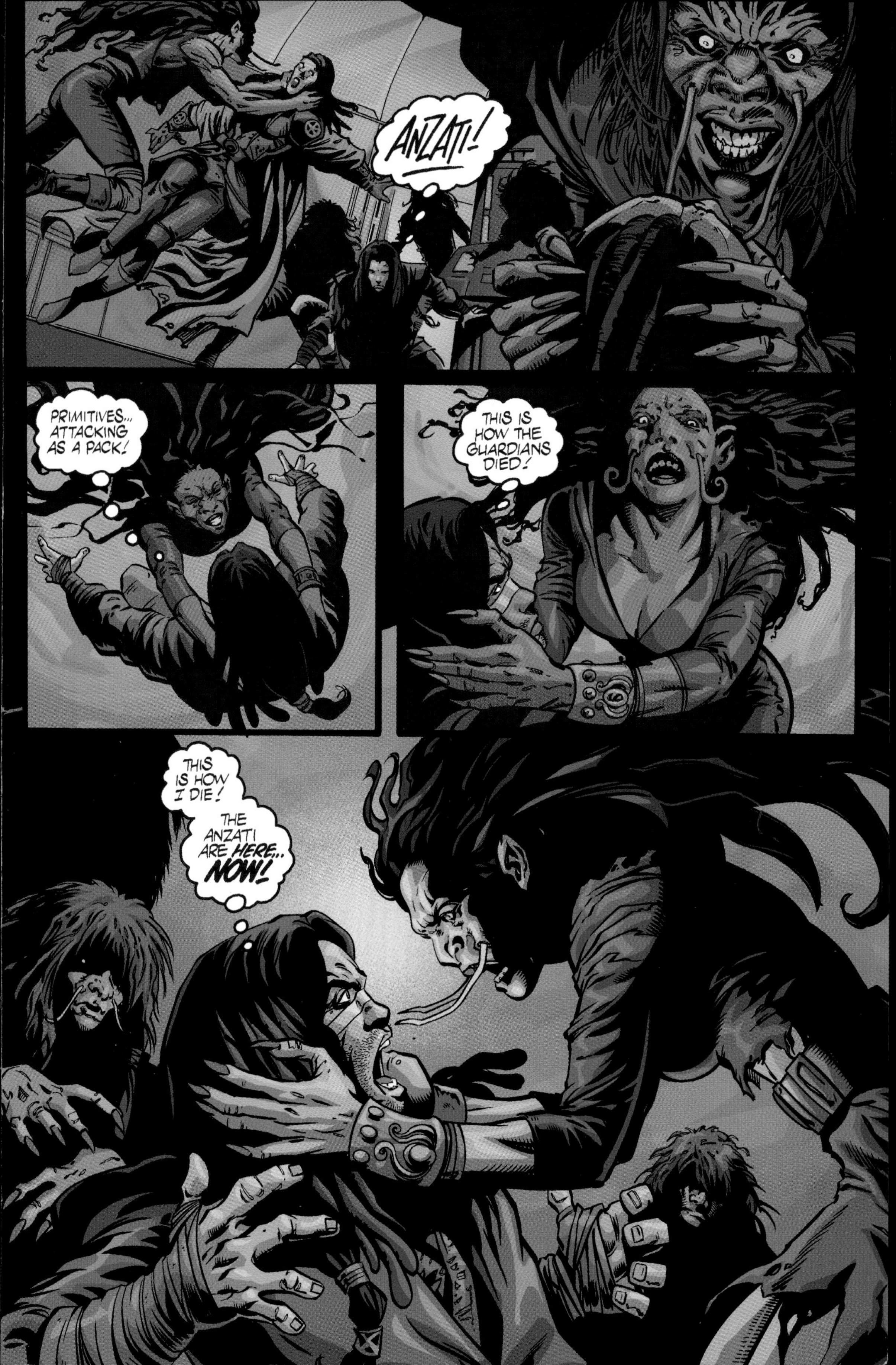
ANZATI!
PRIMITIVES... ATTACKING AS A PACK!
THIS IS HOW THE GUARDIANS DIED!
THIS IS HOW I DIE!
THE ANZATI ARE HERE... NOW!

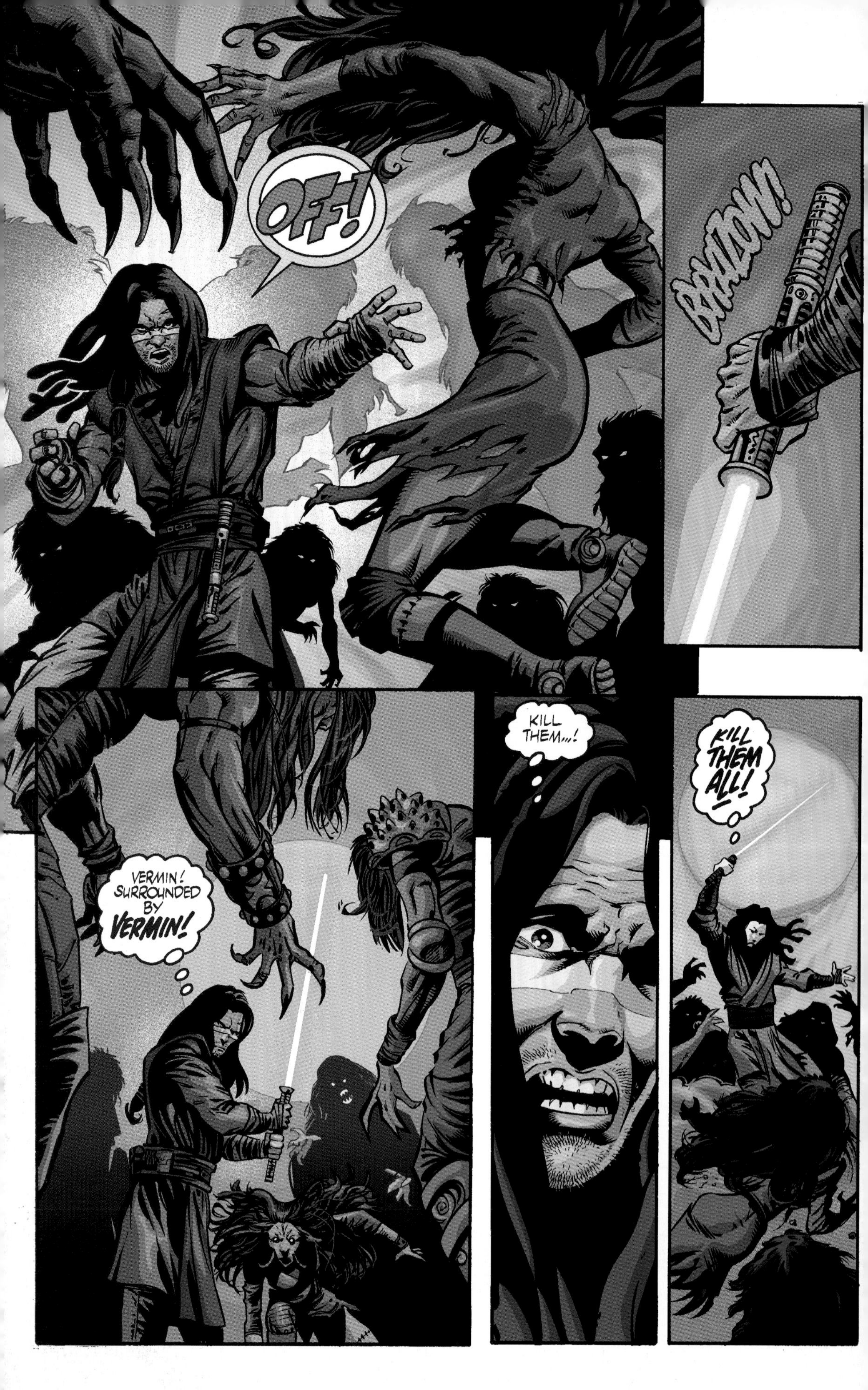
OFF!
BZZZOWN!
VERMIN! SURROUNDED BY VERMIN!
KILL THEM...!
KILL THEM ALL!

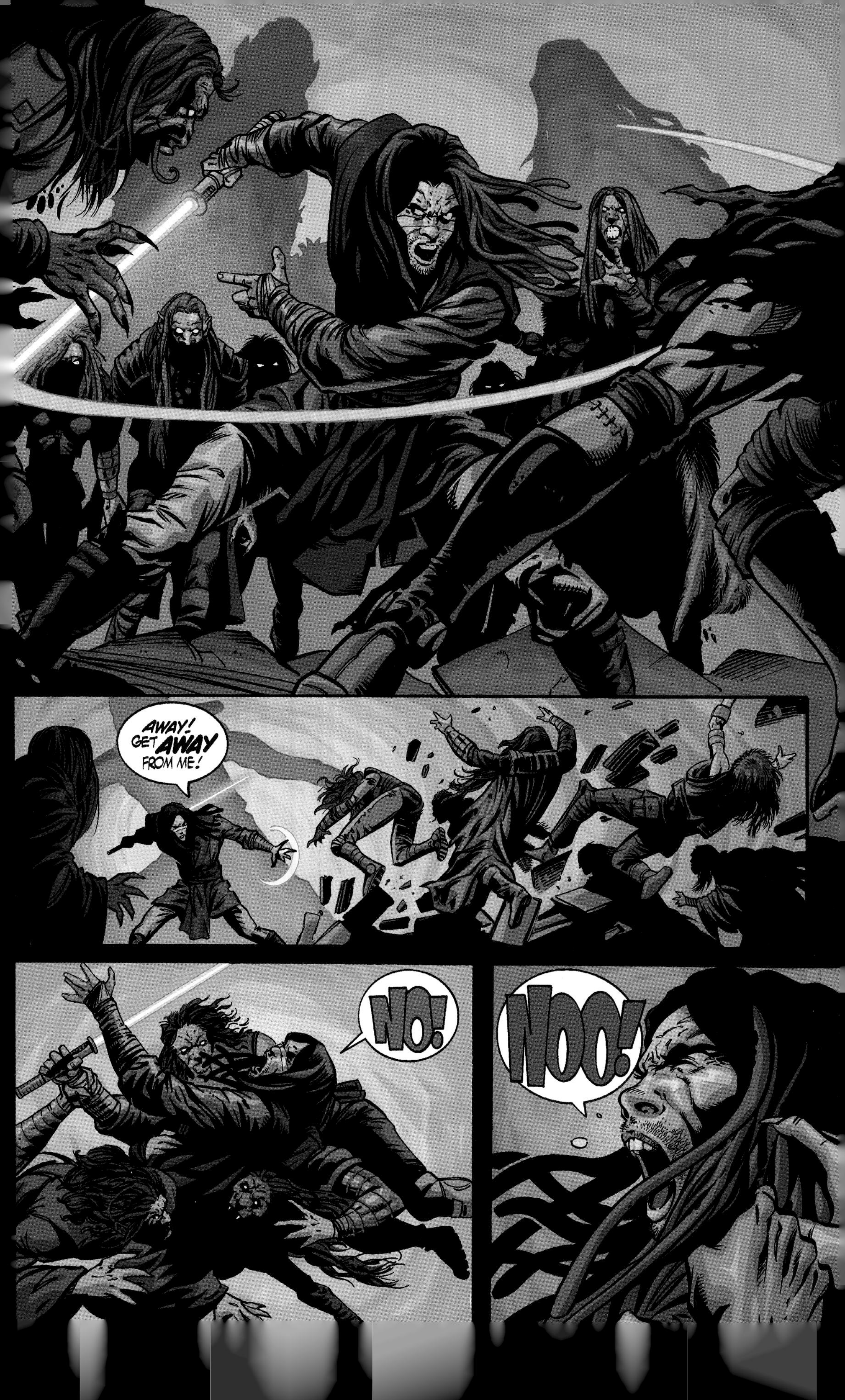
AWAY! GET AWAY FROM ME!
NO!
NOO!

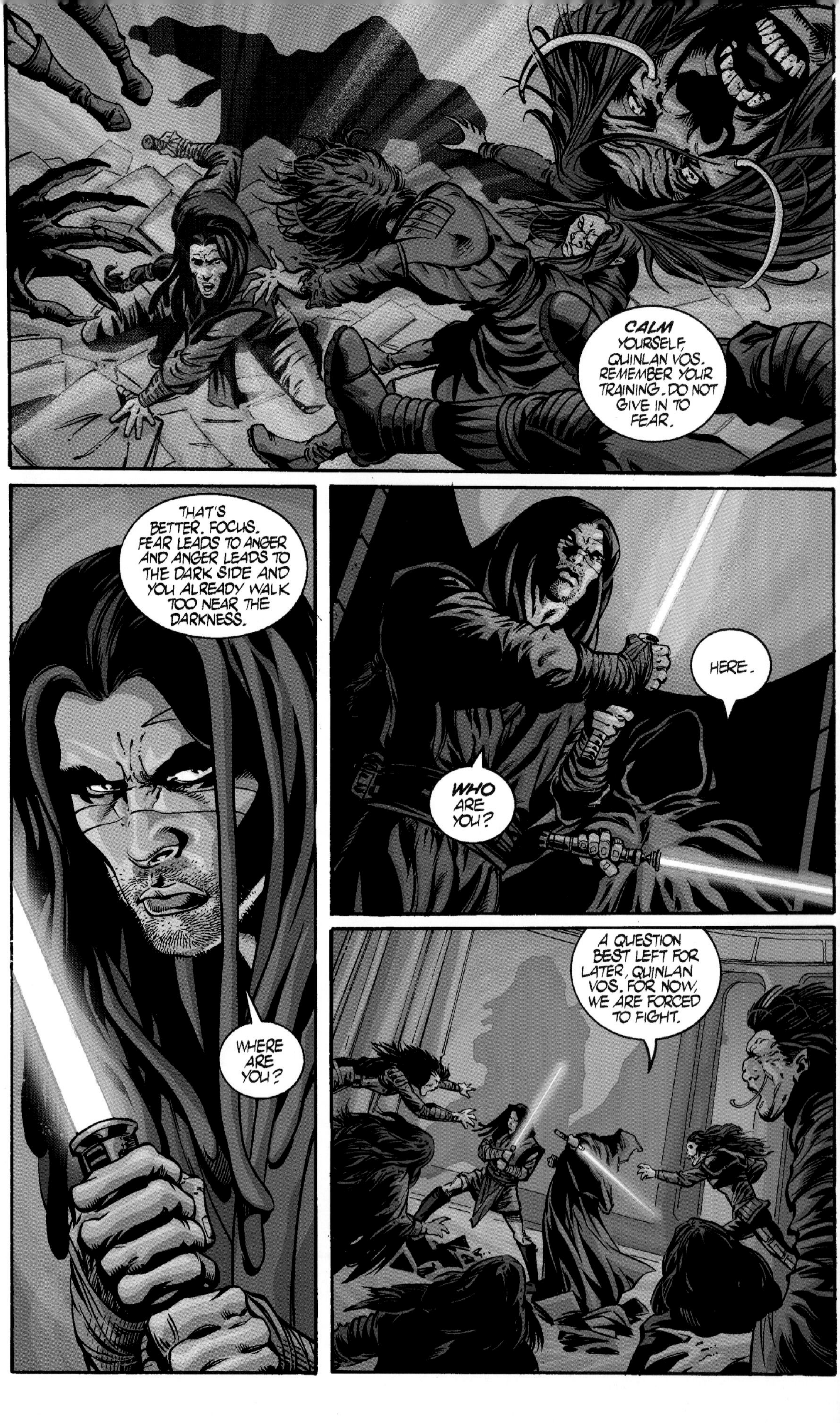
CALM YOURSELF, QUINLAN VOS. REMEMBER YOUR TRAINING. DO NOT GIVE IN TO FEAR.
THAT'S BETTER. FOCUS. FEAR LEADS TO ANGER AND ANGER LEADS TO THE DARK SIDE AND YOU ALREADY WALK TOO NEAR THE DARKNESS.
WHERE ARE YOU?
WHO ARE YOU?
HERE.
A QUESTION BEST LEFT FOR LATER, QUINLAN VOS. FOR NOW, WE ARE FORCED TO FIGHT.

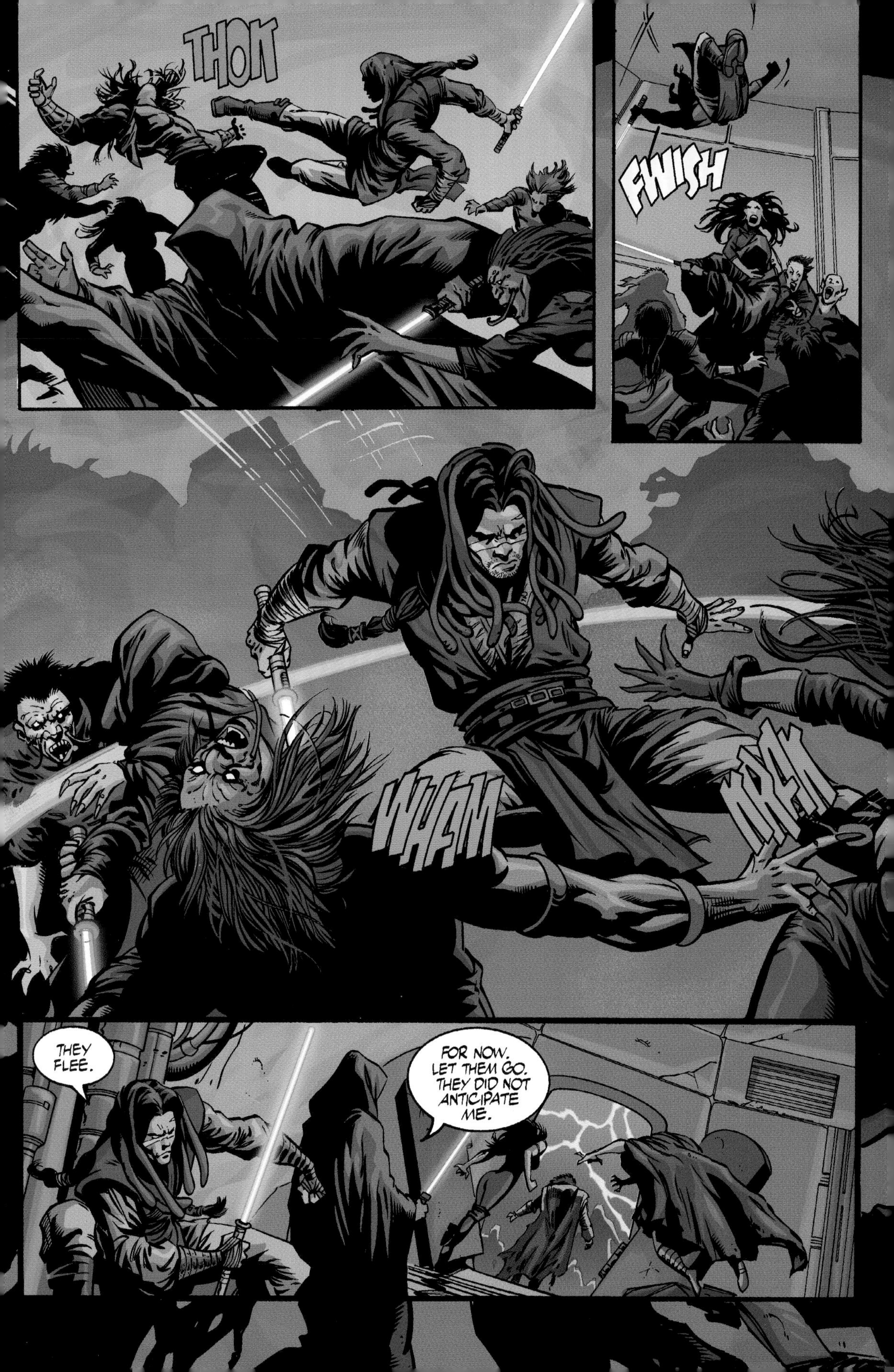
THOM
FWISH
WHAM
THEY FLEE.
FOR NOW. LET THEM GO. THEY DID NOT ANTICIPATE ME.

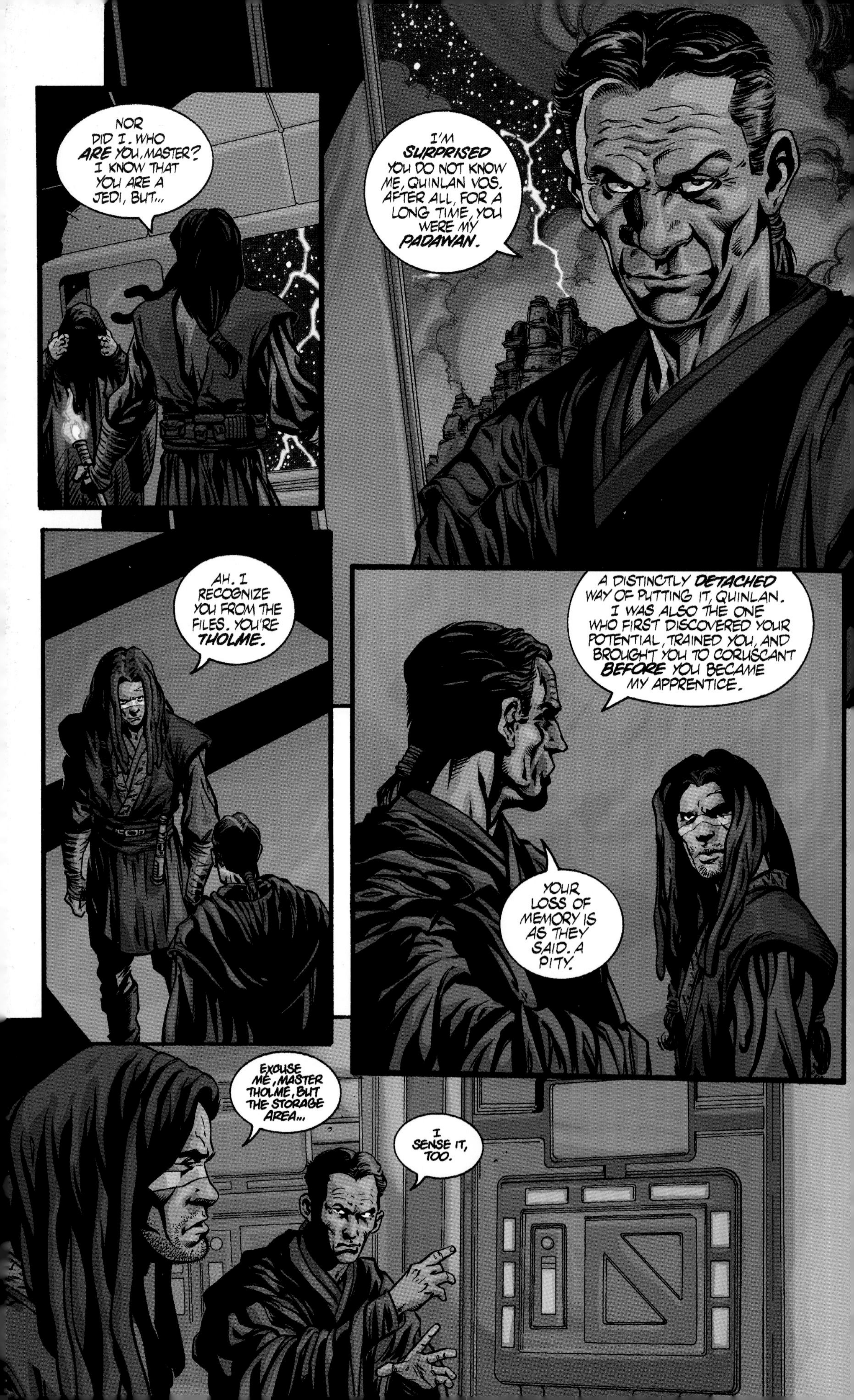
NOR DID I. WHO ARE YOU, MASTER? I KNOW THAT YOU ARE A JEDI, BUT...
I'M SURPRISED YOU DO NOT KNOW ME, QUINLAN VOS. AFTER ALL, FOR A LONG TIME, YOU WERE MY PADAWAN.
AH. I RECOGNIZE YOU FROM THE FILES. YOU'RE THOLME.
A DISTINCTLY DETACHED WAY OF PUTTING IT, QUINLAN. I WAS ALSO THE ONE WHO FIRST DISCOVERED YOUR POTENTIAL, TRAINED YOU, AND BROUGHT YOU TO CORUSCANT BEFORE YOU BECAME MY APPRENTICE.
YOUR LOSS OF MEMORY IS AS THEY SAID. A PITY.
EXCUSE ME, MASTER THOLME, BUT THE STORAGE AREA...
I SENSE IT, TOO.

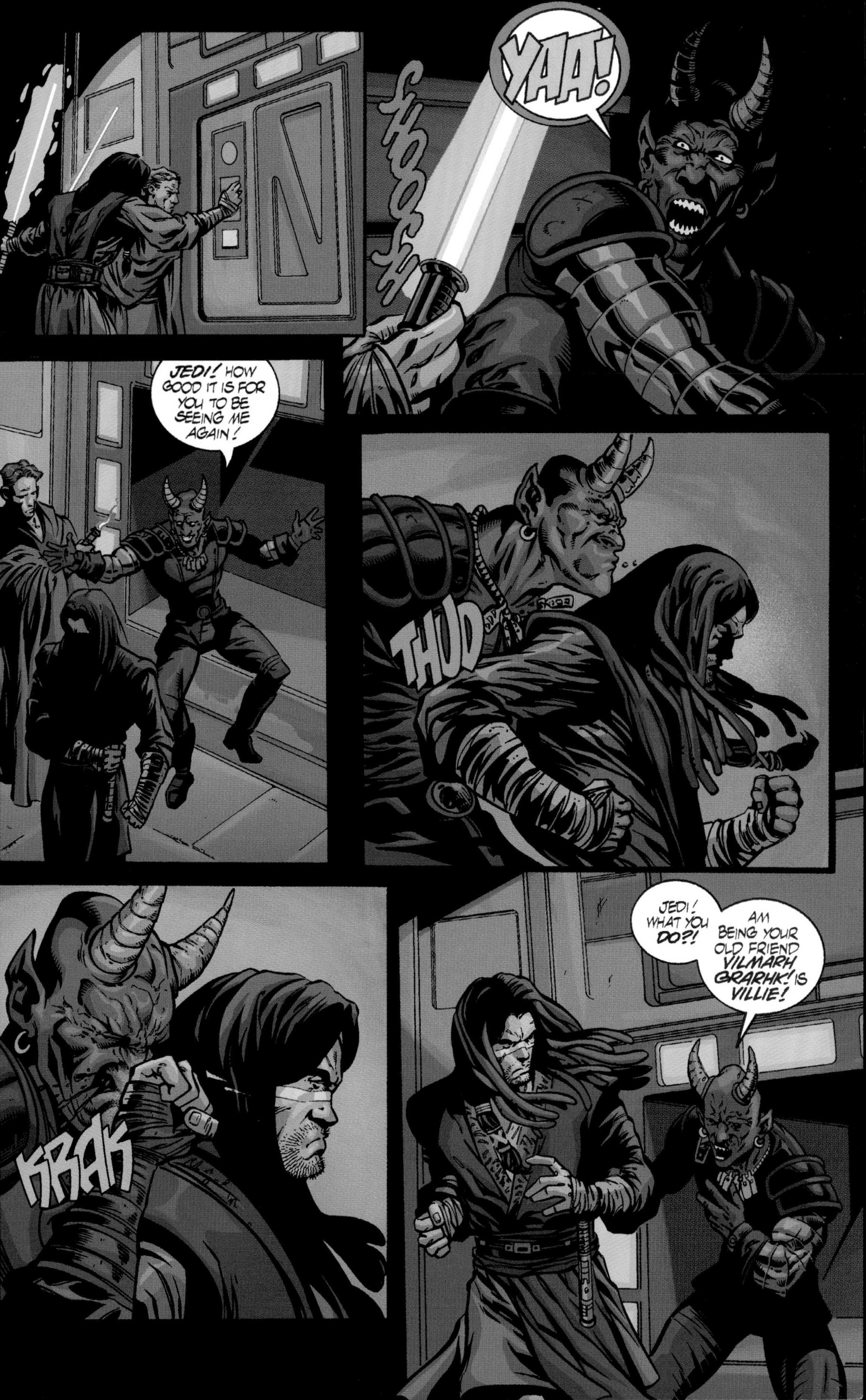
SHOOOSH
YAA!
JEDI! HOW GOOD IT IS FOR YOU TO BE SEEING ME AGAIN!
THUD
KRAK
JEDI! WHAT YOU DO?!
AM BEING YOUR OLD FRIEND VILMARH GRAHK! IS VILLIE!

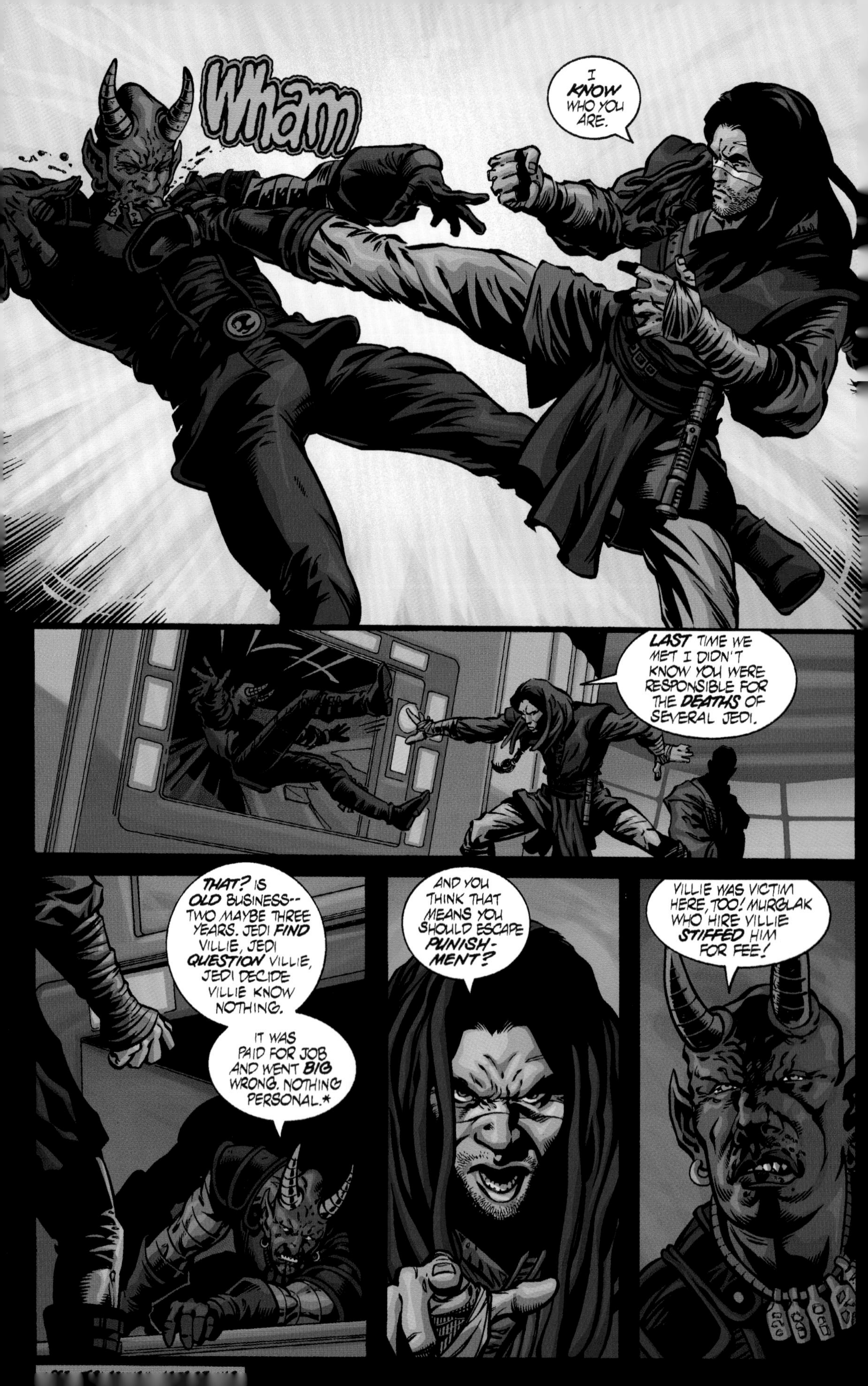
Wham
I KNOW WHO YOU ARE.
LAST TIME WE MET I DIDN'T KNOW YOU WERE RESPONSIBLE FOR THE DEATHS OF SEVERAL JEDI.
THAT? IS OLD BUSINESS-- TWO MAYBE THREE YEARS. JEDI FIND VILLIE, JEDI QUESTION VILLIE, JEDI DECIDE VILLIE KNOW NOTHING.
IT WAS PAID FOR JOB AND WENT BIG WRONG. NOTHING PERSONAL.*
AND YOU THINK THAT MEANS YOU SHOULD ESCAPE PUNISHMENT?
VILLIE WAS VICTIM HERE, TOO! MURGLAK WHO HIRE VILLIE STIFFED HIM FOR FEE!

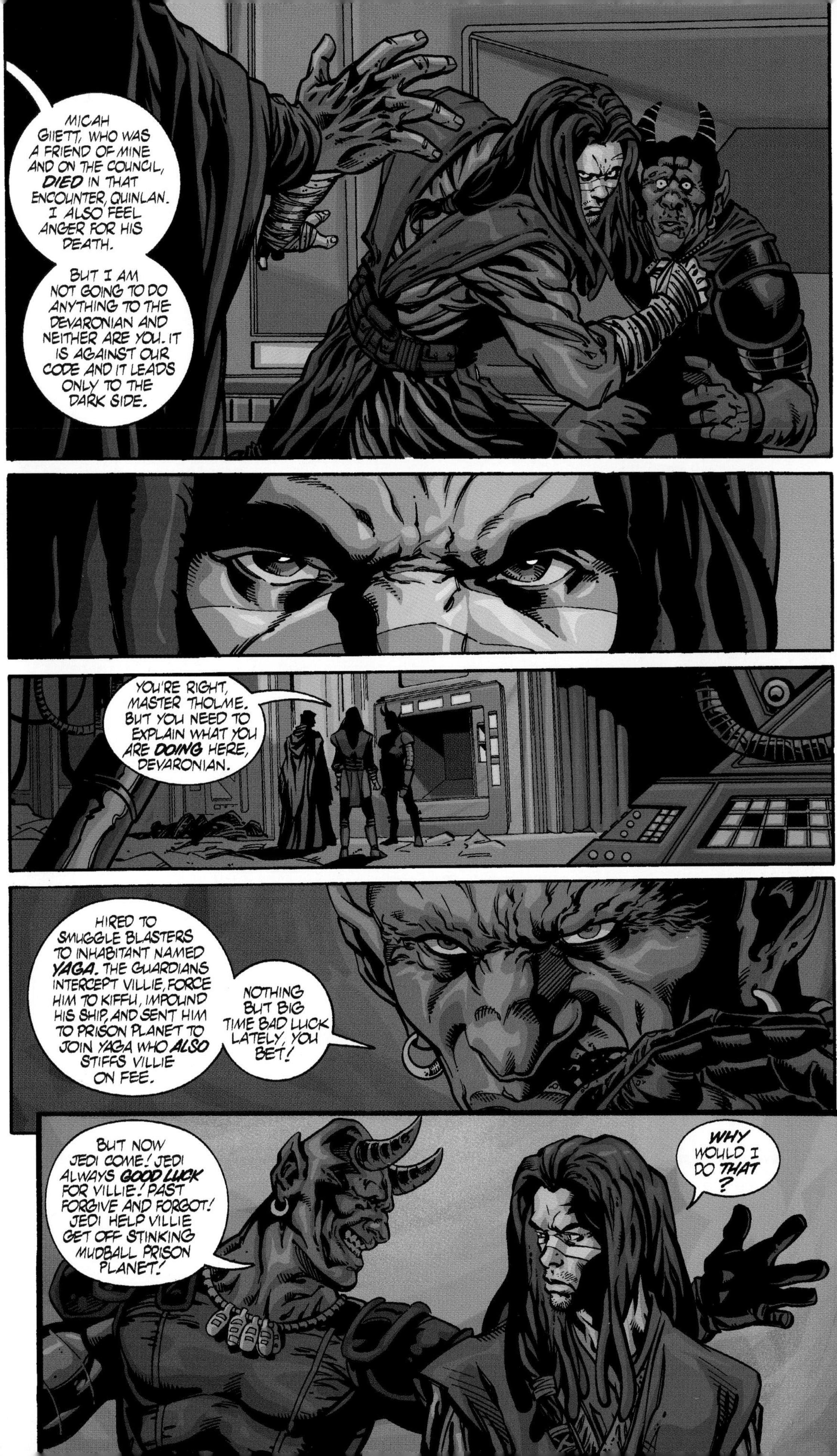
MICAH GIIETT, WHO WAS A FRIEND OF MINE AND ON THE COUNCIL, **DIED** IN THAT ENCOUNTER, QUINLAN. I ALSO FEEL ANGER FOR HIS DEATH.
BUT I AM NOT GOING TO DO ANYTHING TO THE DEVARONIAN AND NEITHER ARE YOU. IT IS AGAINST OUR CODE AND IT LEADS ONLY TO THE DARK SIDE.
YOU'RE RIGHT, MASTER THOLME. BUT YOU NEED TO EXPLAIN WHAT YOU ARE **DOING** HERE, DEVARONIAN.
HIRED TO SMUGGLE BLASTERS TO INHABITANT NAMED **YAGA**. THE GUARDIANS INTERCEPT VILLIE, FORCE HIM TO KIFFU, IMPOUND HIS SHIP, AND SENT HIM TO PRISON PLANET TO JOIN YAGA WHO **ALSO** STIFFS VILLIE ON FEE.
NOTHING BUT BIG TIME BAD LUCK LATELY, YOU BET!
BUT NOW JEDI COME! JEDI ALWAYS **GOOD LUCK** FOR VILLIE! PAST FORGIVE AND FORGOT! JEDI HELP VILLIE GET OFF STINKING MUDBALL PRISON PLANET!
WHY WOULD I DO **THAT**?

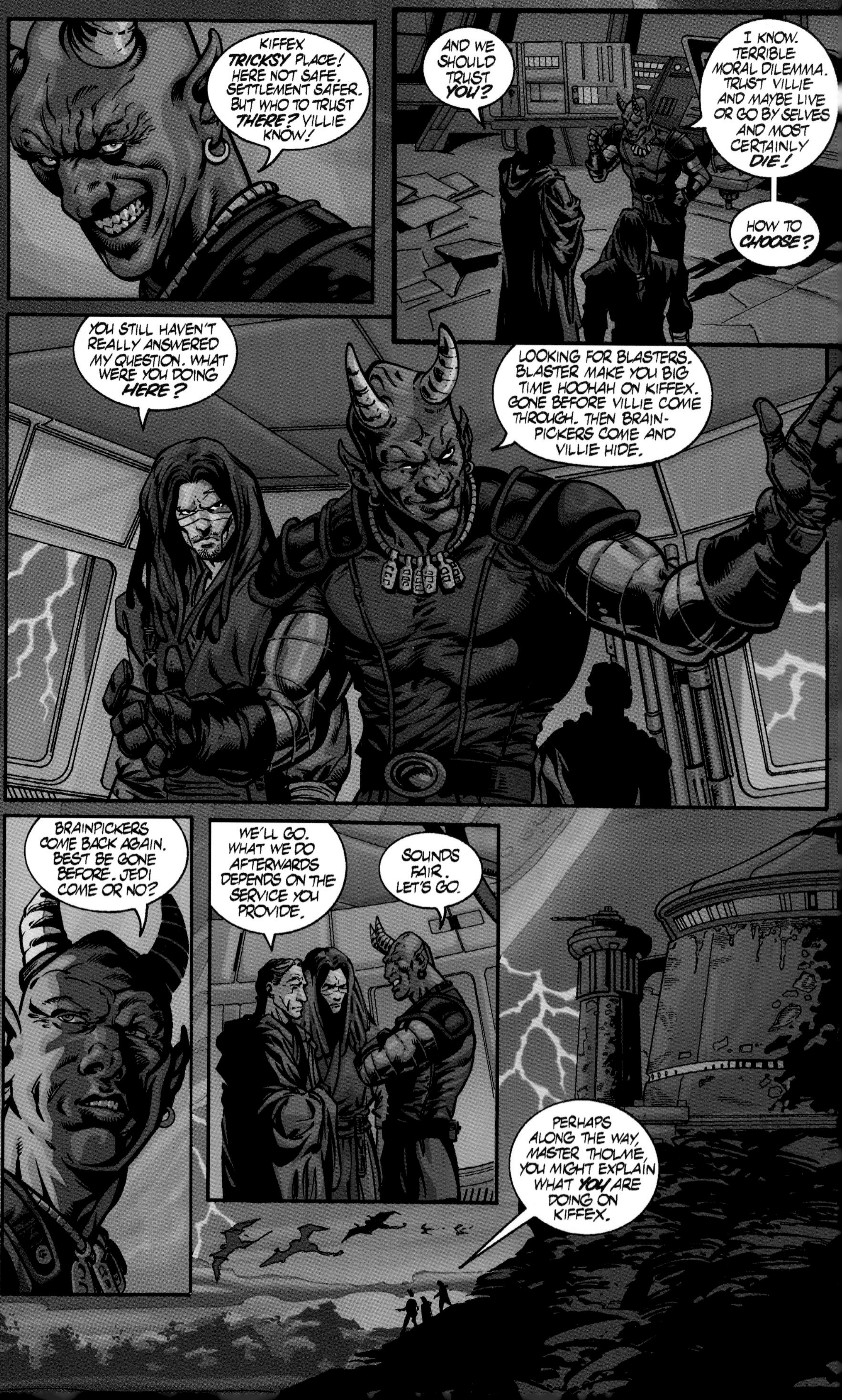
KIFFEX TRICKSY PLACE! HERE NOT SAFE. SETTLEMENT SAFER. BUT WHO TO TRUST THERE? VILLIE KNOW!
AND WE SHOULD TRUST YOU?
I KNOW. TERRIBLE MORAL DILEMMA. TRUST VILLIE AND MAYBE LIVE OR GO BY SELVES AND MOST CERTAINLY DIE!
HOW TO CHOOSE?
YOU STILL HAVEN'T REALLY ANSWERED MY QUESTION. WHAT WERE YOU DOING HERE?
LOOKING FOR BLASTERS. BLASTER MAKE YOU BIG TIME HOOHAH ON KIFFEX. GONE BEFORE VILLIE COME THROUGH. THEN BRAIN-PICKERS COME AND VILLIE HIDE.
BRAINPICKERS COME BACK AGAIN. BEST BE GONE BEFORE. JEDI COME OR NO?
WE'LL GO. WHAT WE DO AFTERWARDS DEPENDS ON THE SERVICE YOU PROVIDE.
SOUNDS FAIR. LET'S GO.
PERHAPS ALONG THE WAY, MASTER THOLME, YOU MIGHT EXPLAIN WHAT YOU ARE DOING ON KIFFEX.

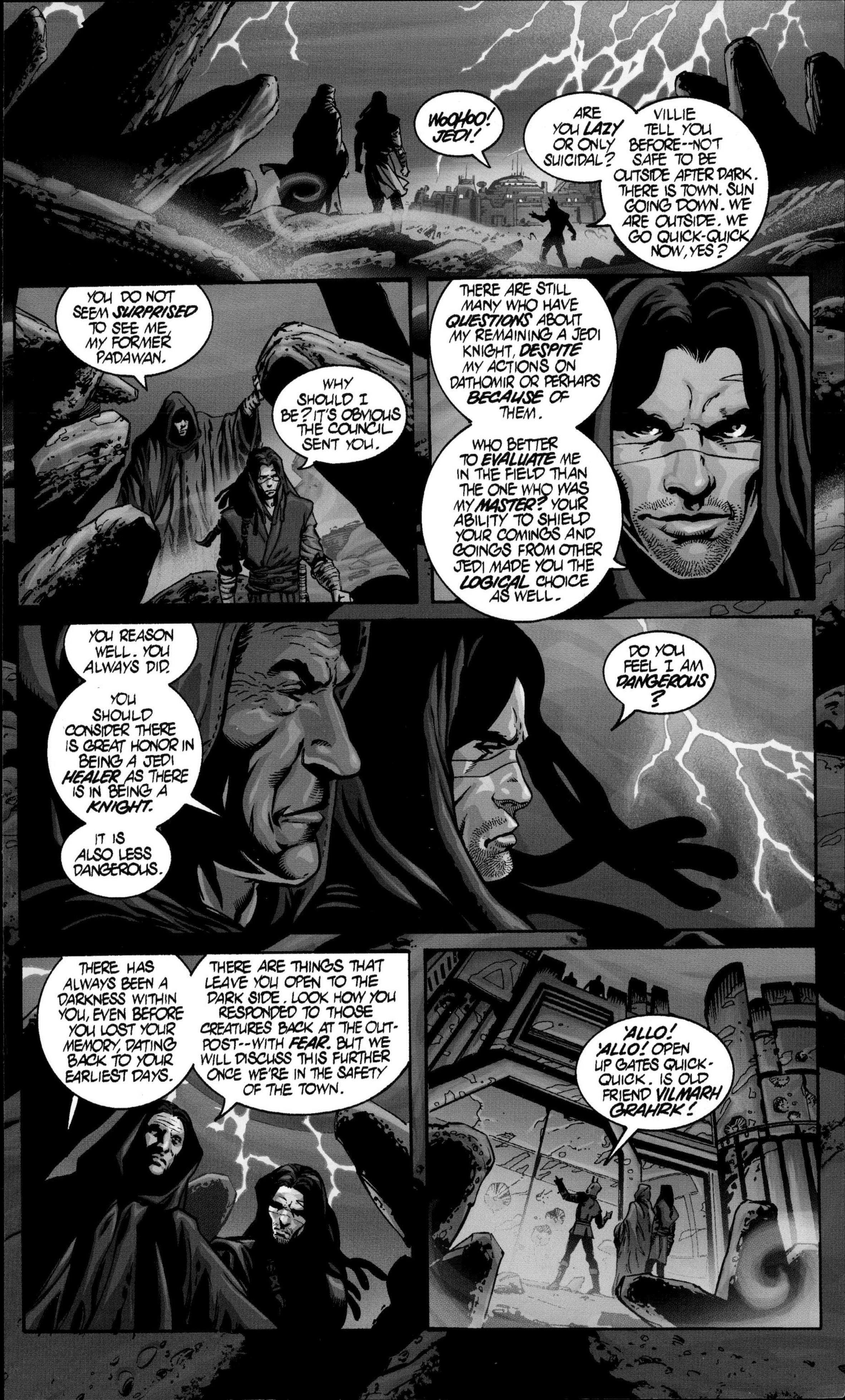
WOOHOO! JEDI!
ARE YOU LAZY OR ONLY SUICIDAL?
VILLIE TELL YOU BEFORE--NOT SAFE TO BE OUTSIDE AFTER DARK. THERE IS TOWN. SUN GOING DOWN. WE ARE OUTSIDE. WE GO QUICK-QUICK NOW, YES?
YOU DO NOT SEEM SURPRISED TO SEE ME, MY FORMER PADAWAN.
WHY SHOULD I BE? IT'S OBVIOUS THE COUNCIL SENT YOU.
THERE ARE STILL MANY WHO HAVE QUESTIONS ABOUT MY REMAINING A JEDI KNIGHT, DESPITE MY ACTIONS ON DATHOMIR OR PERHAPS BECAUSE OF THEM.
WHO BETTER TO EVALUATE ME IN THE FIELD THAN THE ONE WHO WAS MY MASTER? YOUR ABILITY TO SHIELD YOUR COMINGS AND GOINGS FROM OTHER JEDI MADE YOU THE LOGICAL CHOICE AS WELL.
YOU REASON WELL. YOU ALWAYS DID.
YOU SHOULD CONSIDER THERE IS GREAT HONOR IN BEING A JEDI HEALER AS THERE IS IN BEING A KNIGHT.
IT IS ALSO LESS DANGEROUS.
DO YOU FEEL I AM DANGEROUS?
THERE HAS ALWAYS BEEN A DARKNESS WITHIN YOU, EVEN BEFORE YOU LOST YOUR MEMORY, DATING BACK TO YOUR EARLIEST DAYS.
THERE ARE THINGS THAT LEAVE YOU OPEN TO THE DARK SIDE. LOOK HOW YOU RESPONDED TO THOSE CREATURES BACK AT THE OUT-POST--WITH FEAR. BUT WE WILL DISCUSS THIS FURTHER ONCE WE'RE IN THE SAFETY OF THE TOWN.
'ALLO! 'ALLO! OPEN UP GATES QUICK-QUICK. IS OLD FRIEND VILMARH GRAHRK!

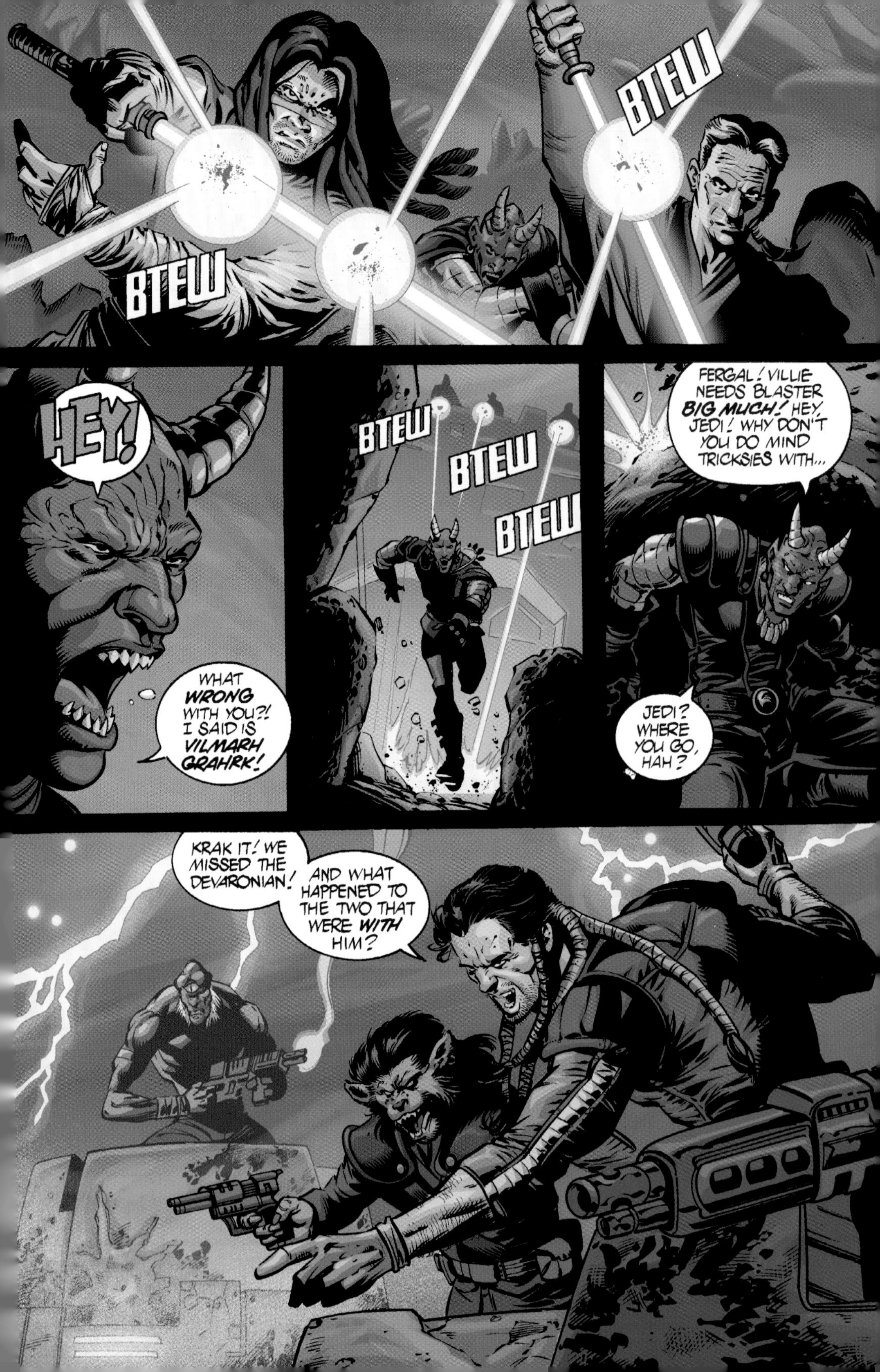
BTEW
BTEW
HEY!
WHAT WRONG WITH YOU?! I SAID IS VILMARH GRAHRK!
BTEW
BTEW
BTEW
FERGAL! VILLIE NEEDS BLASTER BIG MUCH! HEY, JEDI! WHY DON'T YOU DO MIND TRICKSIES WITH...
JEDI? WHERE YOU GO, HAH?
KRAK IT! WE MISSED THE DEVARONIAN!
AND WHAT HAPPENED TO THE TWO THAT WERE WITH HIM?

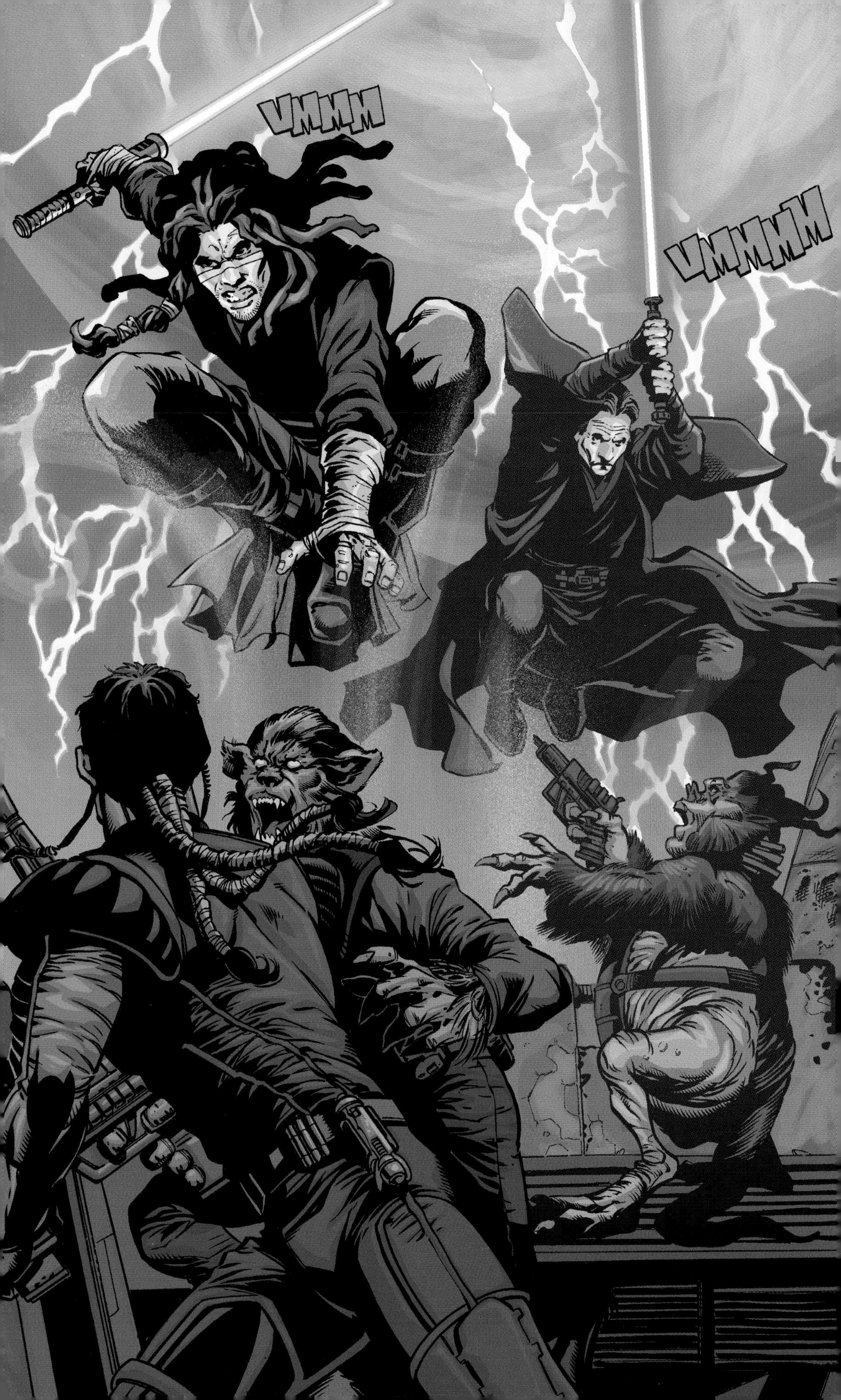

VMMM
VMMMM

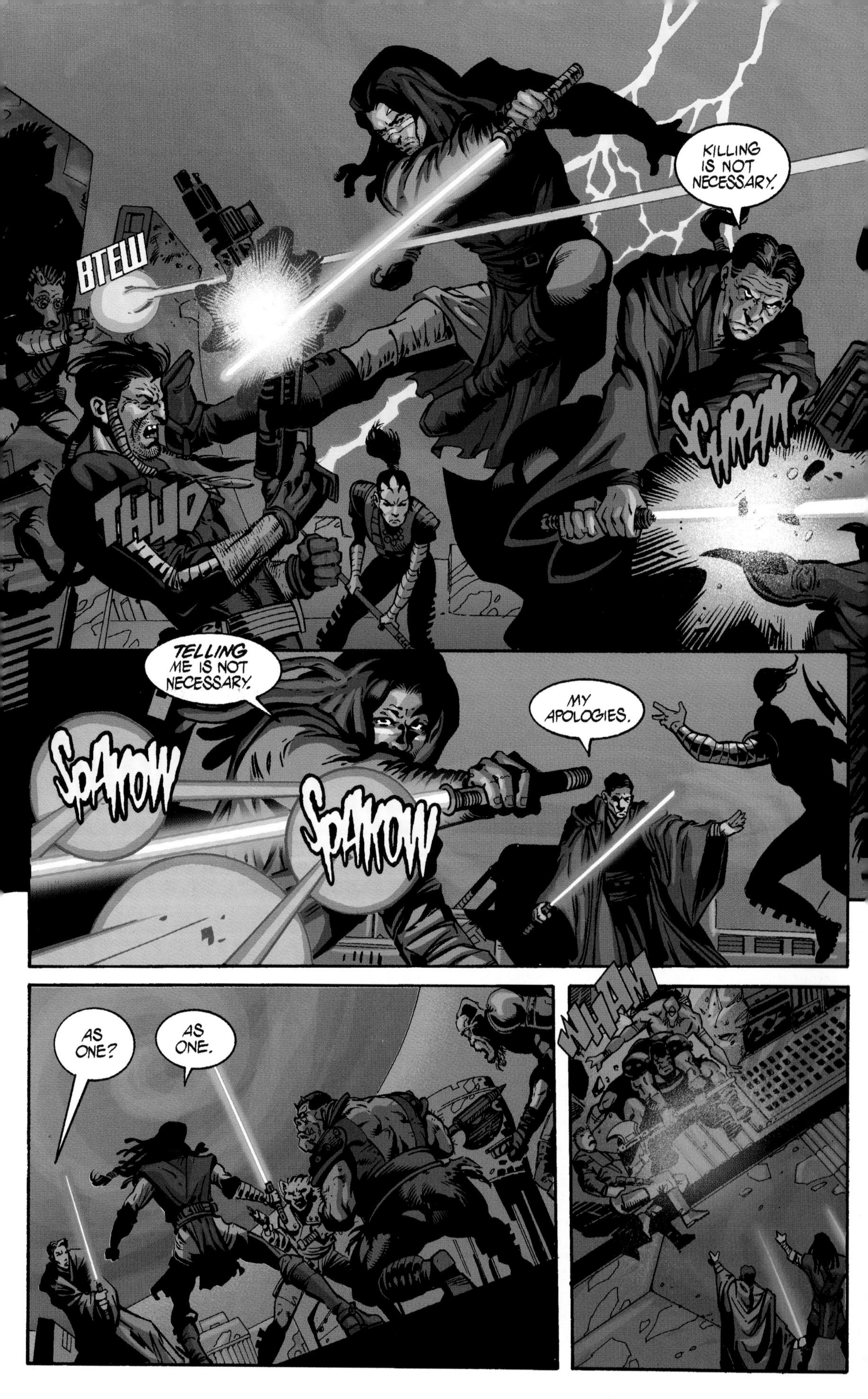
BTEW
KILLING IS NOT NECESSARY.
THUD
SCHRAK
TELLING ME IS NOT NECESSARY.
MY APOLOGIES.
SPAKOW
SPAKOW
AS ONE?
AS ONE.
WHAM

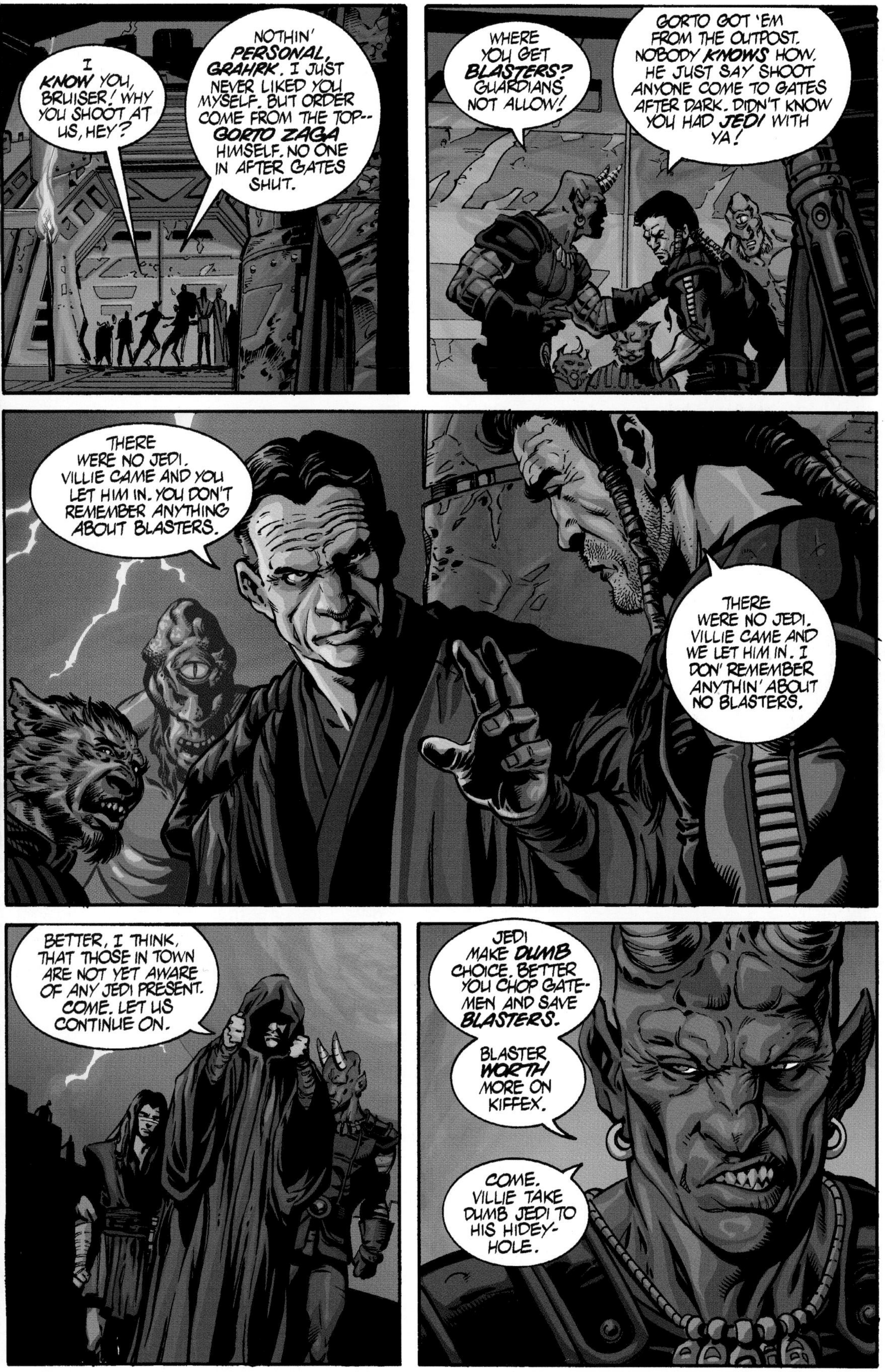
I KNOW YOU, BRUISER! WHY YOU SHOOT AT US, HEY?
NOTHIN' PERSONAL, GRAHRK. I JUST NEVER LIKED YOU MYSELF. BUT ORDER COME FROM THE TOP-- GORTO ZAGA HIMSELF. NO ONE IN AFTER GATES SHUT.
WHERE YOU GET BLASTERS? GUARDIANS NOT ALLOW!
GORTO GOT 'EM FROM THE OUTPOST. NOBODY KNOWS HOW. HE JUST SAY SHOOT ANYONE COME TO GATES AFTER DARK. DIDN'T KNOW YOU HAD JEDI WITH YA!
THERE WERE NO JEDI. VILLIE CAME AND YOU LET HIM IN. YOU DON'T REMEMBER ANYTHING ABOUT BLASTERS.
THERE WERE NO JEDI. VILLIE CAME AND WE LET HIM IN. I DON' REMEMBER ANYTHIN' ABOUT NO BLASTERS.
BETTER, I THINK, THAT THOSE IN TOWN ARE NOT YET AWARE OF ANY JEDI PRESENT. COME. LET US CONTINUE ON.
JEDI MAKE DUMB CHOICE. BETTER YOU CHOP GATE-MEN AND SAVE BLASTERS.
BLASTER WORTH MORE ON KIFFEX.
COME. VILLIE TAKE DUMB JEDI TO HIS HIDEY-HOLE.

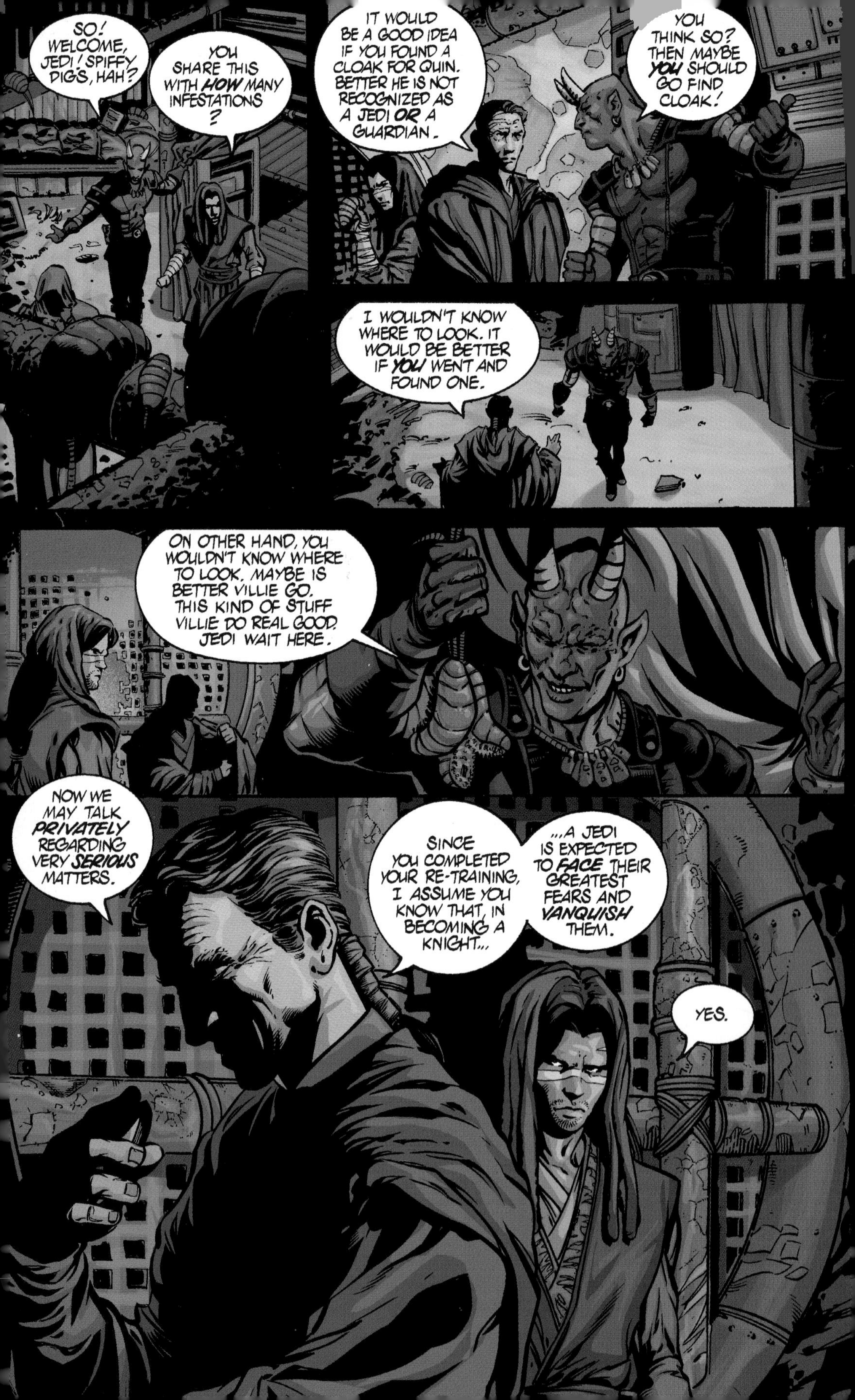
SO! WELCOME, JEDI! SPIFFY DIGS, HAH?
YOU SHARE THIS WITH HOW MANY INFESTATIONS?
IT WOULD BE A GOOD IDEA IF YOU FOUND A CLOAK FOR QUIN. BETTER HE IS NOT RECOGNIZED AS A JEDI OR A GUARDIAN.
YOU THINK SO? THEN MAYBE YOU SHOULD GO FIND CLOAK!
I WOULDN'T KNOW WHERE TO LOOK. IT WOULD BE BETTER IF YOU WENT AND FOUND ONE.
ON OTHER HAND, YOU WOULDN'T KNOW WHERE TO LOOK. MAYBE IS BETTER VILLIE GO. THIS KIND OF STUFF VILLIE DO REAL GOOD. JEDI WAIT HERE.
NOW WE MAY TALK PRIVATELY REGARDING VERY SERIOUS MATTERS.
SINCE YOU COMPLETED YOUR RE-TRAINING, I ASSUME YOU KNOW THAT, IN BECOMING A KNIGHT...
...A JEDI IS EXPECTED TO FACE THEIR GREATEST FEARS AND VANQUISH THEM.
YES.

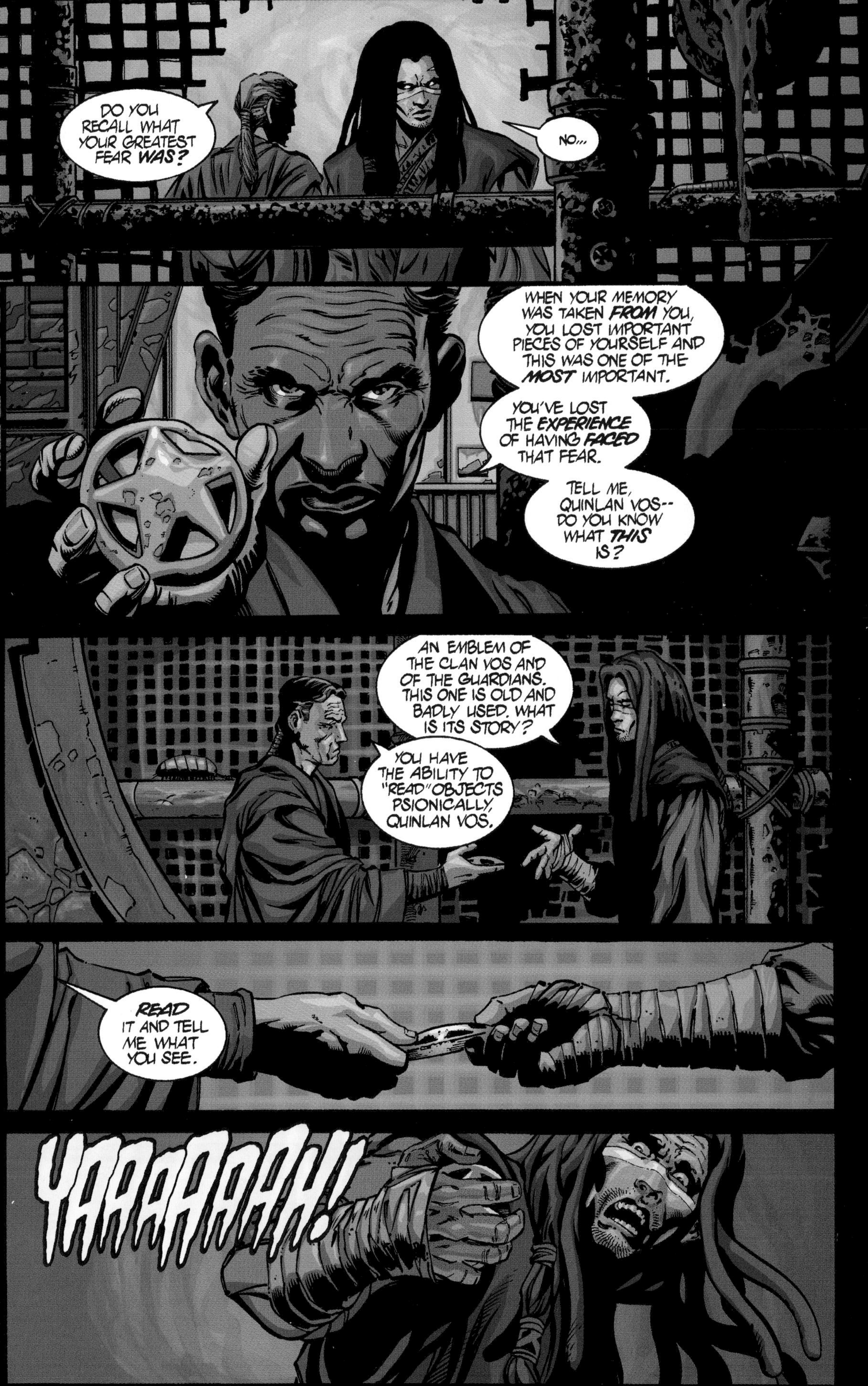
DO YOU RECALL WHAT YOUR GREATEST FEAR WAS?
NO...
WHEN YOUR MEMORY WAS TAKEN FROM YOU, YOU LOST IMPORTANT PIECES OF YOURSELF AND THIS WAS ONE OF THE MOST IMPORTANT.
YOU'VE LOST THE EXPERIENCE OF HAVING FACED THAT FEAR.
TELL ME, QUINLAN VOS-- DO YOU KNOW WHAT THIS IS?
AN EMBLEM OF THE CLAN VOS AND OF THE GUARDIANS. THIS ONE IS OLD AND BADLY USED. WHAT IS ITS STORY?
YOU HAVE THE ABILITY TO "READ" OBJECTS PSIONICALLY, QUINLAN VOS.
READ IT AND TELL ME WHAT YOU SEE.
YAAAAAAAH!

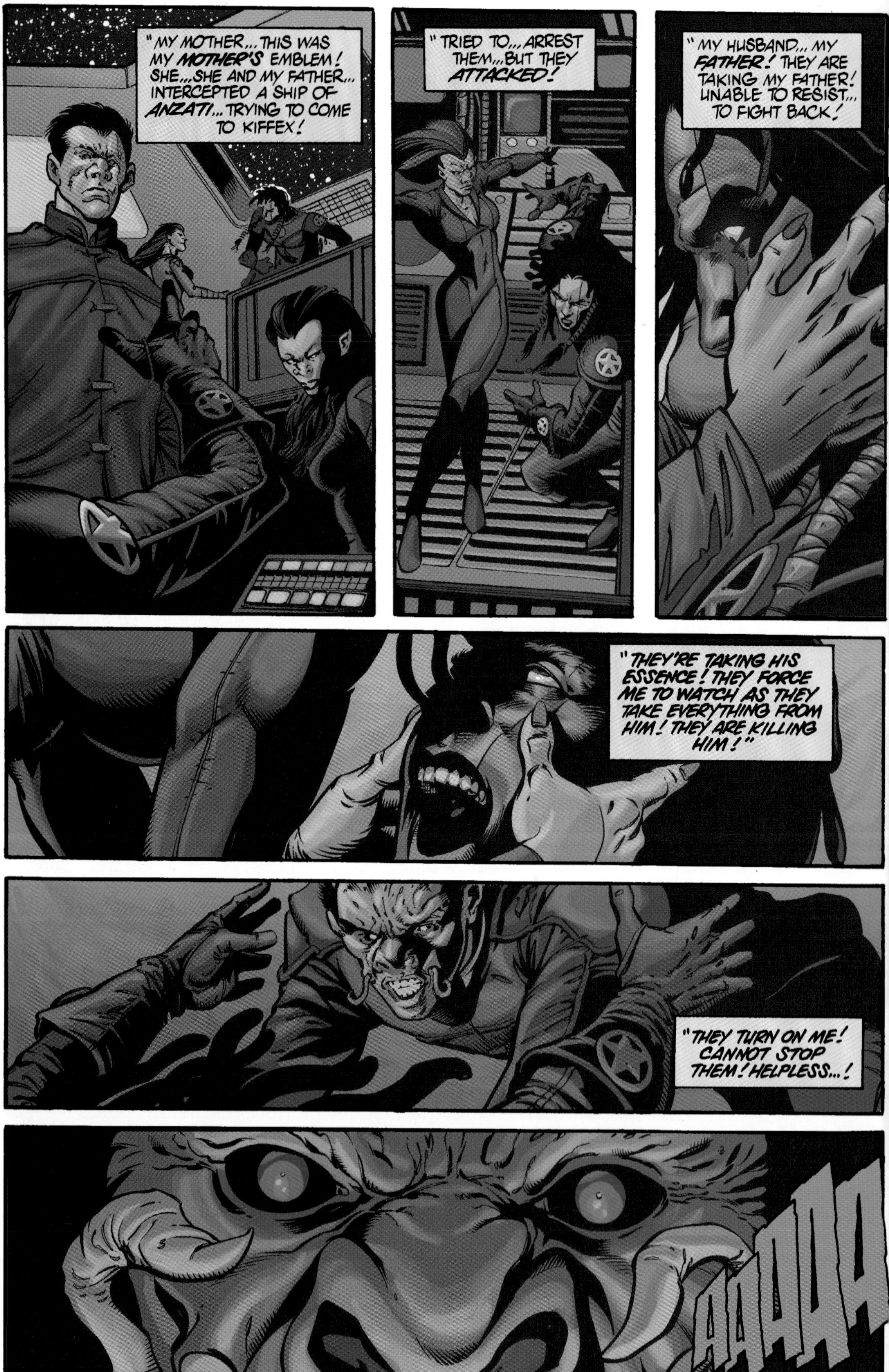
"MY MOTHER... THIS WAS MY MOTHER'S EMBLEM! SHE... SHE AND MY FATHER... INTERCEPTED A SHIP OF ANZATI... TRYING TO COME TO KIFFEX!
"TRIED TO... ARREST THEM... BUT THEY ATTACKED!
"MY HUSBAND... MY FATHER! THEY ARE TAKING MY FATHER! UNABLE TO RESIST... TO FIGHT BACK!
"THEY'RE TAKING HIS ESSENCE! THEY FORCE ME TO WATCH AS THEY TAKE EVERYTHING FROM HIM! THEY ARE KILLING HIM!"
"THEY TURN ON ME! CANNOT STOP THEM! HELPLESS...!
AAAAA

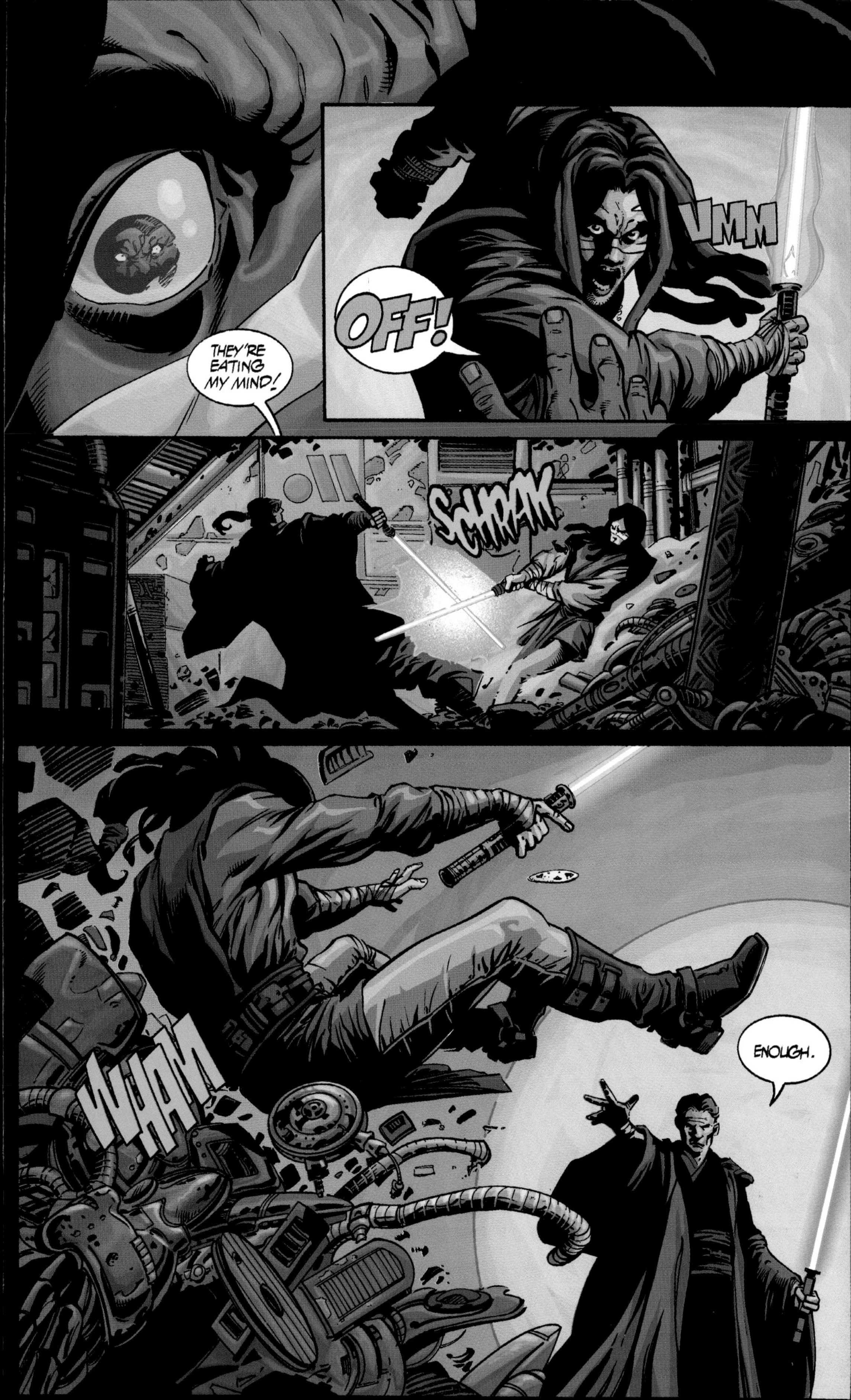
THEY'RE EATING MY MIND!
OFF!
UMM
SCHRAK
WHAM
ENOUGH.

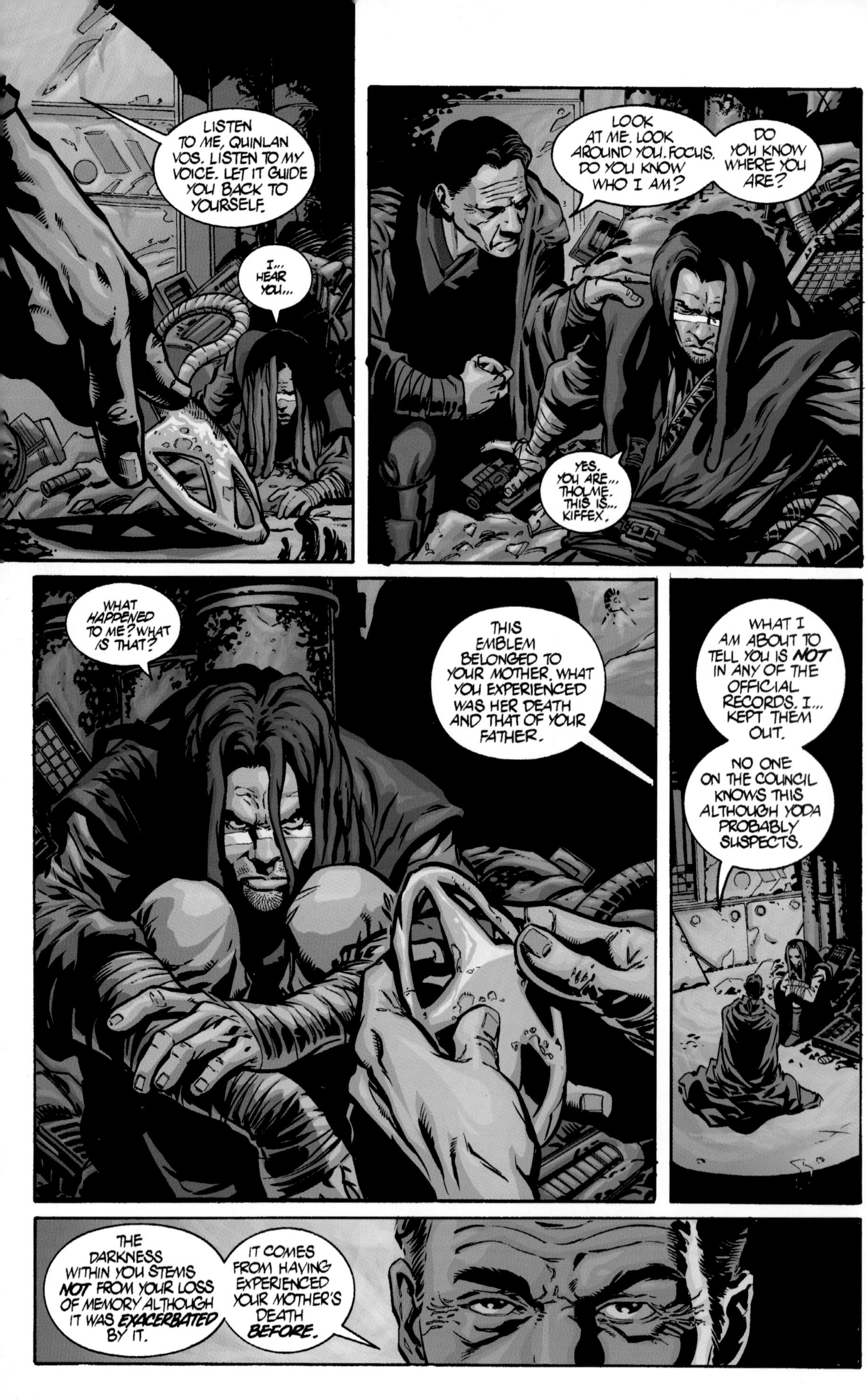
LISTEN TO ME, QUINLAN VOS. LISTEN TO MY VOICE. LET IT GUIDE YOU BACK TO YOURSELF.
I... HEAR YOU...
LOOK AT ME. LOOK AROUND YOU. FOCUS. DO YOU KNOW WHO I AM?
DO YOU KNOW WHERE YOU ARE?
YES. YOU ARE... THOLME. THIS IS... KIFFEX.
WHAT HAPPENED TO ME? WHAT IS THAT?
THIS EMBLEM BELONGED TO YOUR MOTHER. WHAT YOU EXPERIENCED WAS HER DEATH AND THAT OF YOUR FATHER.
WHAT I AM ABOUT TO TELL YOU IS NOT IN ANY OF THE OFFICIAL RECORDS. I... KEPT THEM OUT.
NO ONE ON THE COUNCIL KNOWS THIS ALTHOUGH YODA PROBABLY SUSPECTS.
THE DARKNESS WITHIN YOU STEMS NOT FROM YOUR LOSS OF MEMORY ALTHOUGH IT WAS EXACERBATED BY IT.
IT COMES FROM HAVING EXPERIENCED YOUR MOTHER'S DEATH BEFORE.

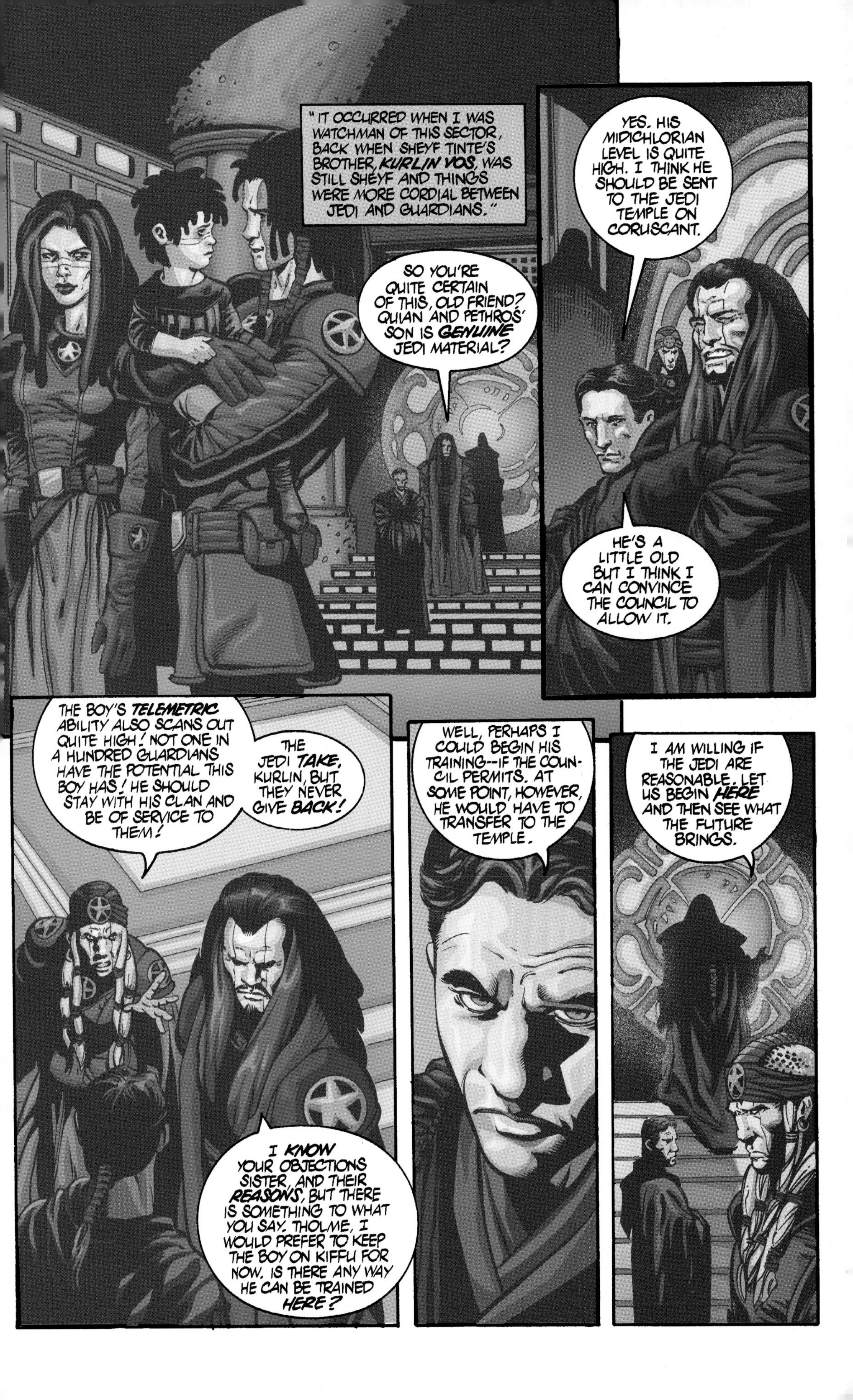
"IT OCCURRED WHEN I WAS WATCHMAN OF THIS SECTOR, BACK WHEN SHEYF TINTE'S BROTHER, KURLIN VOS, WAS STILL SHEYF AND THINGS WERE MORE CORDIAL BETWEEN JEDI AND GUARDIANS."
SO YOU'RE QUITE CERTAIN OF THIS, OLD FRIEND? QUIAN AND PETHROS' SON IS GENUINE JEDI MATERIAL?
YES. HIS MIDICHLORIAN LEVEL IS QUITE HIGH. I THINK HE SHOULD BE SENT TO THE JEDI TEMPLE ON CORUSCANT.
HE'S A LITTLE OLD BUT I THINK I CAN CONVINCE THE COUNCIL TO ALLOW IT.
THE BOY'S TELEMETRIC ABILITY ALSO SCANS OUT QUITE HIGH! NOT ONE IN A HUNDRED GUARDIANS HAVE THE POTENTIAL THIS BOY HAS! HE SHOULD STAY WITH HIS CLAN AND BE OF SERVICE TO THEM!
THE JEDI TAKE, KURLIN, BUT THEY NEVER GIVE BACK!
I KNOW YOUR OBJECTIONS SISTER, AND THEIR REASONS, BUT THERE IS SOMETHING TO WHAT YOU SAY. THOLME, I WOULD PREFER TO KEEP THE BOY ON KIFFU FOR NOW. IS THERE ANY WAY HE CAN BE TRAINED HERE?
WELL, PERHAPS I COULD BEGIN HIS TRAINING--IF THE COUNCIL PERMITS. AT SOME POINT, HOWEVER, HE WOULD HAVE TO TRANSFER TO THE TEMPLE.
I AM WILLING IF THE JEDI ARE REASONABLE. LET US BEGIN HERE AND THEN SEE WHAT THE FUTURE BRINGS.

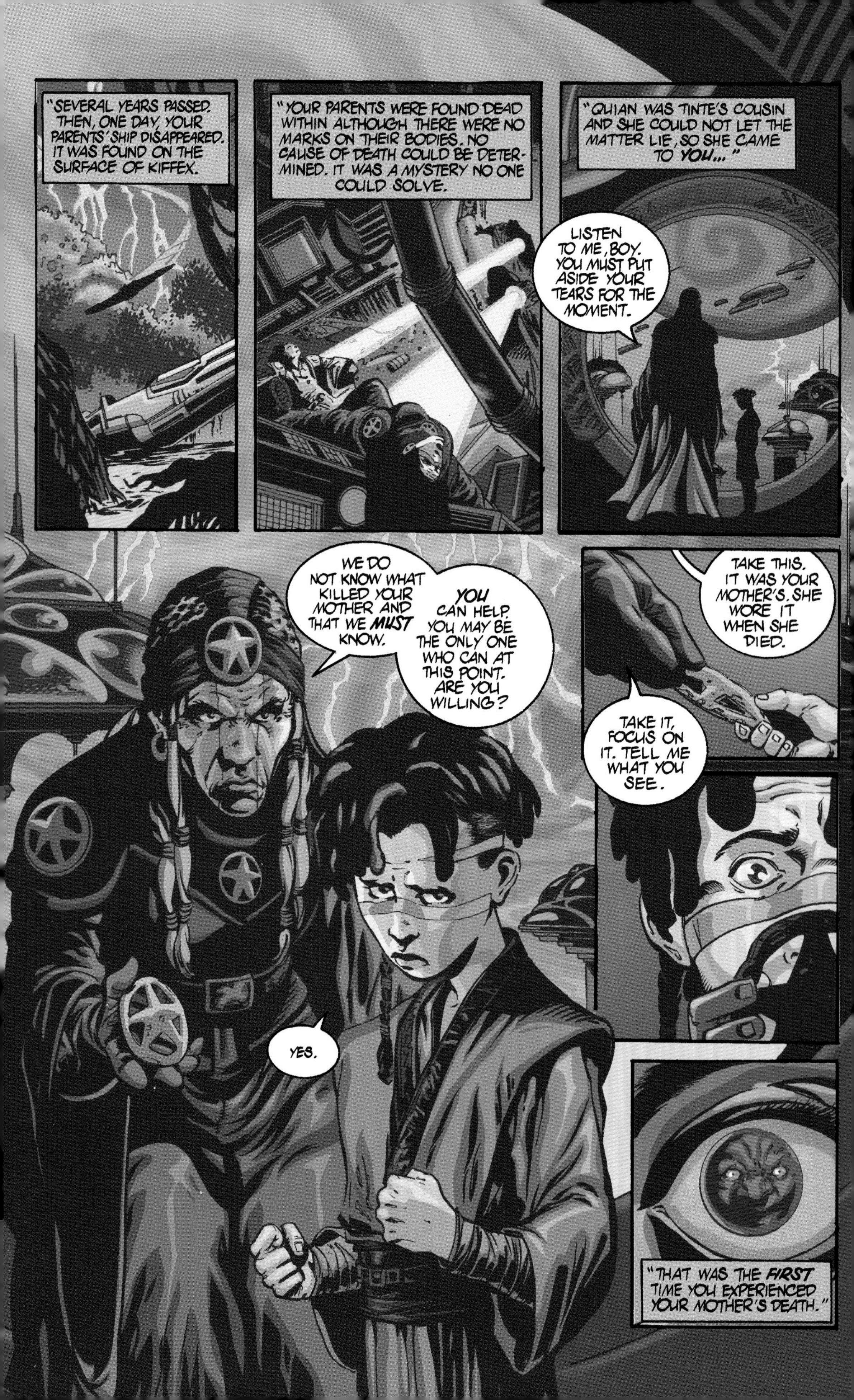
"SEVERAL YEARS PASSED. THEN, ONE DAY, YOUR PARENTS' SHIP DISAPPEARED. IT WAS FOUND ON THE SURFACE OF KIFFEX.
"YOUR PARENTS WERE FOUND DEAD WITHIN ALTHOUGH THERE WERE NO MARKS ON THEIR BODIES. NO CAUSE OF DEATH COULD BE DETERMINED. IT WAS A MYSTERY NO ONE COULD SOLVE.
"QUIAN WAS TINTE'S COUSIN AND SHE COULD NOT LET THE MATTER LIE, SO SHE CAME TO YOU..."
LISTEN TO ME, BOY. YOU MUST PUT ASIDE YOUR TEARS FOR THE MOMENT.
WE DO NOT KNOW WHAT KILLED YOUR MOTHER AND THAT WE MUST KNOW.
YOU CAN HELP. YOU MAY BE THE ONLY ONE WHO CAN AT THIS POINT. ARE YOU WILLING?
YES.
TAKE THIS. IT WAS YOUR MOTHER'S. SHE WORE IT WHEN SHE DIED.
TAKE IT, FOCUS ON IT. TELL ME WHAT YOU SEE.
"THAT WAS THE FIRST TIME YOU EXPERIENCED YOUR MOTHER'S DEATH."

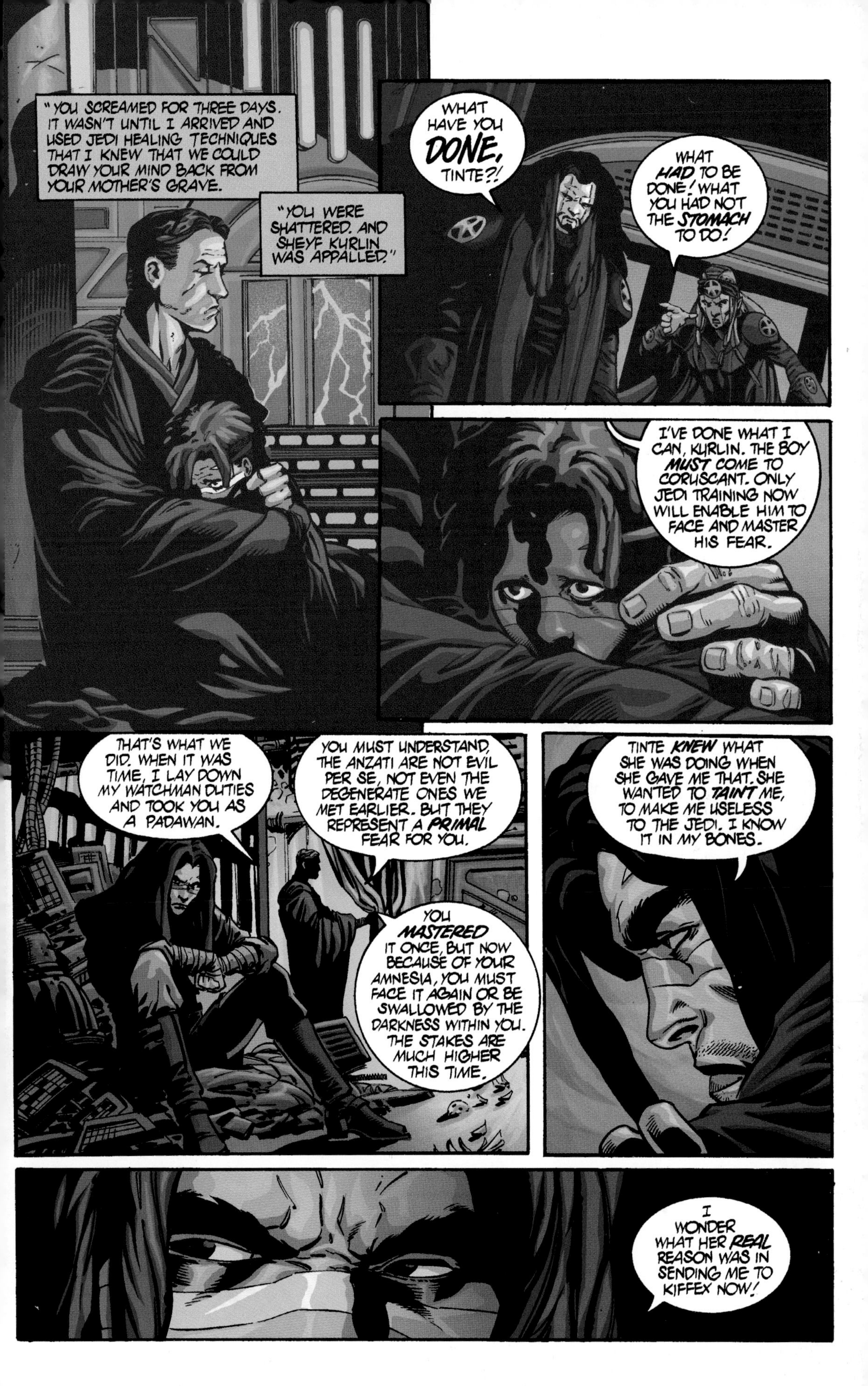
"YOU SCREAMED FOR THREE DAYS. IT WASN'T UNTIL I ARRIVED AND USED JEDI HEALING TECHNIQUES THAT I KNEW THAT WE COULD DRAW YOUR MIND BACK FROM YOUR MOTHER'S GRAVE.
"YOU WERE SHATTERED. AND SHEYF KURLIN WAS APPALLED."
WHAT HAVE YOU DONE, TINTE?!
WHAT HAD TO BE DONE! WHAT YOU HAD NOT THE STOMACH TO DO!
I'VE DONE WHAT I CAN, KURLIN. THE BOY MUST COME TO CORUSCANT. ONLY JEDI TRAINING NOW WILL ENABLE HIM TO FACE AND MASTER HIS FEAR.
THAT'S WHAT WE DID. WHEN IT WAS TIME, I LAY DOWN MY WATCHMAN DUTIES AND TOOK YOU AS A PADAWAN.
YOU MUST UNDERSTAND, THE ANZATI ARE NOT EVIL PER SE, NOT EVEN THE DEGENERATE ONES WE MET EARLIER. BUT THEY REPRESENT A PRIMAL FEAR FOR YOU.
YOU MASTERED IT ONCE, BUT NOW BECAUSE OF YOUR AMNESIA, YOU MUST FACE IT AGAIN OR BE SWALLOWED BY THE DARKNESS WITHIN YOU. THE STAKES ARE MUCH HIGHER THIS TIME.
TINTE KNEW WHAT SHE WAS DOING WHEN SHE GAVE ME THAT. SHE WANTED TO TAINT ME, TO MAKE ME USELESS TO THE JEDI. I KNOW IT IN MY BONES.
I WONDER WHAT HER REAL REASON WAS IN SENDING ME TO KIFFEX NOW!

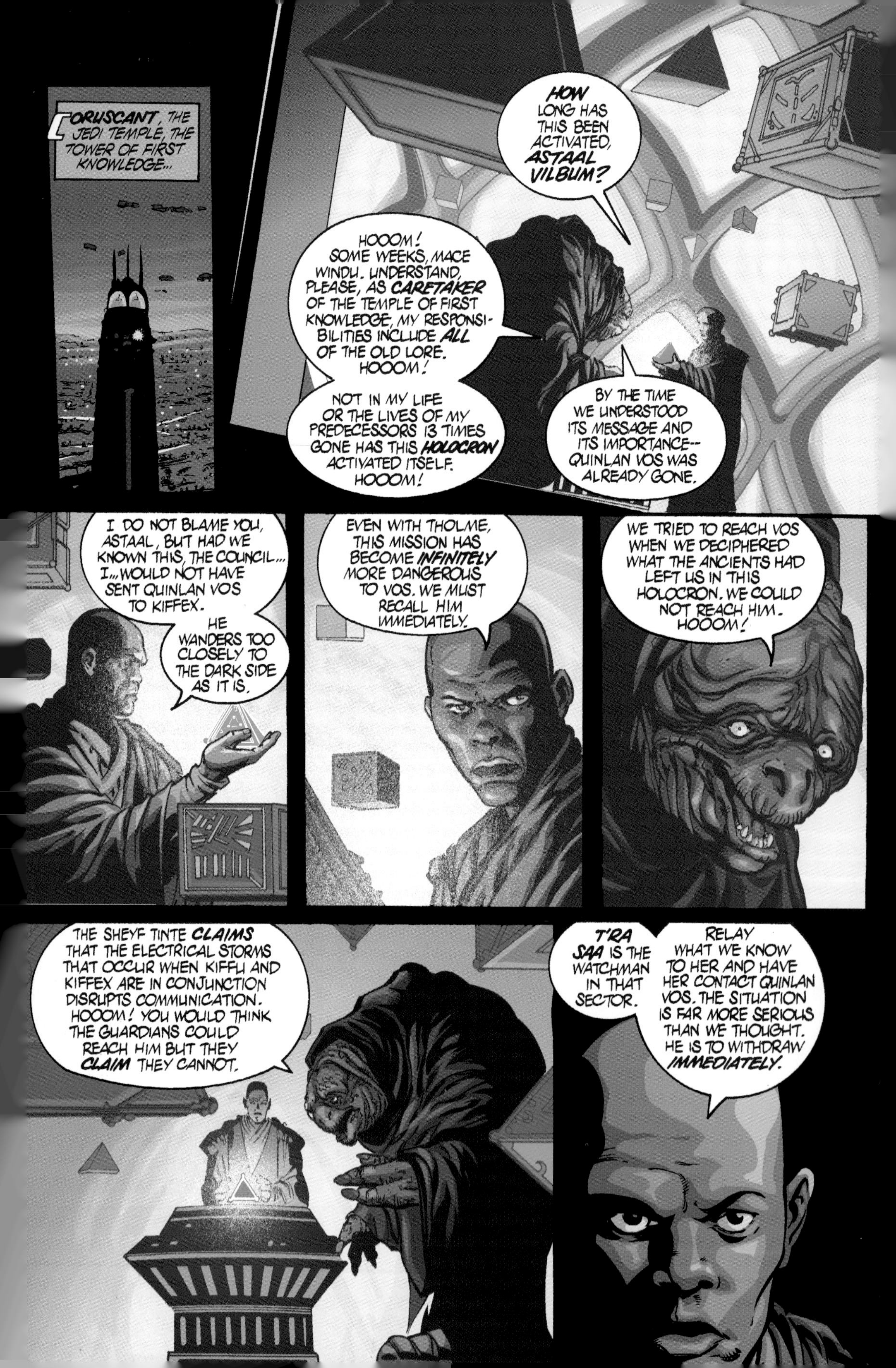
CORUSCANT, THE JEDI TEMPLE, THE TOWER OF FIRST KNOWLEDGE...
HOW LONG HAS THIS BEEN ACTIVATED, ASTAAL VILBUM?
HOOOM! SOME WEEKS, MACE WINDU. UNDERSTAND, PLEASE, AS CARETAKER OF THE TEMPLE OF FIRST KNOWLEDGE, MY RESPONSIBILITIES INCLUDE ALL OF THE OLD LORE. HOOOM!
NOT IN MY LIFE OR THE LIVES OF MY PREDECESSORS 13 TIMES GONE HAS THIS HOLOCRON ACTIVATED ITSELF. HOOOM!
BY THE TIME WE UNDERSTOOD ITS MESSAGE AND ITS IMPORTANCE-- QUINLAN VOS WAS ALREADY GONE.
I DO NOT BLAME YOU, ASTAAL, BUT HAD WE KNOWN THIS, THE COUNCIL... I...WOULD NOT HAVE SENT QUINLAN VOS TO KIFFEX.
HE WANDERS TOO CLOSELY TO THE DARK SIDE AS IT IS.
EVEN WITH THOLME, THIS MISSION HAS BECOME INFINITELY MORE DANGEROUS TO VOS. WE MUST RECALL HIM IMMEDIATELY.
WE TRIED TO REACH VOS WHEN WE DECIPHERED WHAT THE ANCIENTS HAD LEFT US IN THIS HOLOCRON. WE COULD NOT REACH HIM. HOOOM!
THE SHEYF TINTE CLAIMS THAT THE ELECTRICAL STORMS THAT OCCUR WHEN KIFFU AND KIFFEX ARE IN CONJUNCTION DISRUPTS COMMUNICATION. HOOOM! YOU WOULD THINK THE GUARDIANS COULD REACH HIM BUT THEY CLAIM THEY CANNOT.
T'RA SAA IS THE WATCHMAN IN THAT SECTOR.
RELAY WHAT WE KNOW TO HER AND HAVE HER CONTACT QUINLAN VOS. THE SITUATION IS FAR MORE SERIOUS THAN WE THOUGHT. HE IS TO WITHDRAW IMMEDIATELY.

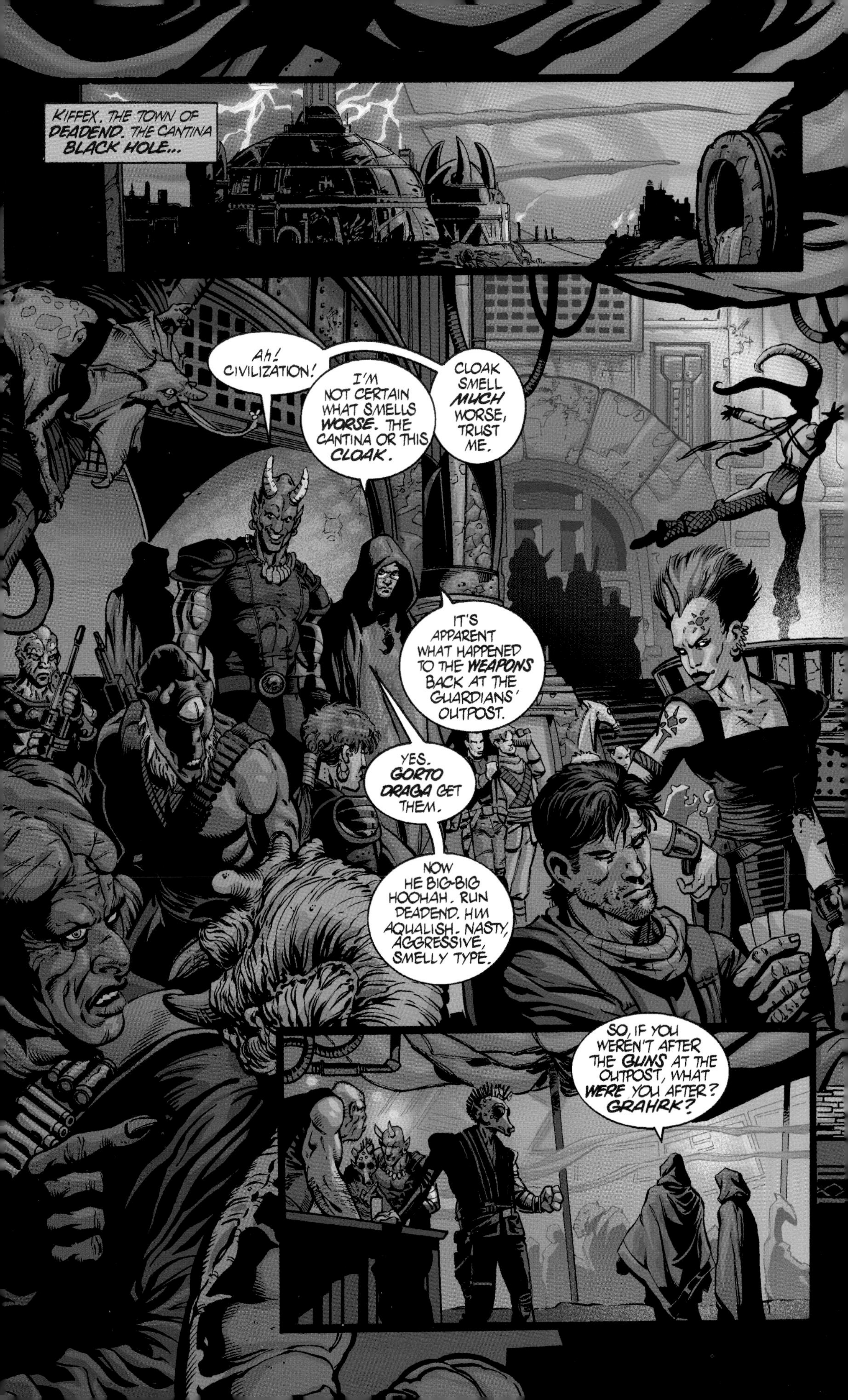
KIFFEX. THE TOWN OF DEADEND. THE CANTINA BLACK HOLE...
Ah! CIVILIZATION!
I'M NOT CERTAIN WHAT SMELLS WORSE. THE CANTINA OR THIS CLOAK.
CLOAK SMELL MUCH WORSE, TRUST ME.
IT'S APPARENT WHAT HAPPENED TO THE WEAPONS BACK AT THE GUARDIANS' OUTPOST.
YES. GORTO DRAGA GET THEM.
NOW HE BIG-BIG HOOHAH. RUN DEADEND. HIM AQUALISH. NASTY, AGGRESSIVE, SMELLY TYPE.
SO, IF YOU WEREN'T AFTER THE GUNS AT THE OUTPOST, WHAT WERE YOU AFTER? GRAHRK?

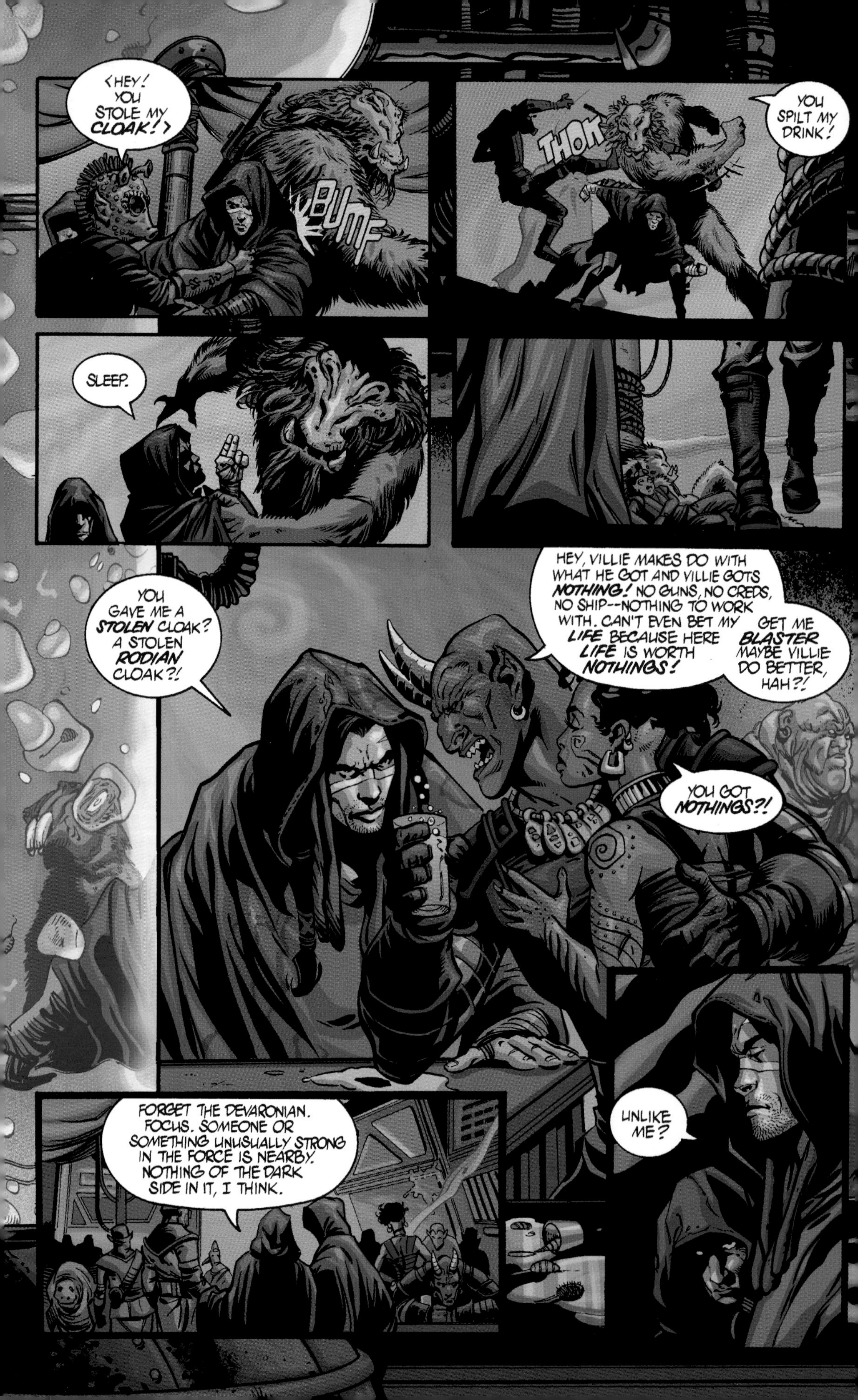
<HEY! YOU STOLE MY CLOAK!>
BUMF
THOK
YOU SPILT MY DRINK!
SLEEP.
YOU GAVE ME A STOLEN CLOAK? A STOLEN RODIAN CLOAK?!
HEY, VILLIE MAKES DO WITH WHAT HE GOT AND VILLIE GOTS NOTHING! NO GUNS, NO CREDS, NO SHIP--NOTHING TO WORK WITH. CAN'T EVEN BET MY LIFE BECAUSE HERE LIFE IS WORTH NOTHINGS!
GET ME BLASTER MAYBE VILLIE DO BETTER, HAH?!
YOU GOT NOTHINGS?!
FORGET THE DEVARONIAN. FOCUS. SOMEONE OR SOMETHING UNUSUALLY STRONG IN THE FORCE IS NEARBY. NOTHING OF THE DARK SIDE IN IT, I THINK.
UNLIKE ME?

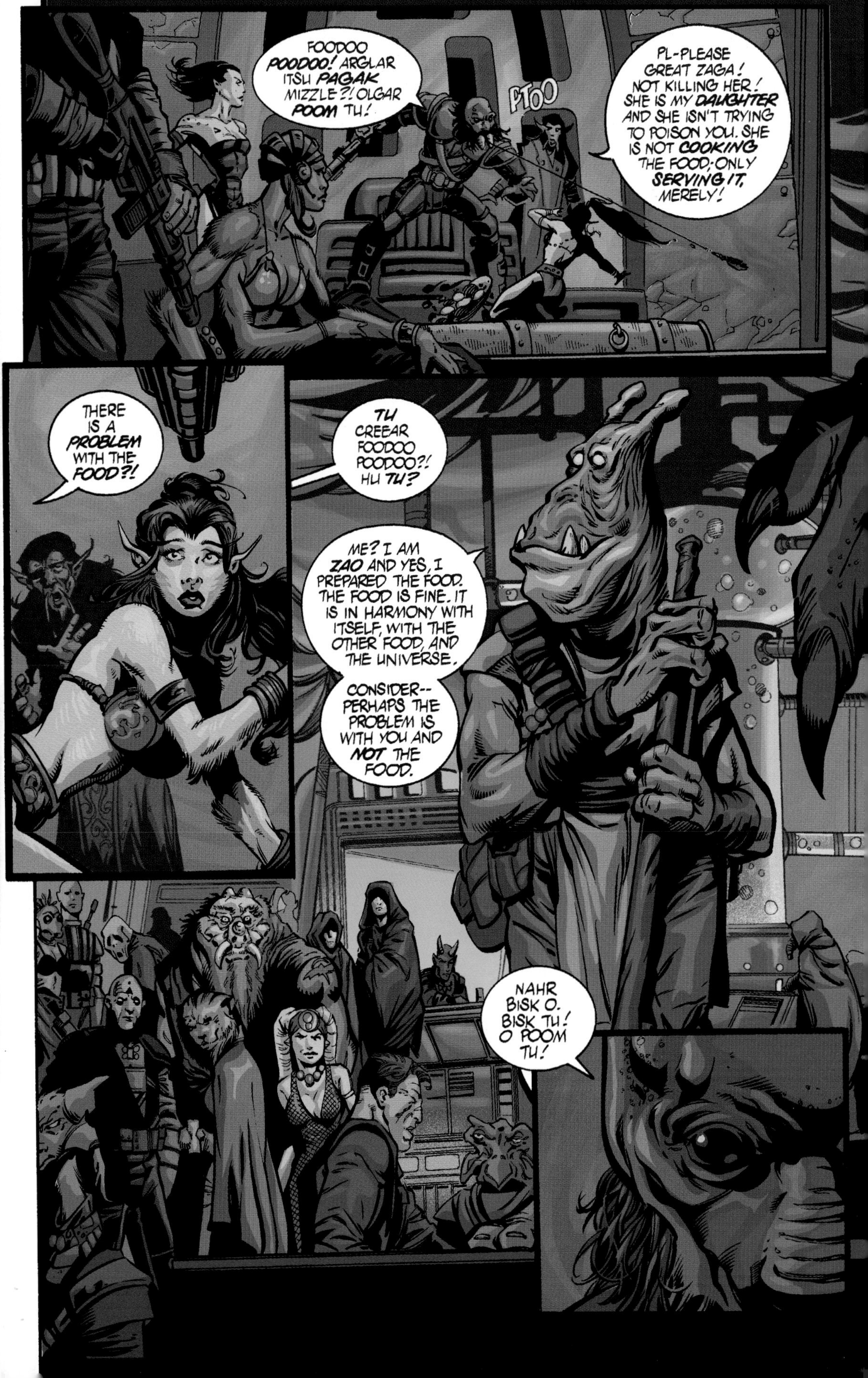
FOODOO POODOO! ARGLAR ITSU PAGAK MIZZLE?! OLGAR POOM TU!
PTOO
PL-PLEASE GREAT ZAGA! NOT KILLING HER! SHE IS MY DAUGHTER AND SHE ISN'T TRYING TO POISON YOU. SHE IS NOT COOKING THE FOOD; ONLY SERVING IT, MERELY!
THERE IS A PROBLEM WITH THE FOOD?!
TU CREEAR FOODOO POODOO?! HU TU?
ME? I AM ZAO AND YES, I PREPARED THE FOOD. THE FOOD IS FINE. IT IS IN HARMONY WITH ITSELF, WITH THE OTHER FOOD, AND THE UNIVERSE.
CONSIDER-- PERHAPS THE PROBLEM IS WITH YOU AND NOT THE FOOD.
NAHR BISK O. BISK TU! O POOM TU!

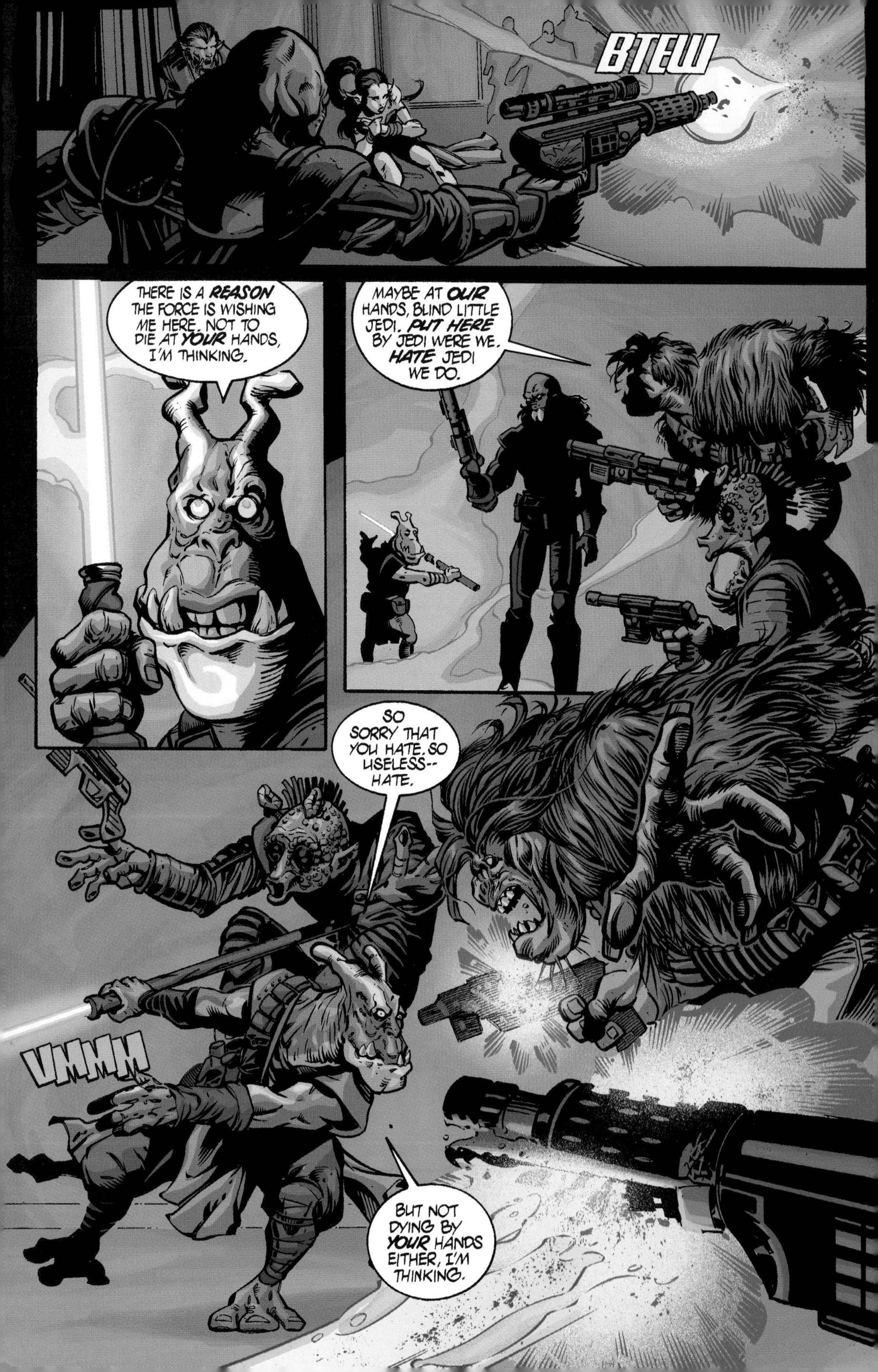
BTEW
THERE IS A REASON THE FORCE IS WISHING ME HERE. NOT TO DIE AT YOUR HANDS, I'M THINKING.
MAYBE AT OUR HANDS, BLIND LITTLE JEDI. PUT HERE BY JEDI WERE WE. HATE JEDI WE DO.
SO SORRY THAT YOU HATE. SO USELESS-- HATE.
UMMM
BUT NOT DYING BY YOUR HANDS EITHER, I'M THINKING.

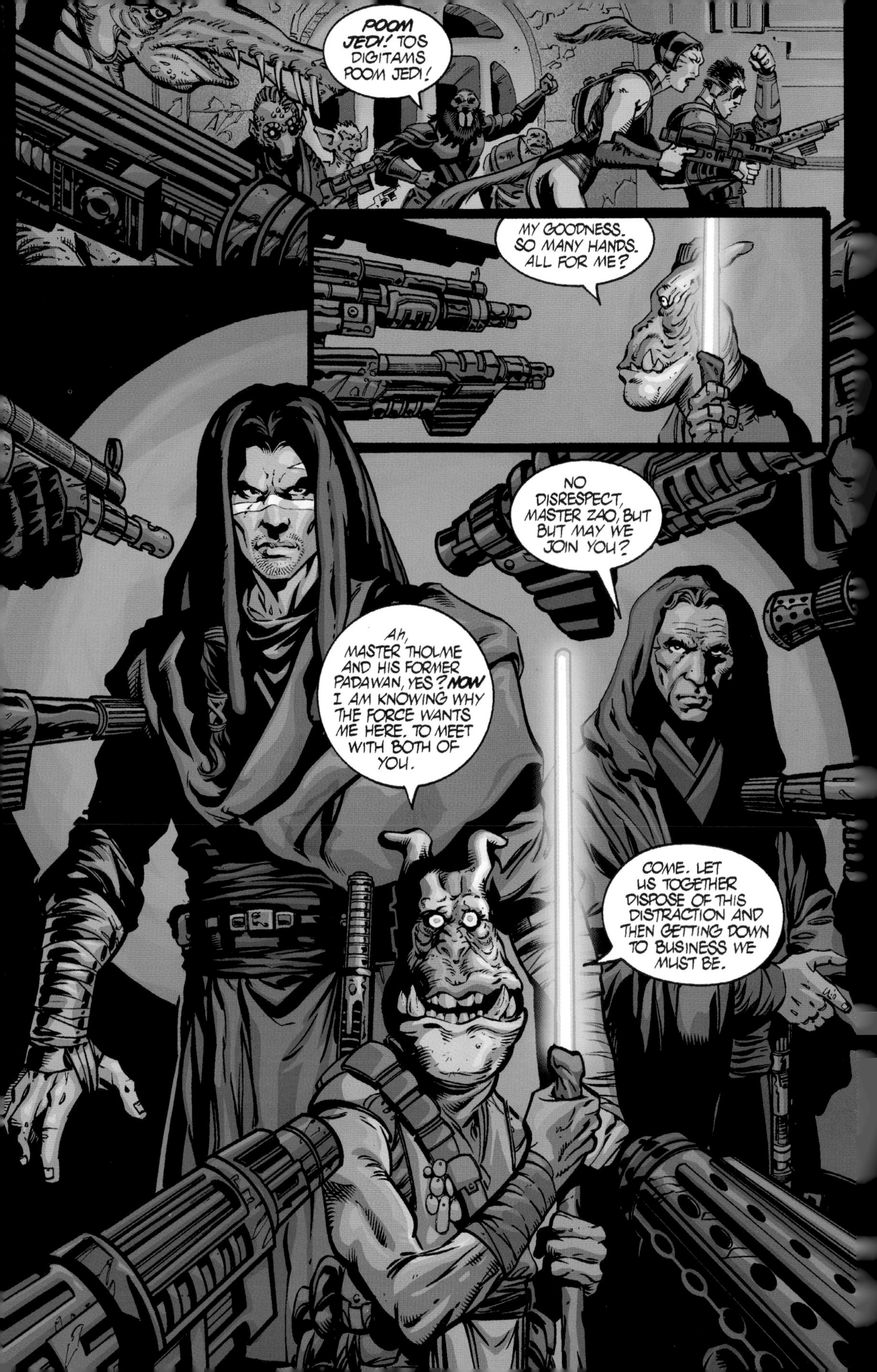
POOM JEDI! TOS DIGITAMS POOM JEDI!
MY GOODNESS. SO MANY HANDS. ALL FOR ME?
NO DISRESPECT, MASTER ZAO, BUT BUT MAY WE JOIN YOU?
Ah, MASTER THOLME AND HIS FORMER PADAWAN, YES? NOW I AM KNOWING WHY THE FORCE WANTS ME HERE. TO MEET WITH BOTH OF YOU.
COME. LET US TOGETHER DISPOSE OF THIS DISTRACTION AND THEN GETTING DOWN TO BUSINESS WE MUST BE.

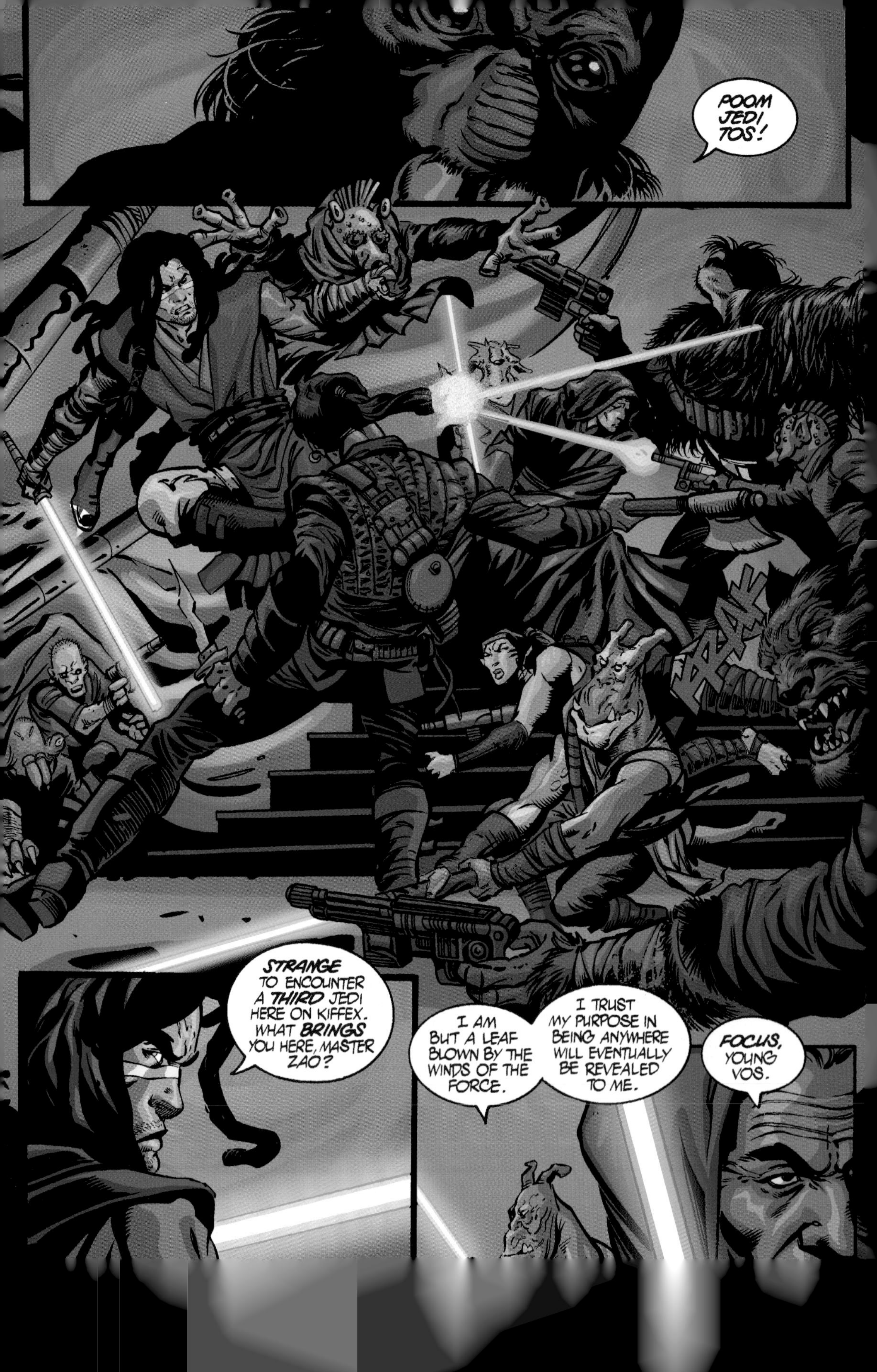
POOM JEDI TOS!
STRANGE TO ENCOUNTER A THIRD JEDI HERE ON KIFFEX. WHAT BRINGS YOU HERE, MASTER ZAO?
I AM BUT A LEAF BLOWN BY THE WINDS OF THE FORCE.
I TRUST MY PURPOSE IN BEING ANYWHERE WILL EVENTUALLY BE REVEALED TO ME.
FOCUS, YOUNG VOS.

THESE SHOULD HARDLY BE A THREAT TO *ONE* JEDI, LET ALONE *THREE*.

BTEW

THIS IS NOT THE *TRUE* BATTLE!

VMMM

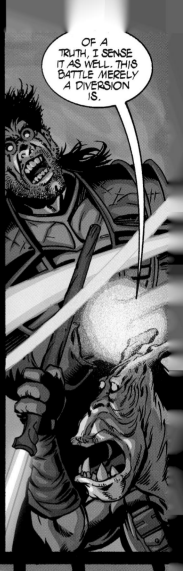

OF A TRUTH, I SENSE IT AS WELL. THIS BATTLE MERELY A DIVERSION IS.

"A GREAT EVIL APPROACHES."

SNUF!

?!

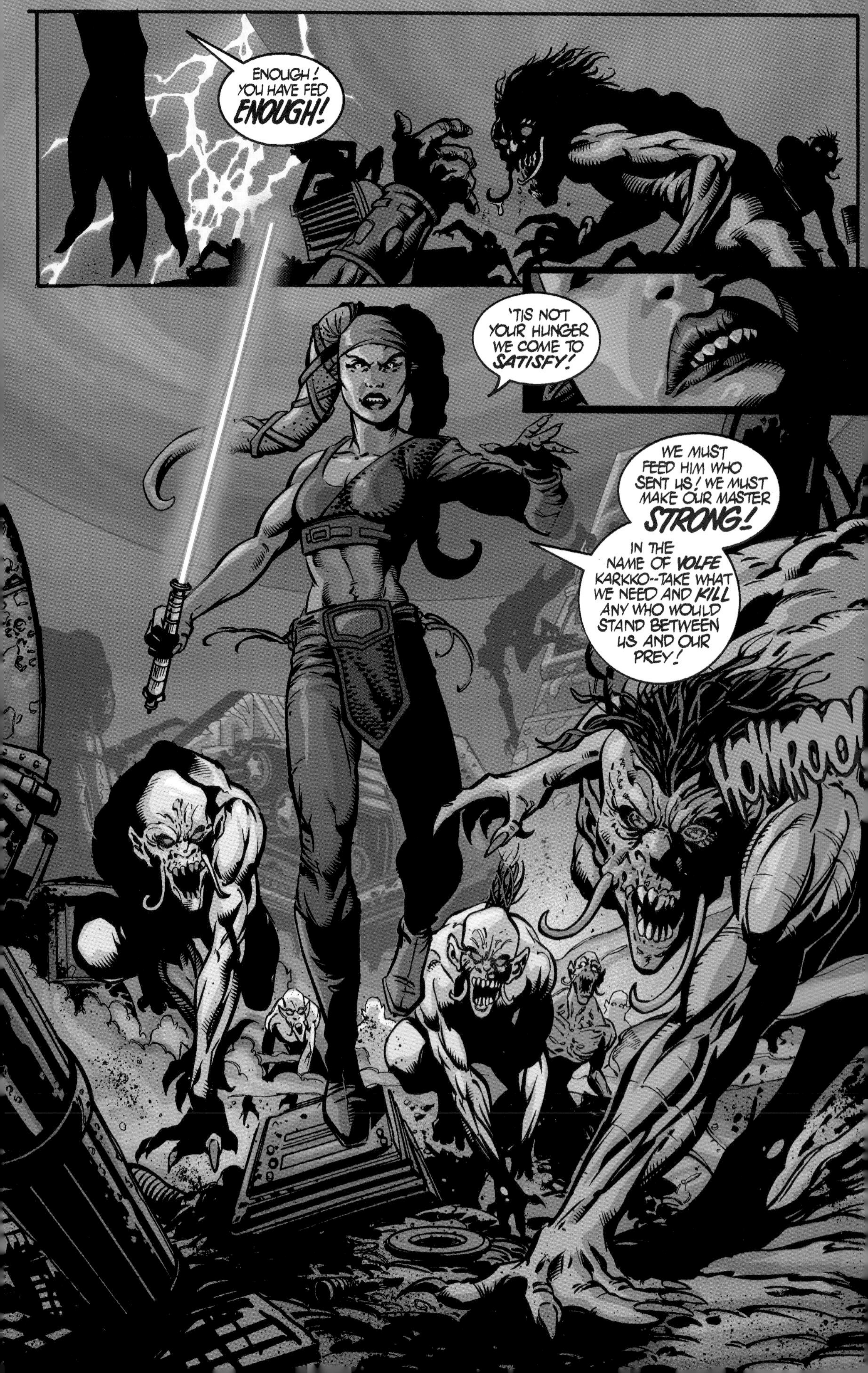
ENOUGH! YOU HAVE FED ENOUGH!
'TIS NOT YOUR HUNGER WE COME TO SATISFY!
WE MUST FEED HIM WHO SENT US! WE MUST MAKE OUR MASTER STRONG!
IN THE NAME OF VOLFE KARKKO--TAKE WHAT WE NEED AND KILL ANY WHO WOULD STAND BETWEEN US AND OUR PREY!
HOWROOO!

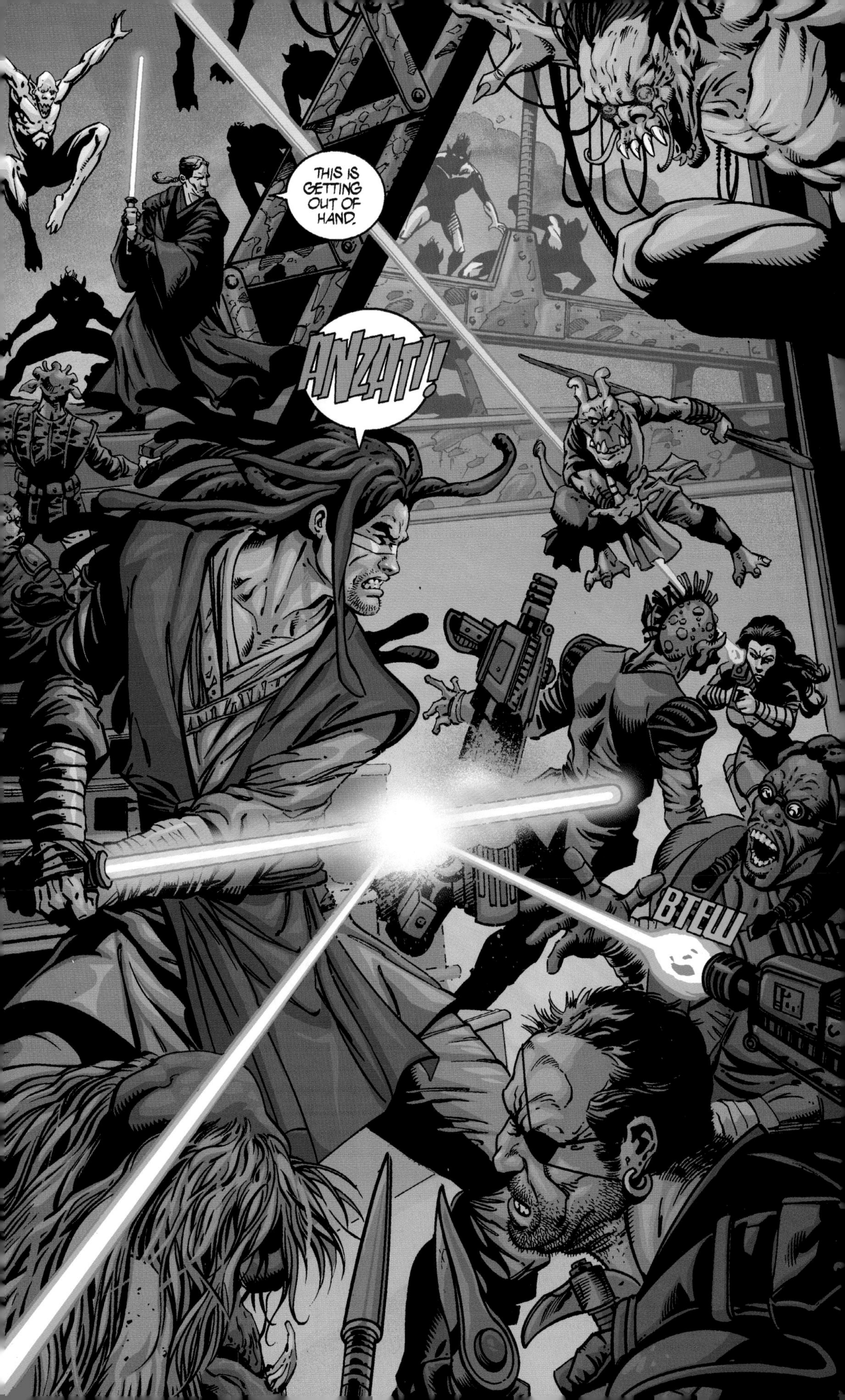
THIS IS GETTING OUT OF HAND.
ANZATI!
BTEW

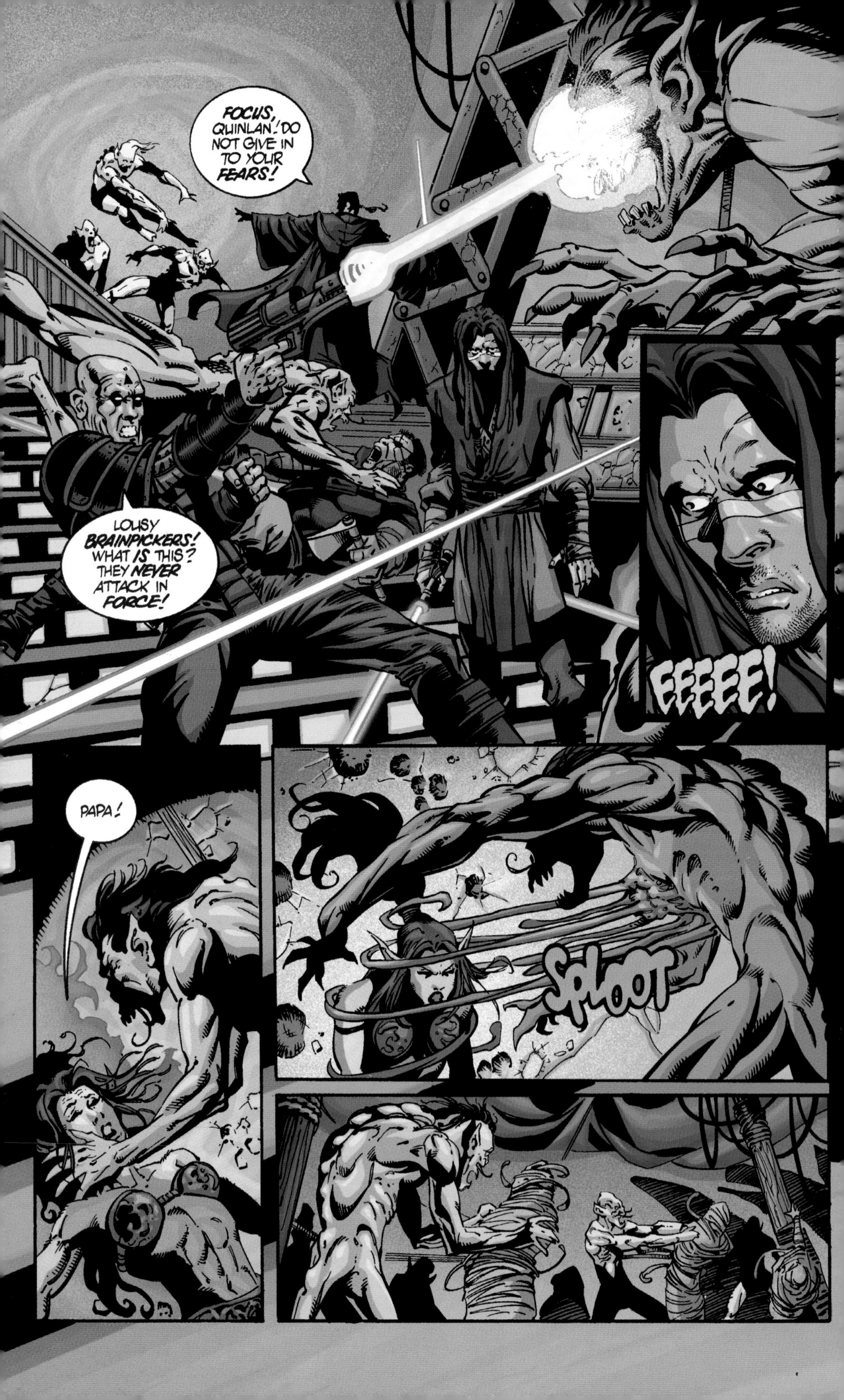
FOCUS, QUINLAN! DO NOT GIVE IN TO YOUR FEARS!
LOUSY BRAINPICKERS! WHAT IS THIS? THEY NEVER ATTACK IN FORCE!
EEEEE!
PAPA!
SPLOOT

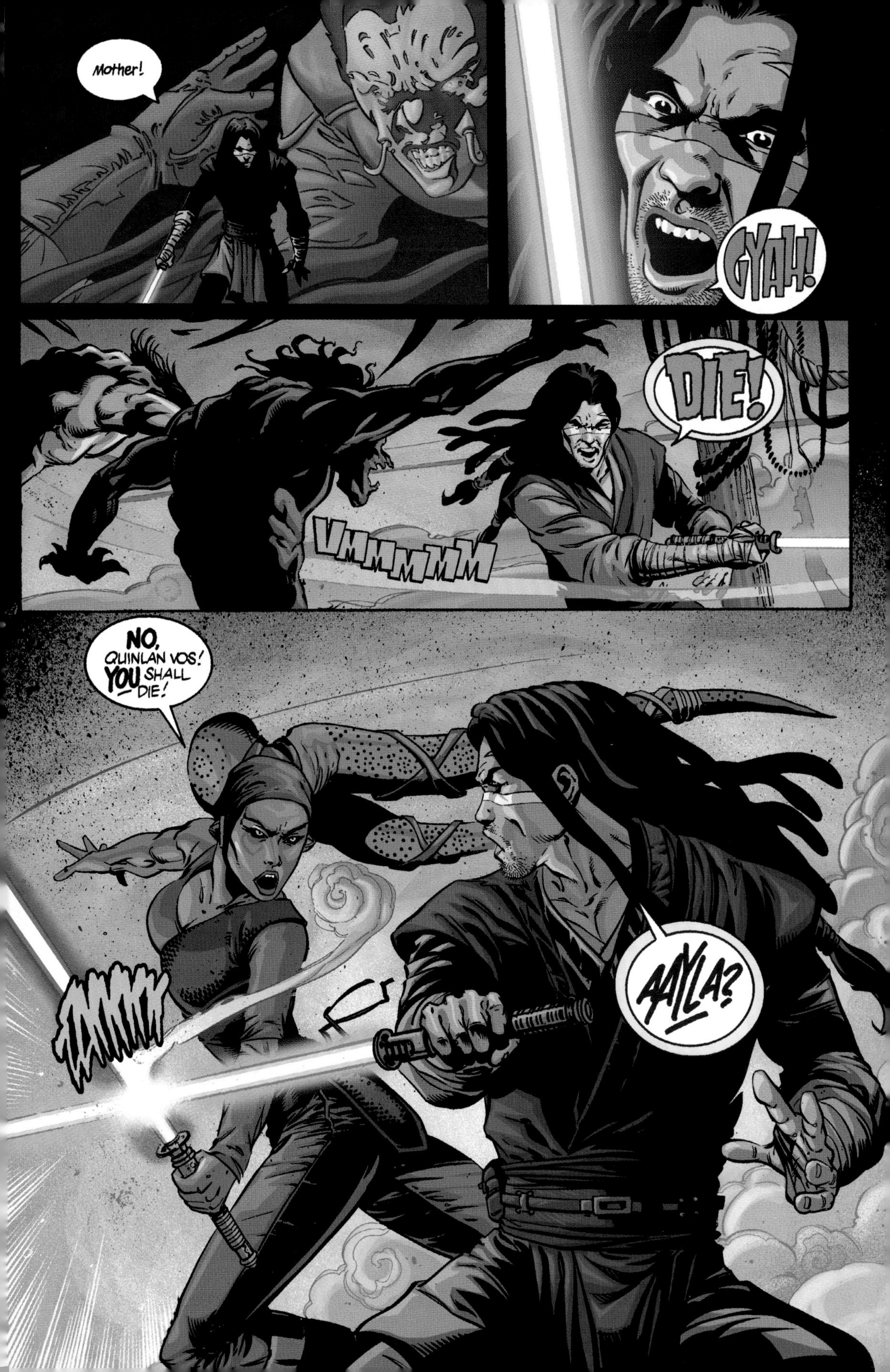
Mother!
GYAH!
DIE!
VMMMMMM
NO, QUINLAN VOS! YOU SHALL DIE!
AAYLA?

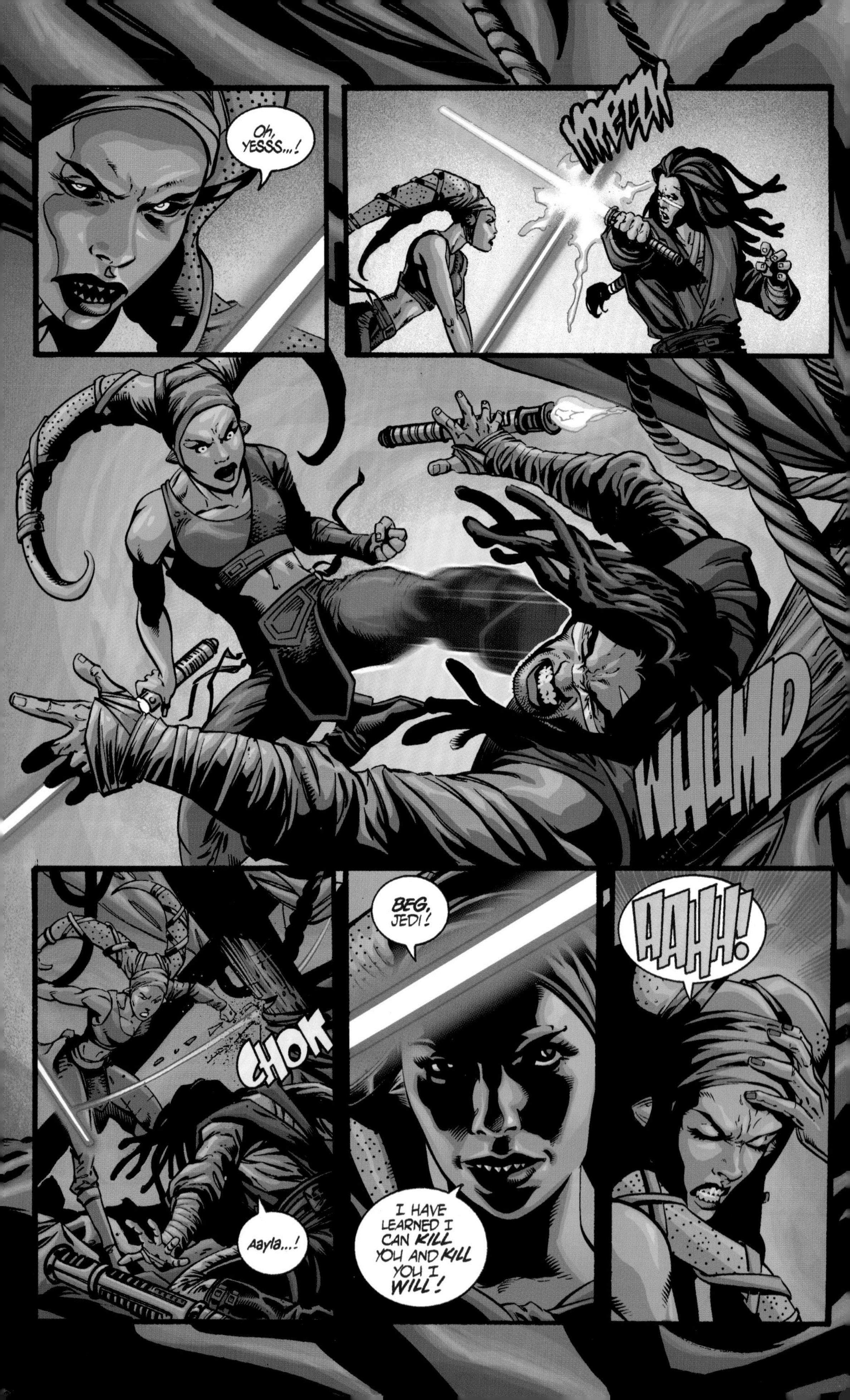
Oh, YESSS...!
WHEEOW
WHUMP
CHOK
Aayla...!
BEG, JEDI!
I HAVE LEARNED I CAN KILL YOU AND KILL YOU I WILL!
AAHH!

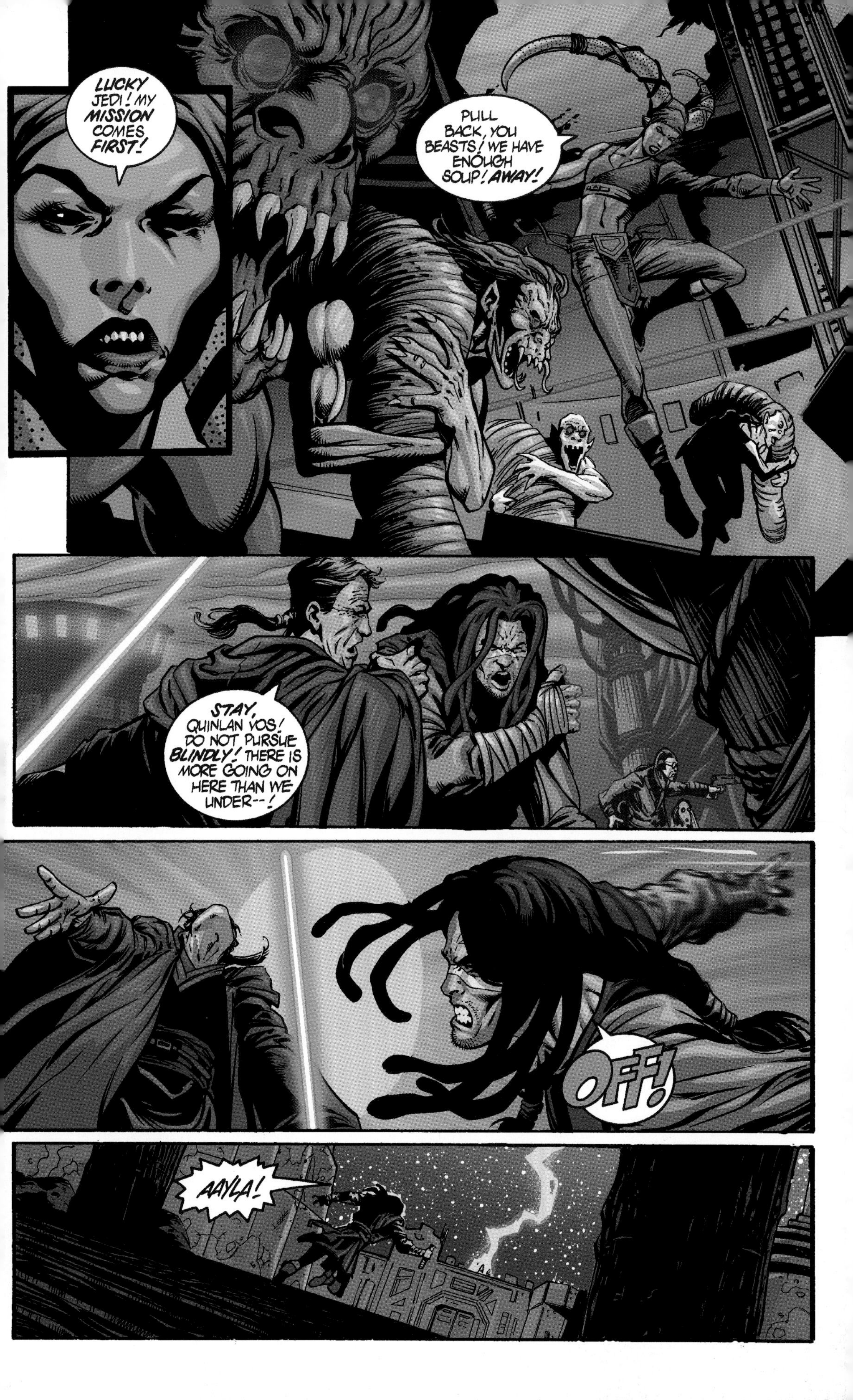
LUCKY JEDI! MY MISSION COMES FIRST!
PULL BACK, YOU BEASTS! WE HAVE ENOUGH SOUP! AWAY!
STAY, QUINLAN VOS! DO NOT PURSUE BLINDLY! THERE IS MORE GOING ON HERE THAN WE UNDER--!
OFF!
AAYLA!

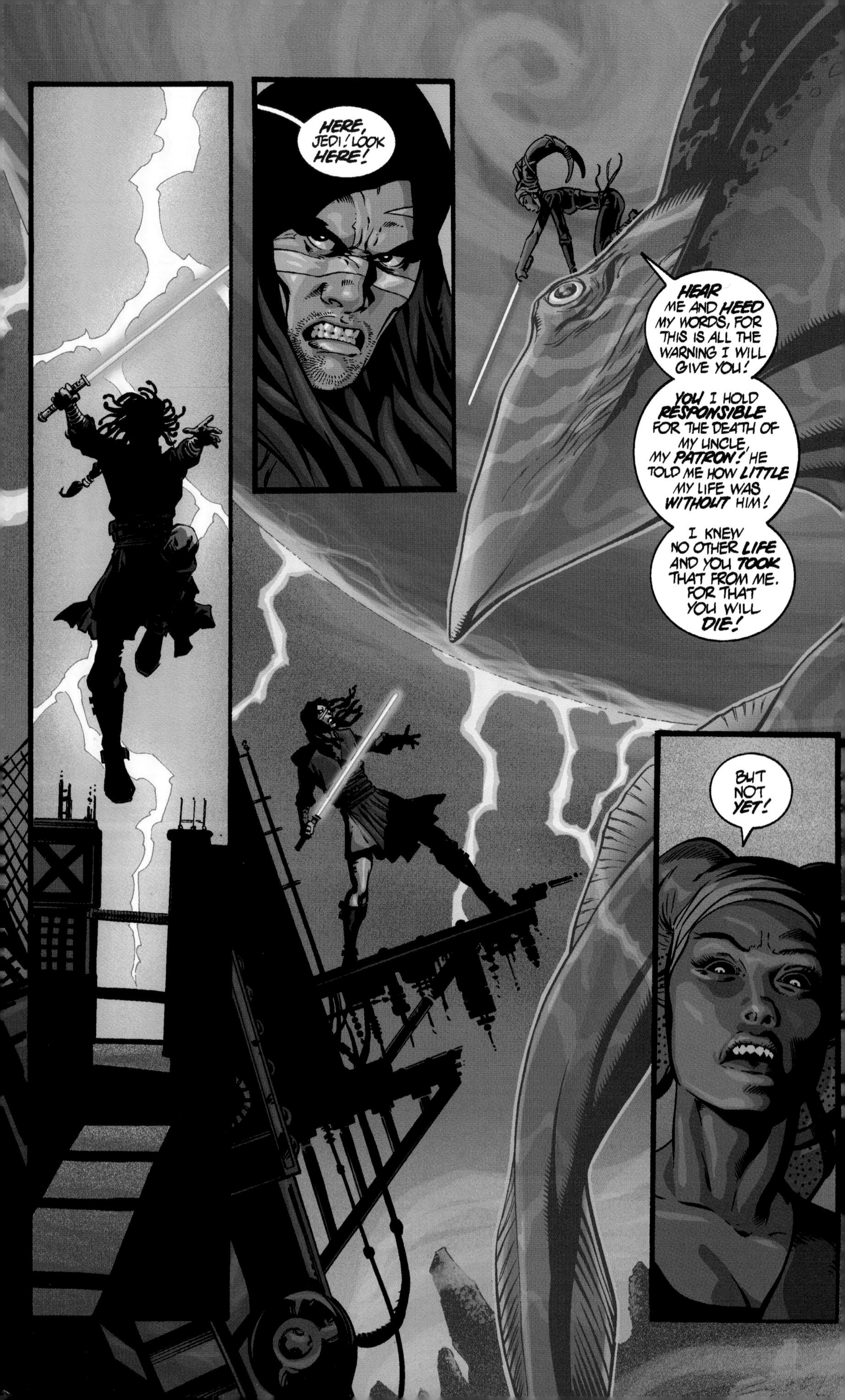

HERE, JEDI! LOOK HERE!
HEAR ME AND HEED MY WORDS, FOR THIS IS ALL THE WARNING I WILL GIVE YOU!
YOU I HOLD RESPONSIBLE FOR THE DEATH OF MY UNCLE, MY PATRON! HE TOLD ME HOW LITTLE MY LIFE WAS WITHOUT HIM!
I KNEW NO OTHER LIFE AND YOU TOOK THAT FROM ME. FOR THAT YOU WILL DIE!
BUT NOT YET!

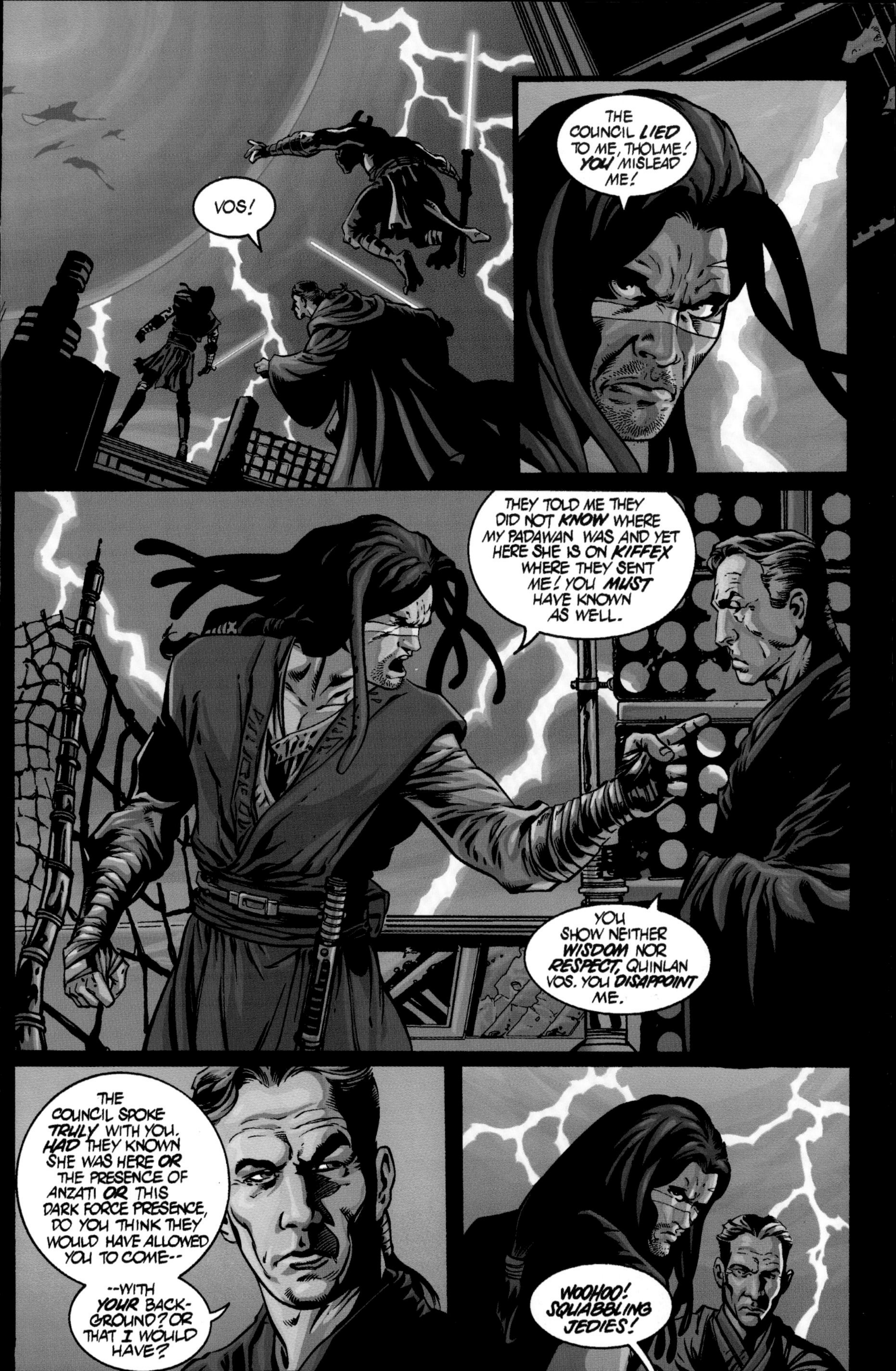
VOS!
THE COUNCIL LIED TO ME, THOLME! YOU MISLEAD ME!
THEY TOLD ME THEY DID NOT KNOW WHERE MY PADAWAN WAS AND YET HERE SHE IS ON KIFFEX WHERE THEY SENT ME! YOU MUST HAVE KNOWN AS WELL.
YOU SHOW NEITHER WISDOM NOR RESPECT, QUINLAN VOS. YOU DISAPPOINT ME.
THE COUNCIL SPOKE TRULY WITH YOU. HAD THEY KNOWN SHE WAS HERE OR THE PRESENCE OF ANZATI OR THIS DARK FORCE PRESENCE, DO YOU THINK THEY WOULD HAVE ALLOWED YOU TO COME--
--WITH YOUR BACK-GROUND? OR THAT I WOULD HAVE?
WOOHOO! SQUABBLING JEDIES!

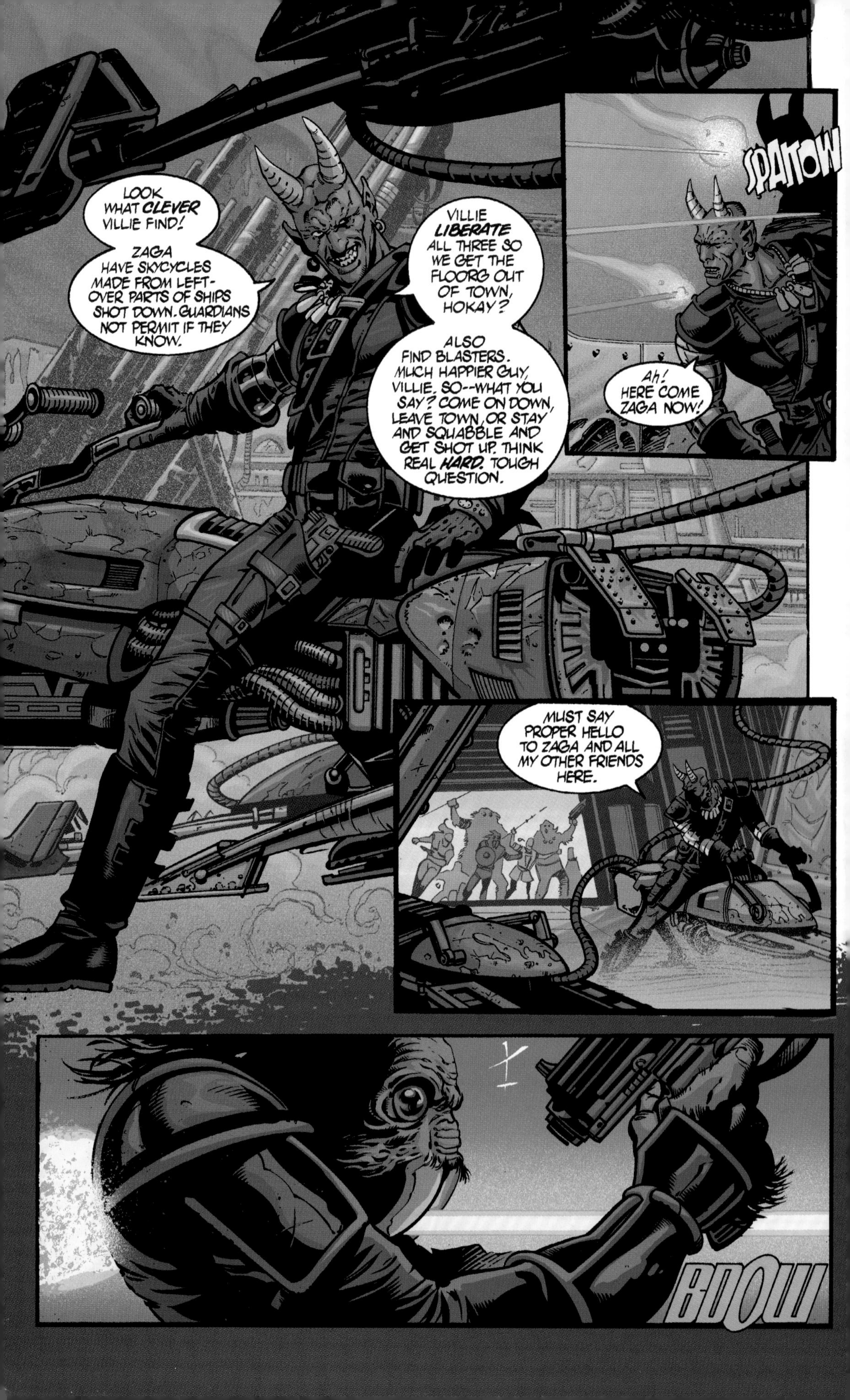
LOOK WHAT CLEVER VILLIE FIND!
ZAGA HAVE SKYCYCLES MADE FROM LEFT-OVER PARTS OF SHIPS SHOT DOWN. GUARDIANS NOT PERMIT IF THEY KNOW.
VILLIE LIBERATE ALL THREE SO WE GET THE FLOORG OUT OF TOWN, HOKAY?
ALSO FIND BLASTERS. MUCH HAPPIER GUY, VILLIE. SO--WHAT YOU SAY? COME ON DOWN, LEAVE TOWN, OR STAY AND SQUABBLE AND GET SHOT UP. THINK REAL HARD. TOUGH QUESTION.
SPATOW
Ah! HERE COME ZAGA NOW!
MUST SAY PROPER HELLO TO ZAGA AND ALL MY OTHER FRIENDS HERE.
BDOW

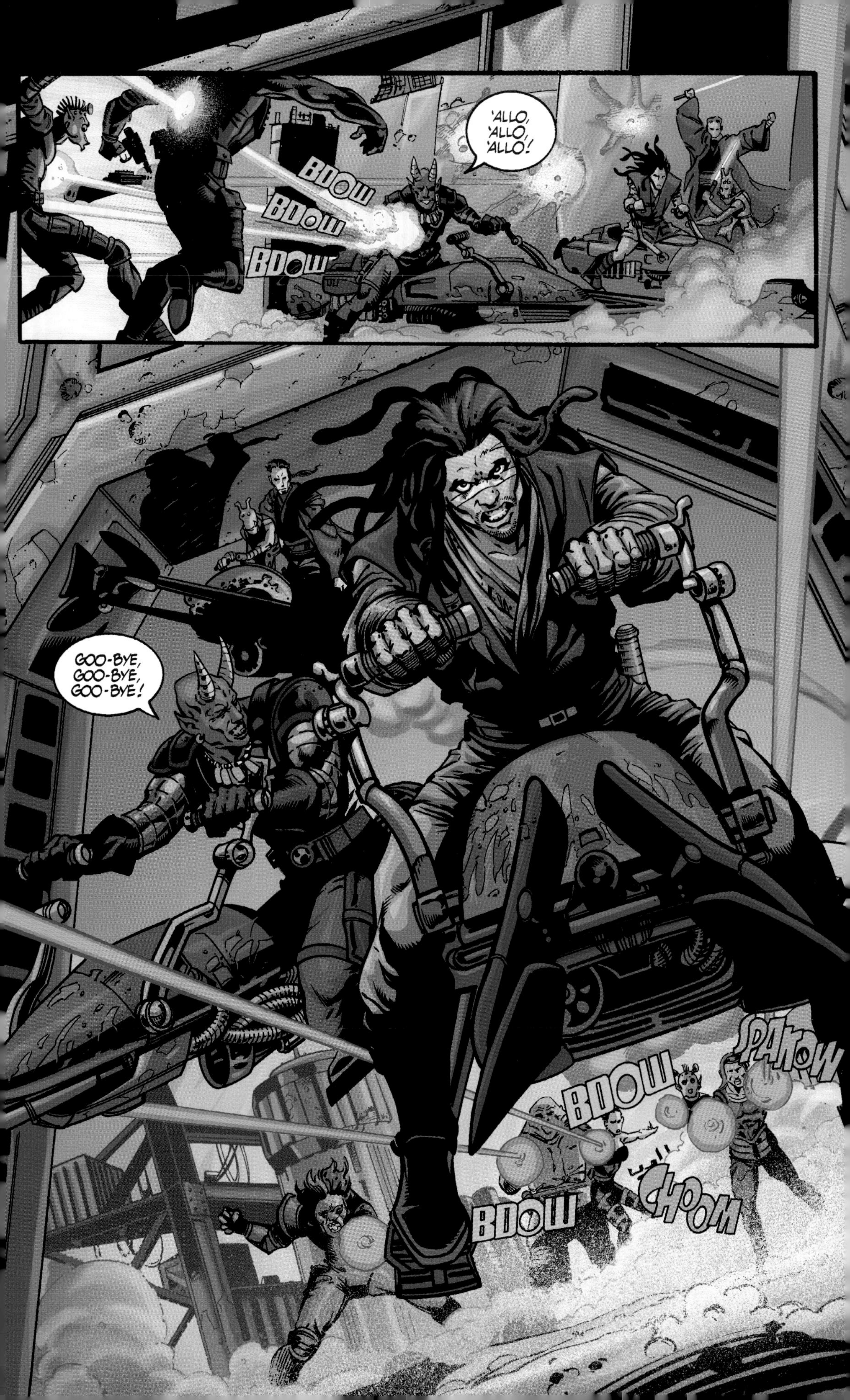
BDOW
BDOW
BDOW
'ALLO, 'ALLO, 'ALLO!
GOO-BYE, GOO-BYE, GOO-BYE!
SPAKOW
BDOW
CHOOM
BDOW

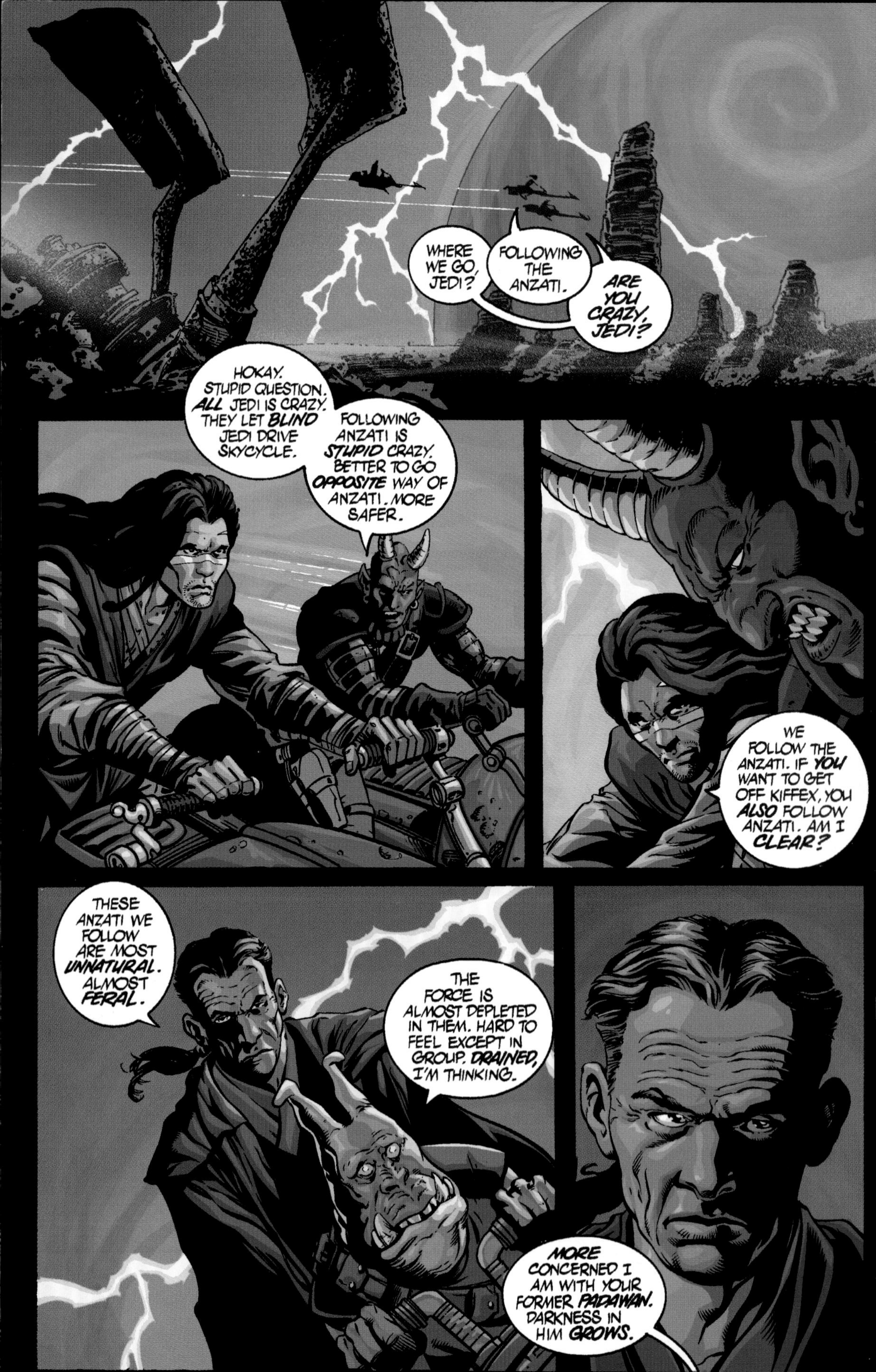

WHERE WE GO, JEDI?
FOLLOWING THE ANZATI.
ARE YOU CRAZY, JEDI?
HOKAY. STUPID QUESTION. ALL JEDI IS CRAZY. THEY LET BLIND JEDI DRIVE SKYCYCLE.
FOLLOWING ANZATI IS STUPID CRAZY. BETTER TO GO OPPOSITE WAY OF ANZATI. MORE SAFER.
WE FOLLOW THE ANZATI. IF YOU WANT TO GET OFF KIFFEX, YOU ALSO FOLLOW ANZATI. AM I CLEAR?
THESE ANZATI WE FOLLOW ARE MOST UNNATURAL. ALMOST FERAL.
THE FORCE IS ALMOST DEPLETED IN THEM. HARD TO FEEL EXCEPT IN GROUP. DRAINED, I'M THINKING.
MORE CONCERNED I AM WITH YOUR FORMER PADAWAN. DARKNESS IN HIM GROWS.

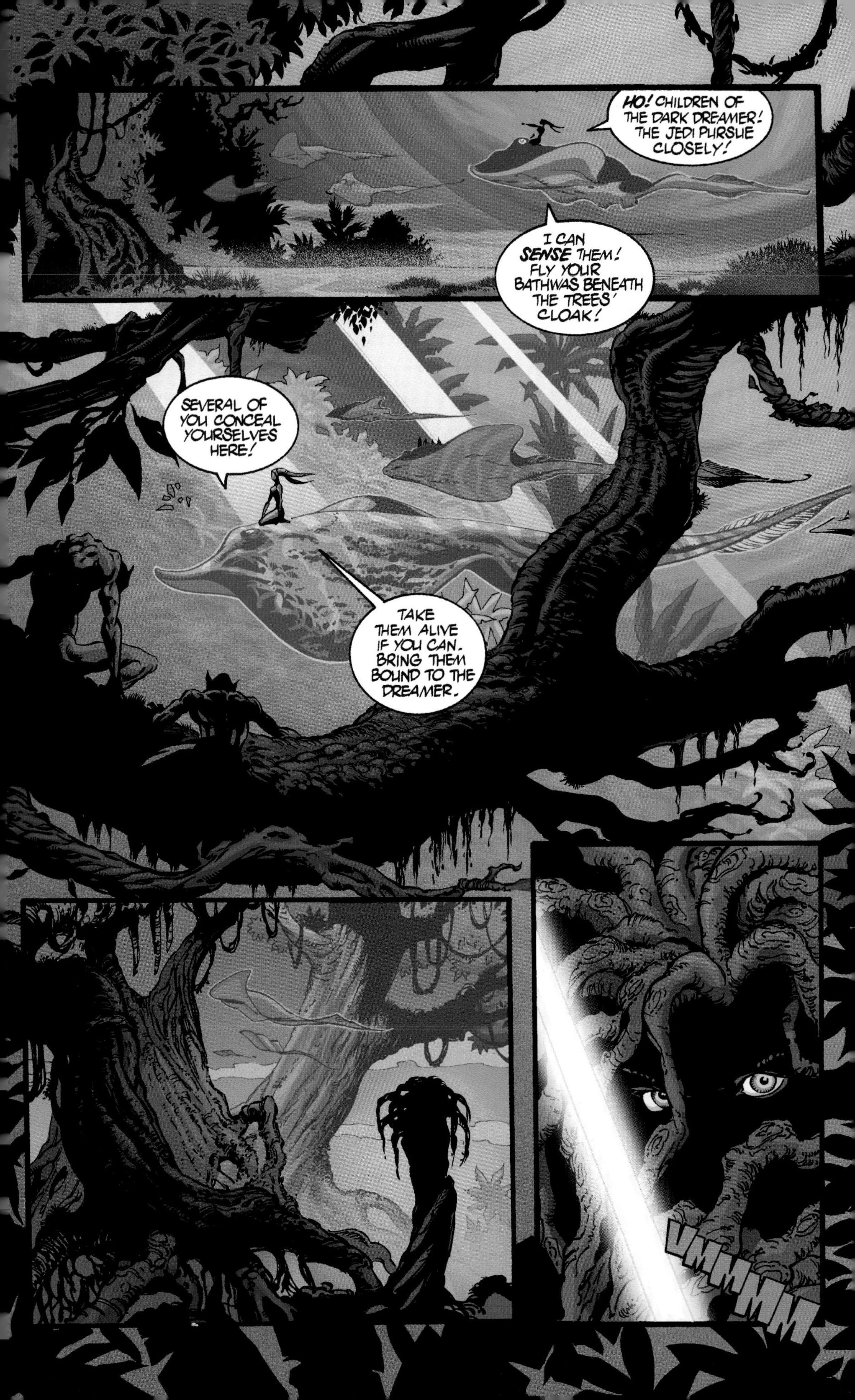

HO! CHILDREN OF THE DARK DREAMER! THE JEDI PURSUE CLOSELY!
I CAN SENSE THEM! FLY YOUR BATHWAS BENEATH THE TREES' CLOAK!
SEVERAL OF YOU CONCEAL YOURSELVES HERE!
TAKE THEM ALIVE IF YOU CAN. BRING THEM BOUND TO THE DREAMER.
VMMMMM

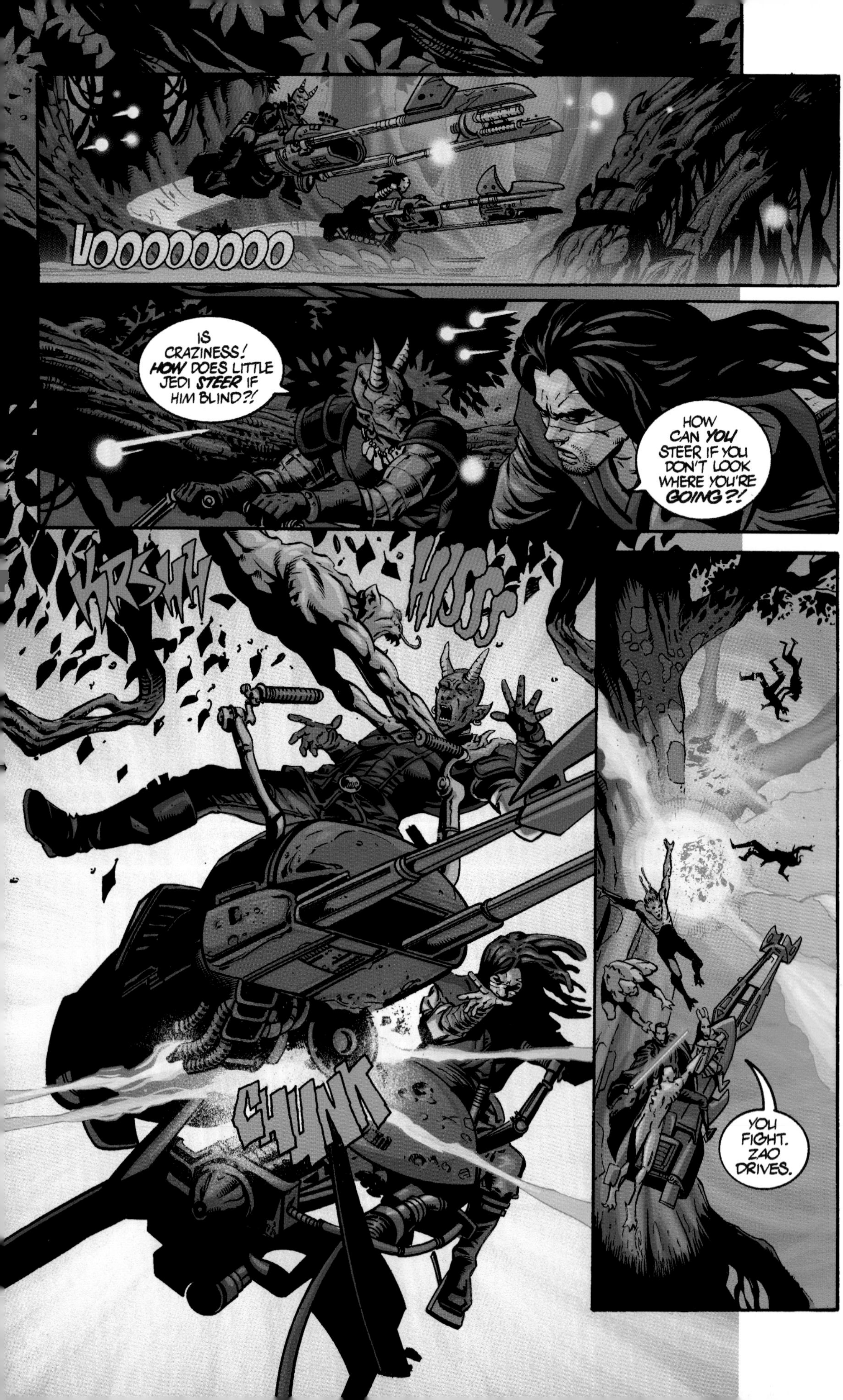
VOOOOOOOO
IS CRAZINESS! HOW DOES LITTLE JEDI STEER IF HIM BLIND?!
HOW CAN YOU STEER IF YOU DON'T LOOK WHERE YOU'RE GOING?!
KRSHH
HISSS
CHUNK
YOU FIGHT. ZAO DRIVES.

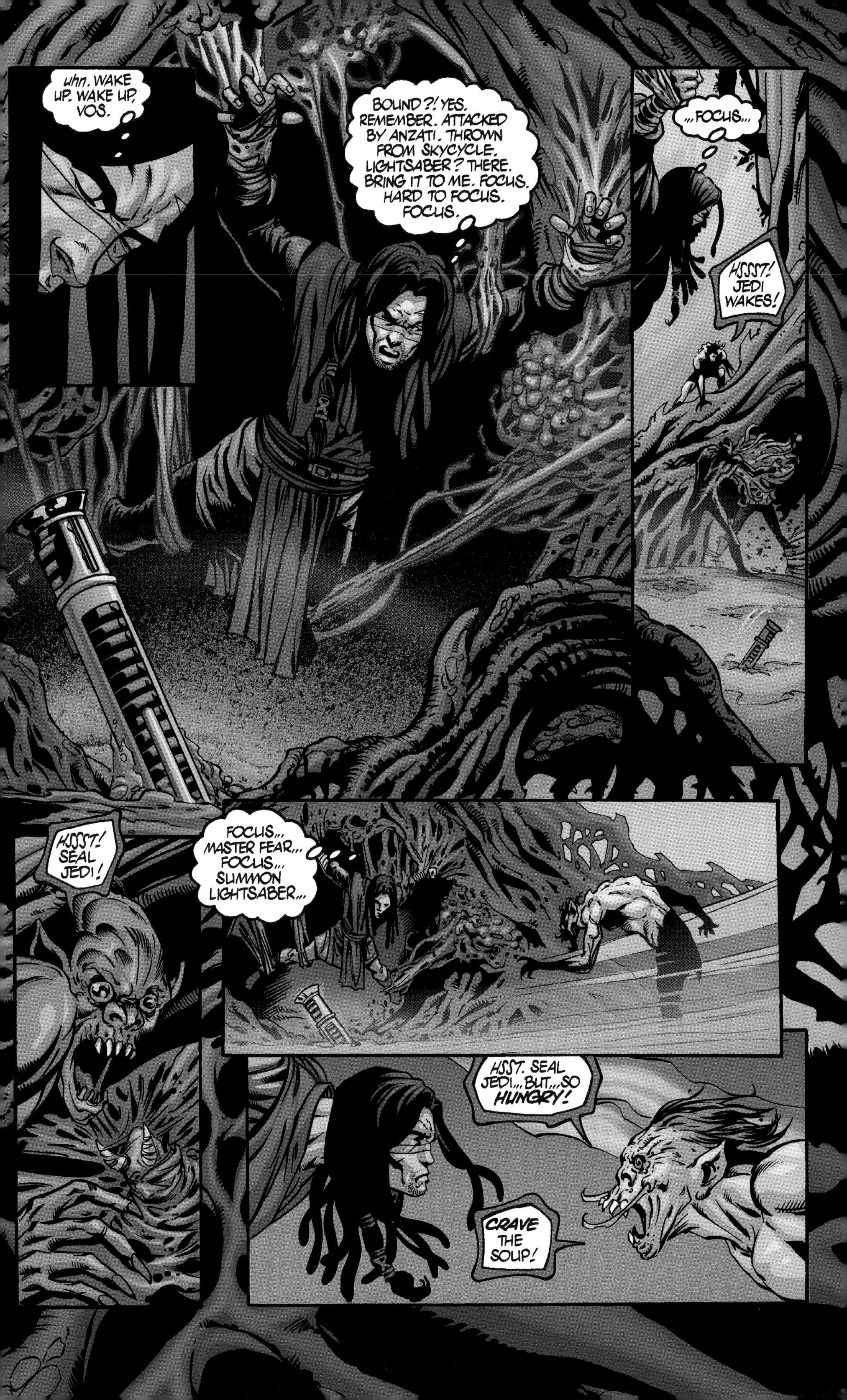
UHN. WAKE UP. WAKE UP, VOS.
BOUND?! YES. REMEMBER. ATTACKED BY ANZATI. THROWN FROM SKYCYCLE. LIGHTSABER? THERE. BRING IT TO ME. FOCUS. HARD TO FOCUS. FOCUS.
...FOCUS...
HSSST! JEDI WAKES!
HSSST! SEAL JEDI!
FOCUS... MASTER FEAR... FOCUS... SUMMON LIGHTSABER...
HSST. SEAL JEDI... BUT... SO HUNGRY!
CRAVE THE SOUP!

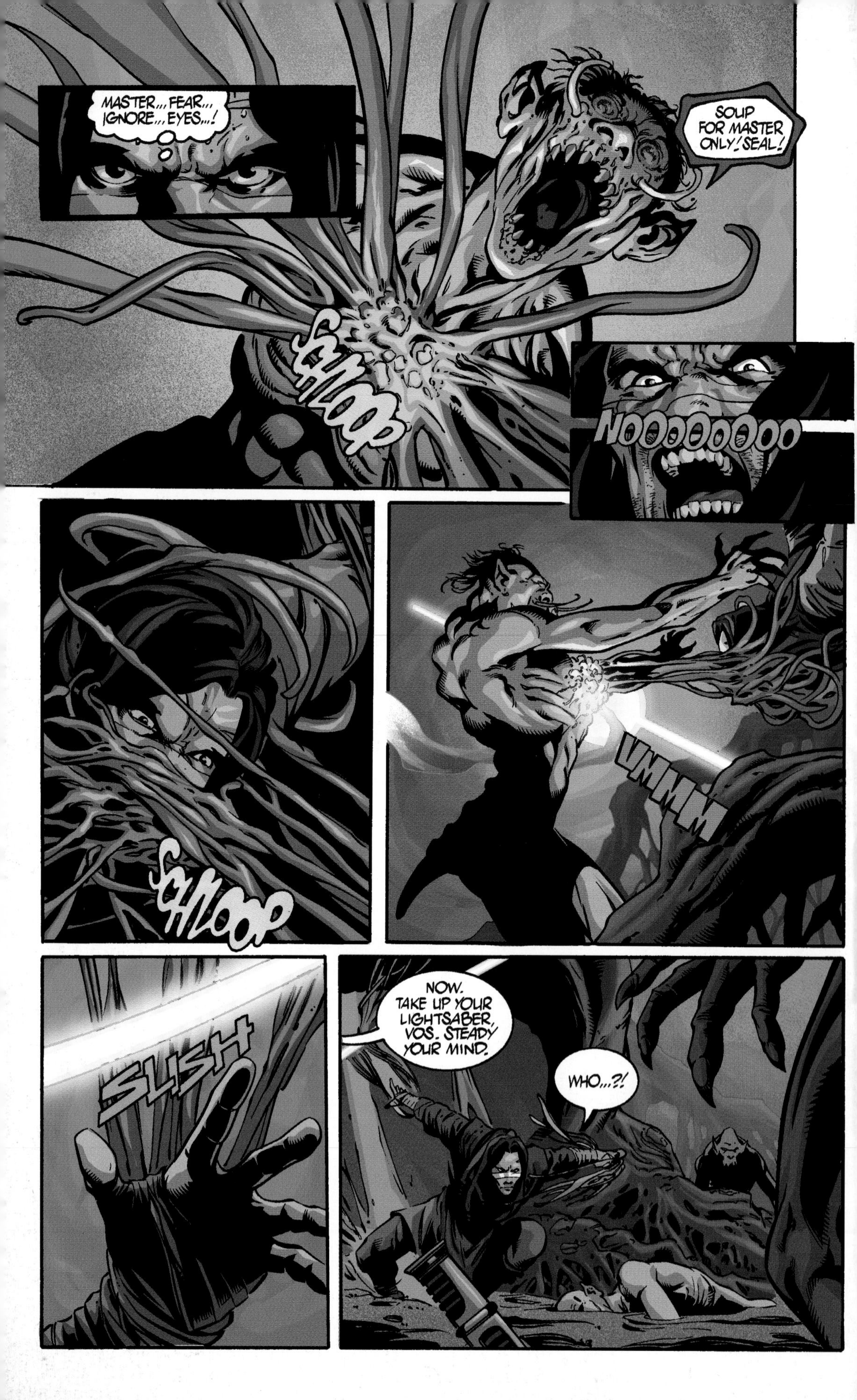
MASTER... FEAR... IGNORE... EYES...!
SOUP FOR MASTER ONLY! SEAL!
SCHLOOP
NOOOOOOOOO
SCHLOOP
UMMM
SLISH
NOW. TAKE UP YOUR LIGHTSABER, VOS. STEADY YOUR MIND.
WHO...?!

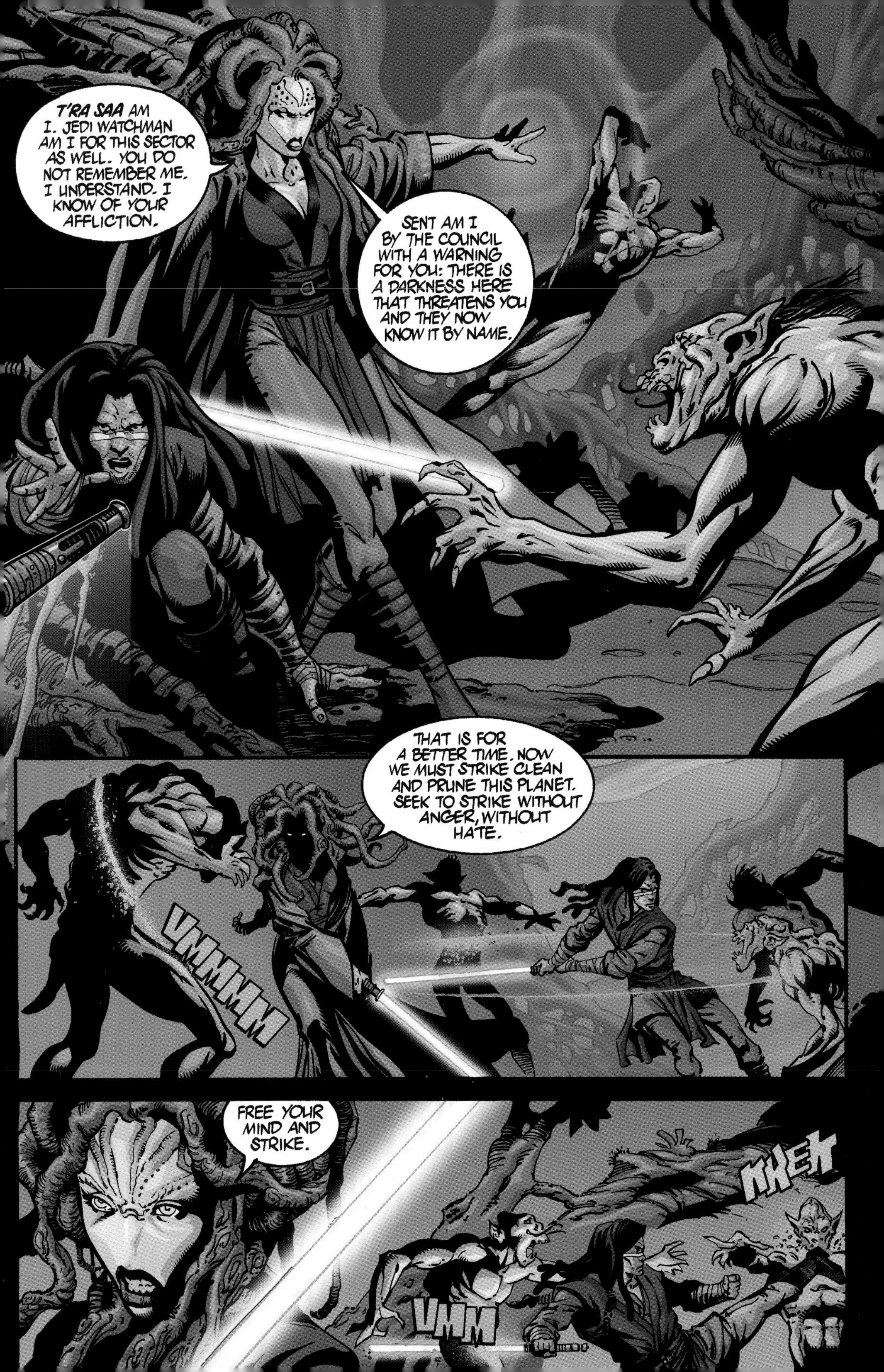
T'RA SAA AM I. JEDI WATCHMAN AM I FOR THIS SECTOR AS WELL. YOU DO NOT REMEMBER ME. I UNDERSTAND. I KNOW OF YOUR AFFLICTION.
SENT AM I BY THE COUNCIL WITH A WARNING FOR YOU: THERE IS A DARKNESS HERE THAT THREATENS YOU AND THEY NOW KNOW IT BY NAME.
THAT IS FOR A BETTER TIME. NOW WE MUST STRIKE CLEAN AND PRUNE THIS PLANET. SEEK TO STRIKE WITHOUT ANGER, WITHOUT HATE.
VMMMMM
FREE YOUR MIND AND STRIKE.
KHEK
VMM

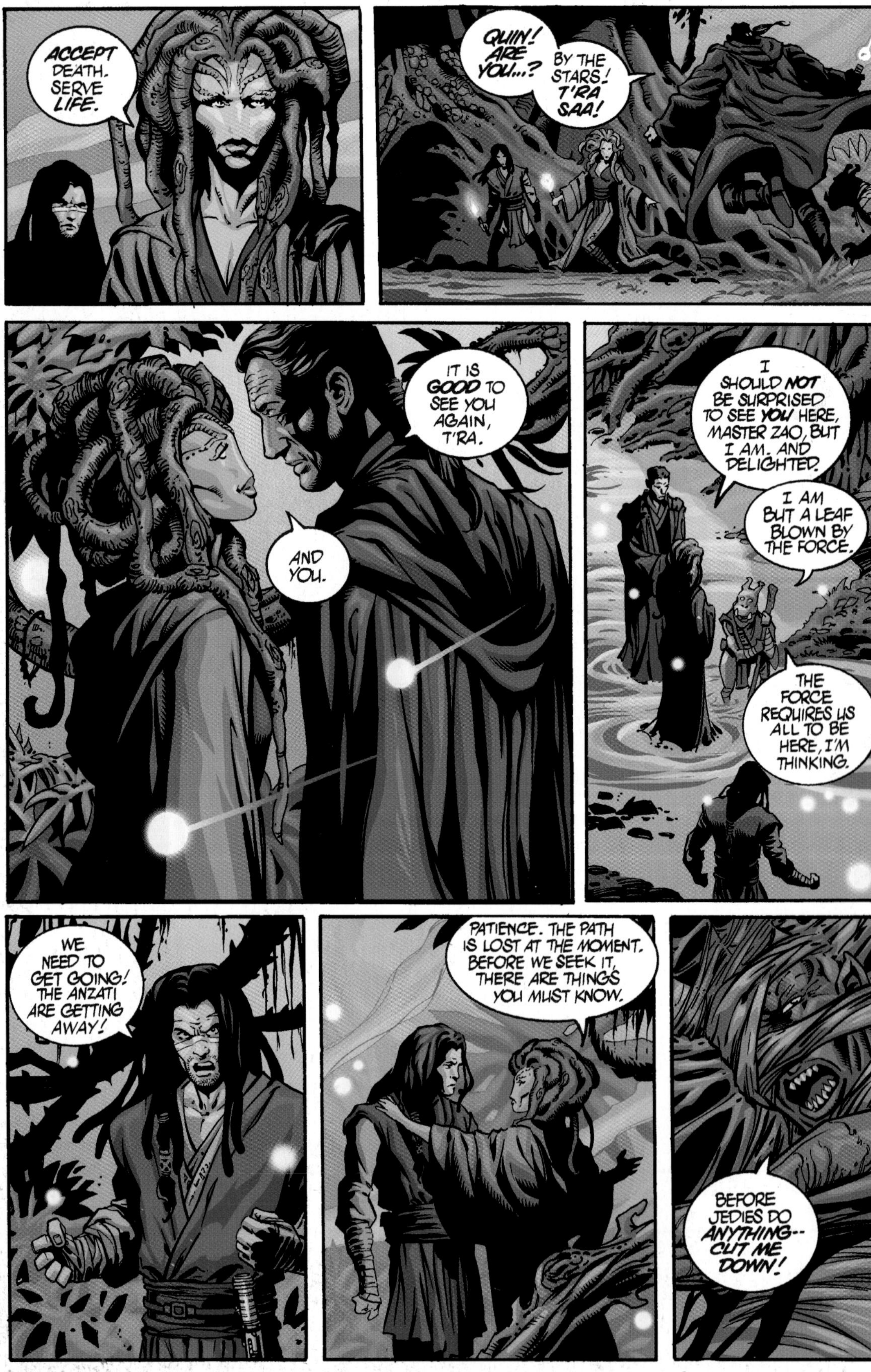
ACCEPT DEATH. SERVE LIFE.
QUIN! ARE YOU...?
BY THE STARS! T'RA SAA!
IT IS GOOD TO SEE YOU AGAIN, T'RA.
AND YOU.
I SHOULD NOT BE SURPRISED TO SEE YOU HERE, MASTER ZAO, BUT I AM. AND DELIGHTED.
I AM BUT A LEAF BLOWN BY THE FORCE.
THE FORCE REQUIRES US ALL TO BE HERE, I'M THINKING.
WE NEED TO GET GOING! THE ANZATI ARE GETTING AWAY!
PATIENCE. THE PATH IS LOST AT THE MOMENT. BEFORE WE SEEK IT, THERE ARE THINGS YOU MUST KNOW.
BEFORE JEDIES DO ANYTHING-- CUT ME DOWN!

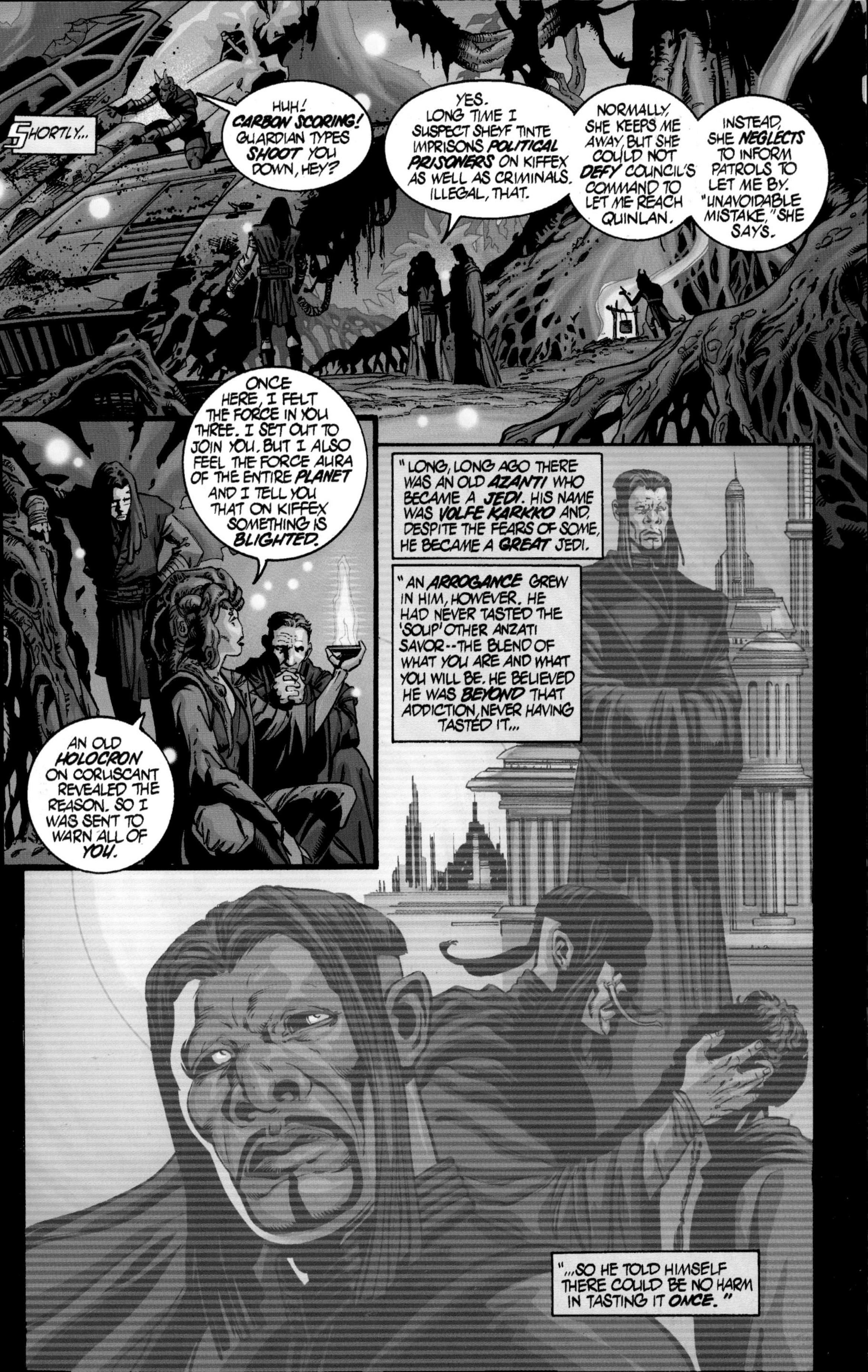
SHORTLY...
HUH! CARBON SCORING! GUARDIAN TYPES SHOOT YOU DOWN, HEY?
YES. LONG TIME I SUSPECT SHEYF TINTE IMPRISONS POLITICAL PRISONERS ON KIFFEX AS WELL AS CRIMINALS. ILLEGAL, THAT.
NORMALLY, SHE KEEPS ME AWAY, BUT SHE COULD NOT DEFY COUNCIL'S COMMAND TO LET ME REACH QUINLAN.
INSTEAD, SHE NEGLECTS TO INFORM PATROLS TO LET ME BY. "UNAVOIDABLE MISTAKE," SHE SAYS.
ONCE HERE, I FELT THE FORCE IN YOU THREE. I SET OUT TO JOIN YOU. BUT I ALSO FEEL THE FORCE AURA OF THE ENTIRE PLANET AND I TELL YOU THAT ON KIFFEX SOMETHING IS BLIGHTED.
AN OLD HOLOCRON ON CORUSCANT REVEALED THE REASON. SO I WAS SENT TO WARN ALL OF YOU.
"LONG, LONG AGO THERE WAS AN OLD AZANTI WHO BECAME A JEDI. HIS NAME WAS VOLFE KARKKO AND, DESPITE THE FEARS OF SOME, HE BECAME A GREAT JEDI.
"AN ARROGANCE GREW IN HIM, HOWEVER. HE HAD NEVER TASTED THE 'SOUP' OTHER ANZATI SAVOR--THE BLEND OF WHAT YOU ARE AND WHAT YOU WILL BE. HE BELIEVED HE WAS BEYOND THAT ADDICTION, NEVER HAVING TASTED IT...
"...SO HE TOLD HIMSELF THERE COULD BE NO HARM IN TASTING IT ONCE."

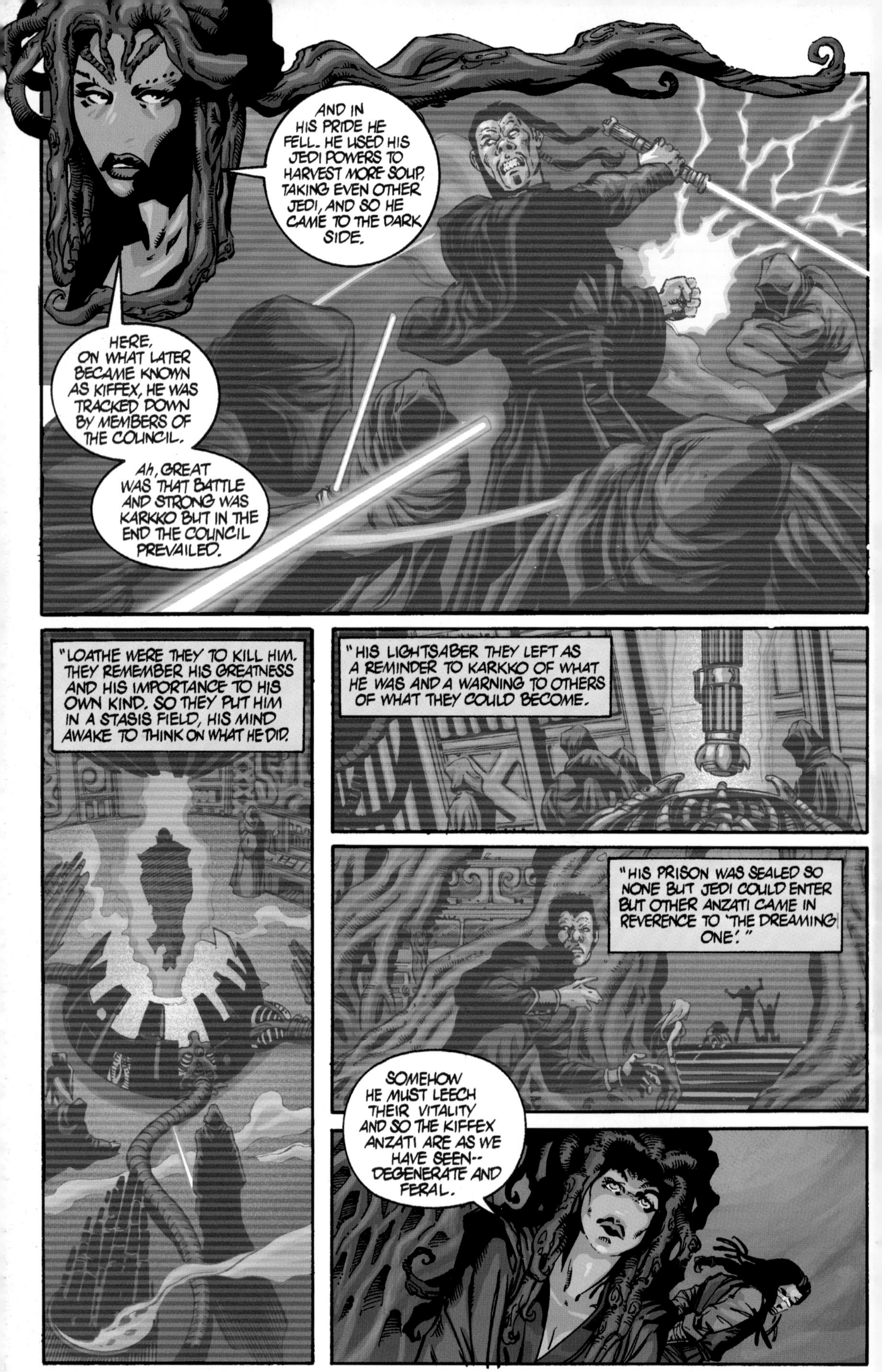
AND IN HIS PRIDE HE FELL. HE USED HIS JEDI POWERS TO HARVEST MORE SOUP, TAKING EVEN OTHER JEDI, AND SO HE CAME TO THE DARK SIDE.
HERE, ON WHAT LATER BECAME KNOWN AS KIFFEX, HE WAS TRACKED DOWN BY MEMBERS OF THE COUNCIL.
Ah, GREAT WAS THAT BATTLE AND STRONG WAS KARKKO BUT IN THE END THE COUNCIL PREVAILED.
"LOATHE WERE THEY TO KILL HIM. THEY REMEMBER HIS GREATNESS AND HIS IMPORTANCE TO HIS OWN KIND. SO THEY PUT HIM IN A STASIS FIELD, HIS MIND AWAKE TO THINK ON WHAT HE DID.
"HIS LIGHTSABER THEY LEFT AS A REMINDER TO KARKKO OF WHAT HE WAS AND A WARNING TO OTHERS OF WHAT THEY COULD BECOME.
"HIS PRISON WAS SEALED SO NONE BUT JEDI COULD ENTER BUT OTHER ANZATI CAME IN REVERENCE TO 'THE DREAMING ONE'."
SOMEHOW HE MUST LEECH THEIR VITALITY AND SO THE KIFFEX ANZATI ARE AS WE HAVE SEEN-- DEGENERATE AND FERAL.

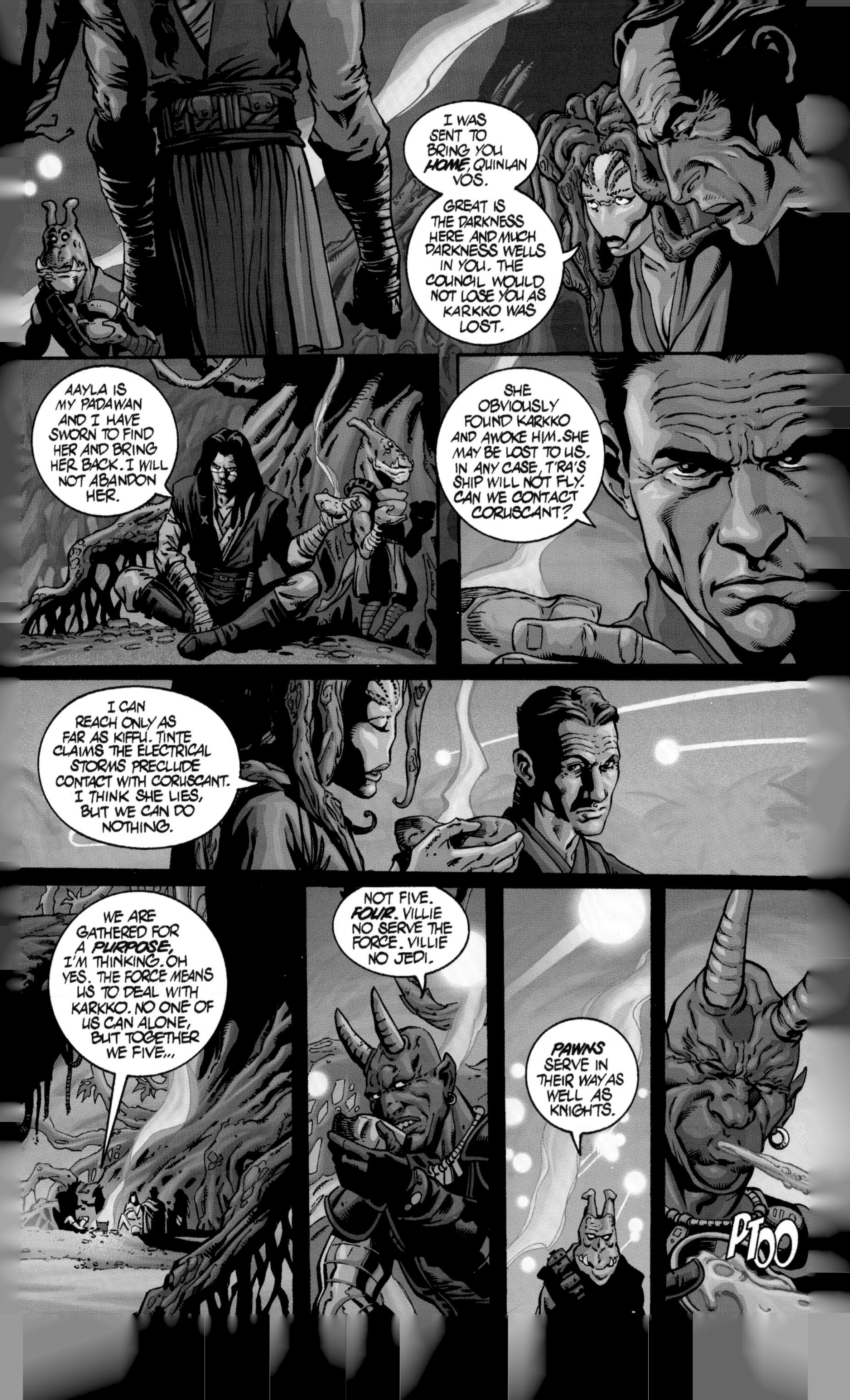
I WAS SENT TO BRING YOU HOME, QUINLAN VOS.
GREAT IS THE DARKNESS HERE AND MUCH DARKNESS WELLS IN YOU. THE COUNCIL WOULD NOT LOSE YOU AS KARKKO WAS LOST.
AAYLA IS MY PADAWAN AND I HAVE SWORN TO FIND HER AND BRING HER BACK. I WILL NOT ABANDON HER.
SHE OBVIOUSLY FOUND KARKKO AND AWOKE HIM. SHE MAY BE LOST TO US. IN ANY CASE, T'RA'S SHIP WILL NOT FLY. CAN WE CONTACT CORUSCANT?
I CAN REACH ONLY AS FAR AS KIFFU. TINTE CLAIMS THE ELECTRICAL STORMS PRECLUDE CONTACT WITH CORUSCANT. I THINK SHE LIES, BUT WE CAN DO NOTHING.
WE ARE GATHERED FOR A PURPOSE, I'M THINKING. OH YES. THE FORCE MEANS US TO DEAL WITH KARKKO. NO ONE OF US CAN ALONE, BUT TOGETHER WE FIVE...
NOT FIVE. FOUR. VILLIE NO SERVE THE FORCE. VILLIE NO JEDI.
PAWNS SERVE IN THEIR WAY AS WELL AS KNIGHTS.
PTOO

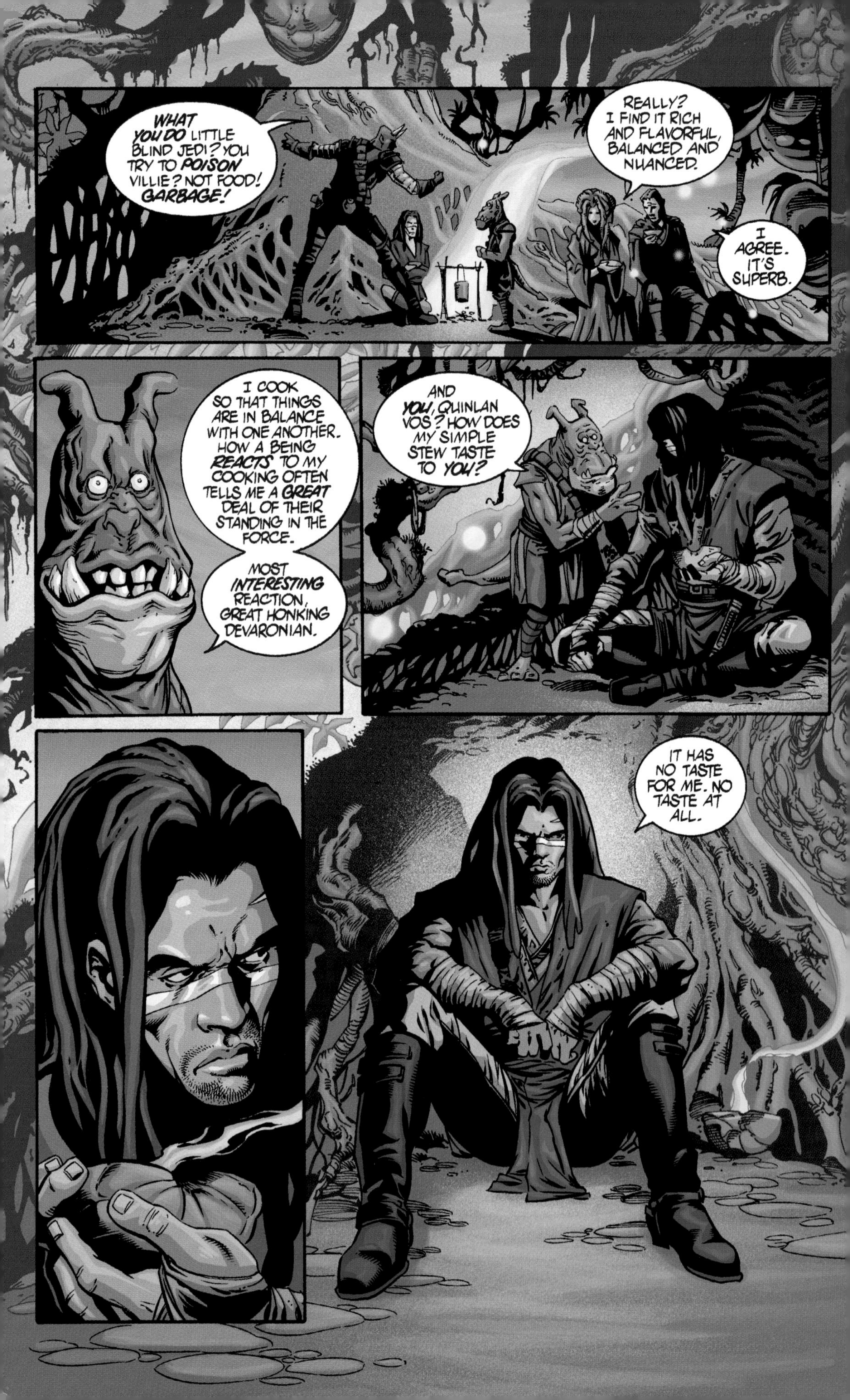
WHAT YOU DO LITTLE BLIND JEDI? YOU TRY TO POISON VILLIE? NOT FOOD! GARBAGE!
REALLY? I FIND IT RICH AND FLAVORFUL, BALANCED AND NUANCED.
I AGREE. IT'S SUPERB.
I COOK SO THAT THINGS ARE IN BALANCE WITH ONE ANOTHER. HOW A BEING REACTS TO MY COOKING OFTEN TELLS ME A GREAT DEAL OF THEIR STANDING IN THE FORCE.
MOST INTERESTING REACTION, GREAT HONKING DEVARONIAN.
AND YOU, QUINLAN VOS? HOW DOES MY SIMPLE STEW TASTE TO YOU?
IT HAS NO TASTE FOR ME. NO TASTE AT ALL.

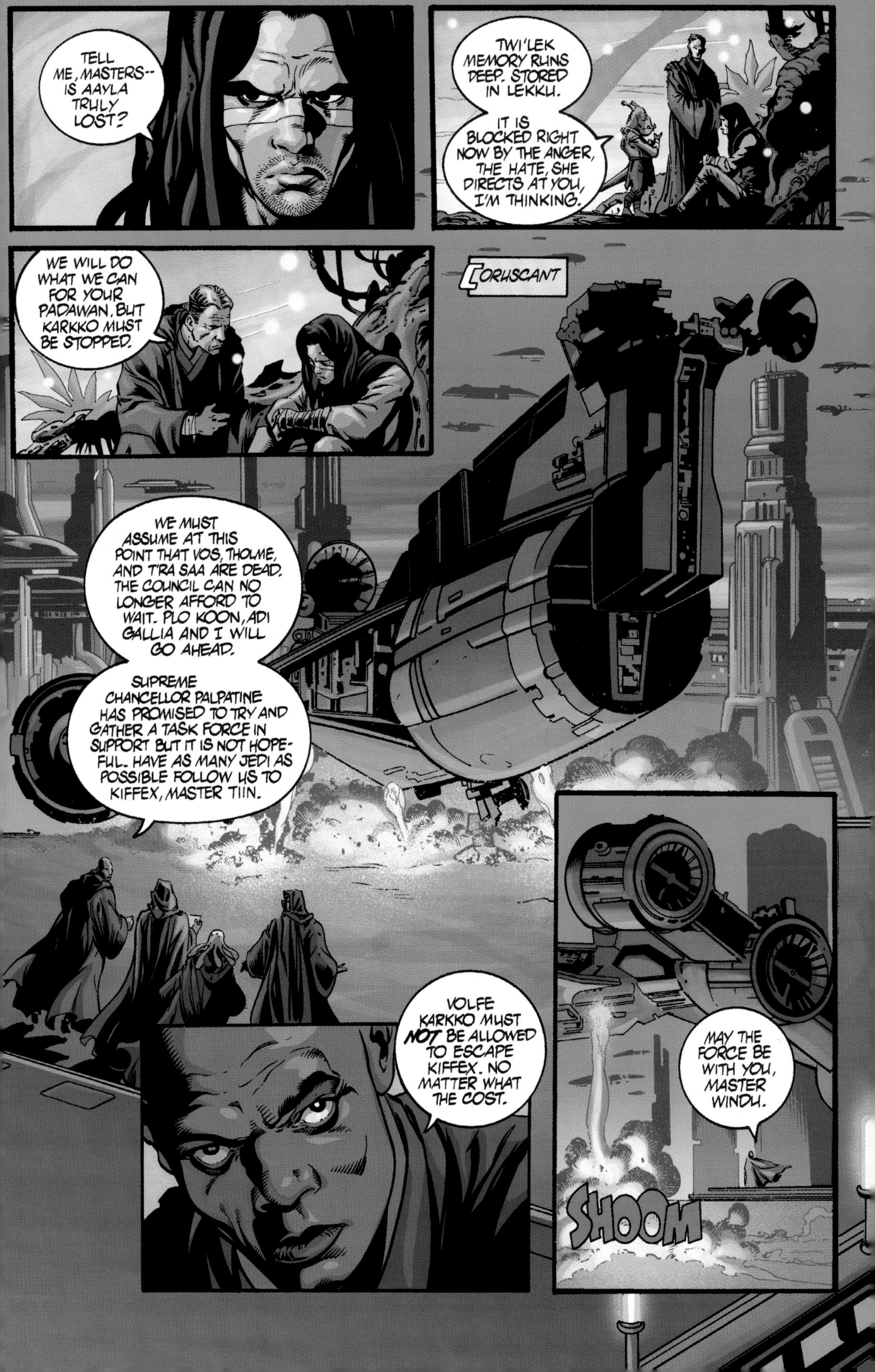
TELL ME, MASTERS-- IS AAYLA TRULY LOST?
TWI'LEK MEMORY RUNS DEEP. STORED IN LEKKU.
IT IS BLOCKED RIGHT NOW BY THE ANGER, THE HATE, SHE DIRECTS AT YOU, I'M THINKING.
WE WILL DO WHAT WE CAN FOR YOUR PADAWAN, BUT KARKKO MUST BE STOPPED.
CORUSCANT
WE MUST ASSUME AT THIS POINT THAT VOS, THOLME, AND T'RA SAA ARE DEAD. THE COUNCIL CAN NO LONGER AFFORD TO WAIT. PLO KOON, ADI GALLIA AND I WILL GO AHEAD.
SUPREME CHANCELLOR PALPATINE HAS PROMISED TO TRY AND GATHER A TASK FORCE IN SUPPORT BUT IT IS NOT HOPEFUL. HAVE AS MANY JEDI AS POSSIBLE FOLLOW US TO KIFFEX, MASTER TIIN.
VOLFE KARKKO MUST NOT BE ALLOWED TO ESCAPE KIFFEX. NO MATTER WHAT THE COST.
MAY THE FORCE BE WITH YOU, MASTER WINDU.
SHOOM

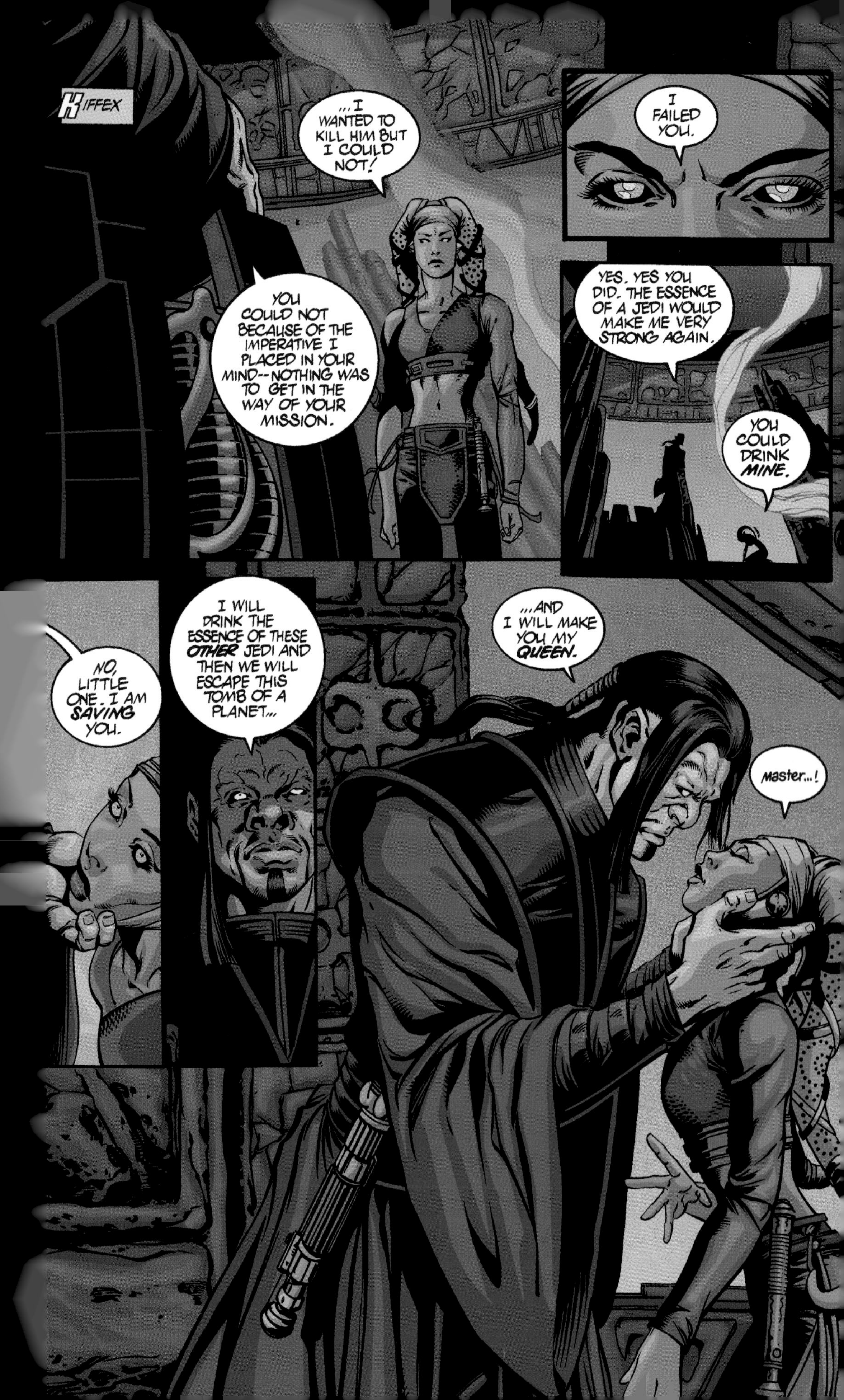
RIFFEX
...I WANTED TO KILL HIM BUT I COULD NOT!
YOU COULD NOT BECAUSE OF THE IMPERATIVE I PLACED IN YOUR MIND--NOTHING WAS TO GET IN THE WAY OF YOUR MISSION.
I FAILED YOU.
YES. YES YOU DID. THE ESSENCE OF A JEDI WOULD MAKE ME VERY STRONG AGAIN.
YOU COULD DRINK MINE.
NO, LITTLE ONE. I AM SAVING YOU.
I WILL DRINK THE ESSENCE OF THESE OTHER JEDI AND THEN WE WILL ESCAPE THIS TOMB OF A PLANET...
...AND I WILL MAKE YOU MY QUEEN.
Master...!

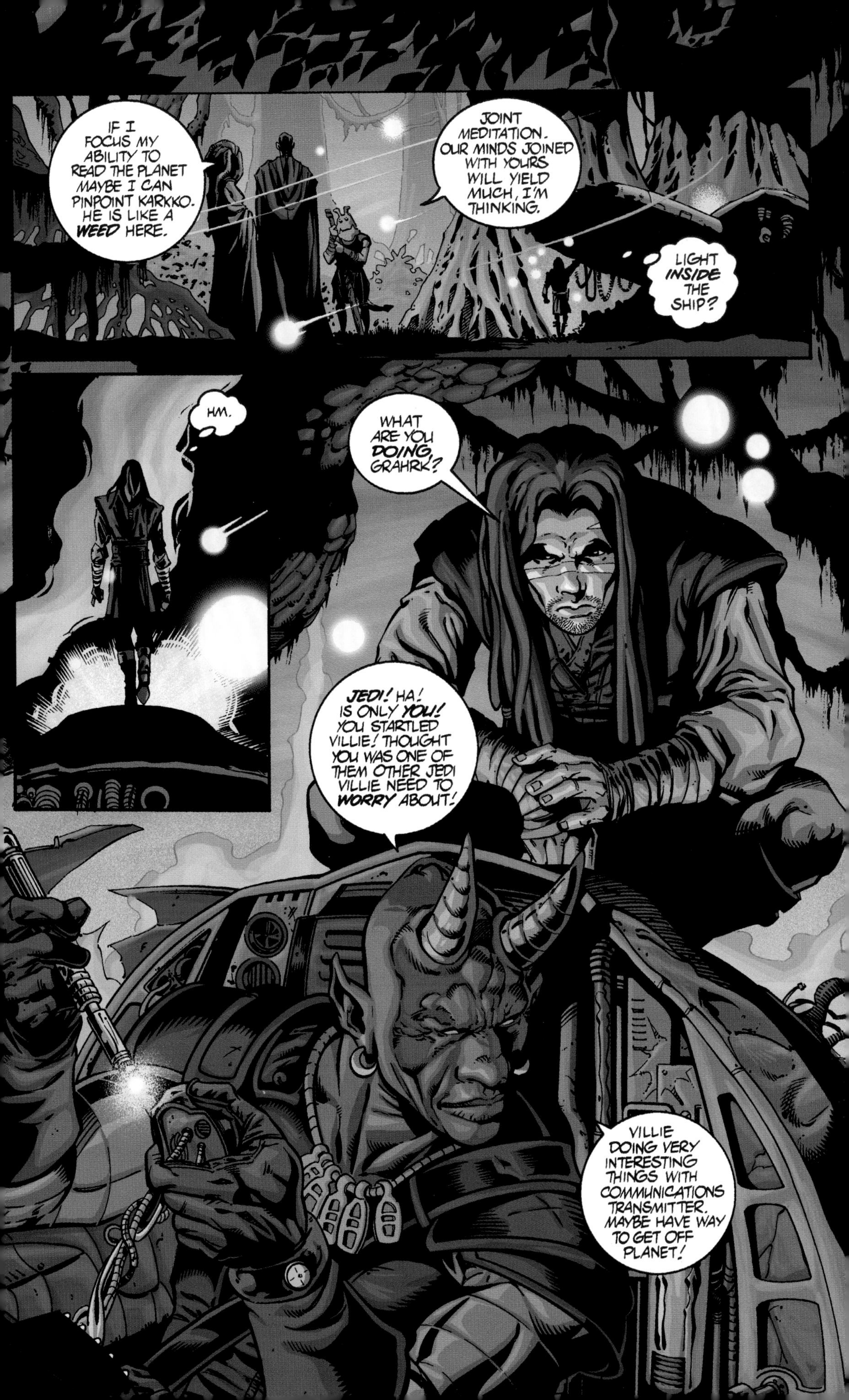
IF I FOCUS MY ABILITY TO READ THE PLANET MAYBE I CAN PINPOINT KARKKO. HE IS LIKE A WEED HERE.
JOINT MEDITATION. OUR MINDS JOINED WITH YOURS WILL YIELD MUCH, I'M THINKING.
LIGHT INSIDE THE SHIP?
HM.
WHAT ARE YOU DOING, GRAHRK?
JEDI! HA! IS ONLY YOU! YOU STARTLED VILLIE! THOUGHT YOU WAS ONE OF THEM OTHER JEDI VILLIE NEED TO WORRY ABOUT!
VILLIE DOING VERY INTERESTING THINGS WITH COMMUNICATIONS TRANSMITTER. MAYBE HAVE WAY TO GET OFF PLANET!

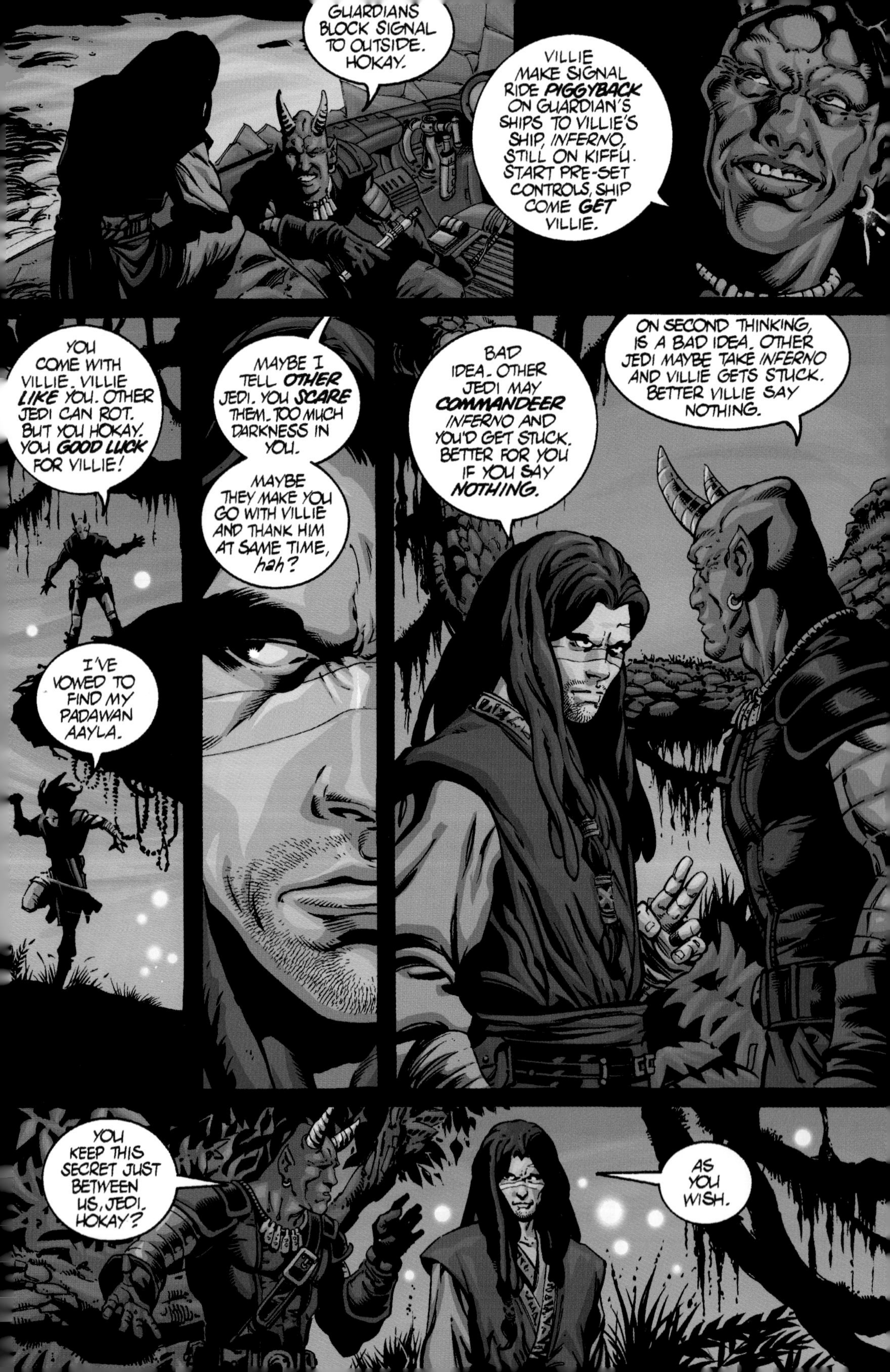
GUARDIANS BLOCK SIGNAL TO OUTSIDE. HOKAY.
VILLIE MAKE SIGNAL RIDE PIGGYBACK ON GUARDIAN'S SHIPS TO VILLIE'S SHIP, INFERNO, STILL ON KIFFU. START PRE-SET CONTROLS, SHIP COME GET VILLIE.
YOU COME WITH VILLIE. VILLIE LIKE YOU. OTHER JEDI CAN ROT. BUT YOU HOKAY. YOU GOOD LUCK FOR VILLIE!
MAYBE I TELL OTHER JEDI. YOU SCARE THEM. TOO MUCH DARKNESS IN YOU.
MAYBE THEY MAKE YOU GO WITH VILLIE AND THANK HIM AT SAME TIME, hah?
I'VE VOWED TO FIND MY PADAWAN AAYLA.
BAD IDEA. OTHER JEDI MAY COMMANDEER INFERNO AND YOU'D GET STUCK. BETTER FOR YOU IF YOU SAY NOTHING.
ON SECOND THINKING, IS A BAD IDEA. OTHER JEDI MAYBE TAKE INFERNO AND VILLIE GETS STUCK. BETTER VILLIE SAY NOTHING.
YOU KEEP THIS SECRET JUST BETWEEN US, JEDI. HOKAY?
AS YOU WISH.

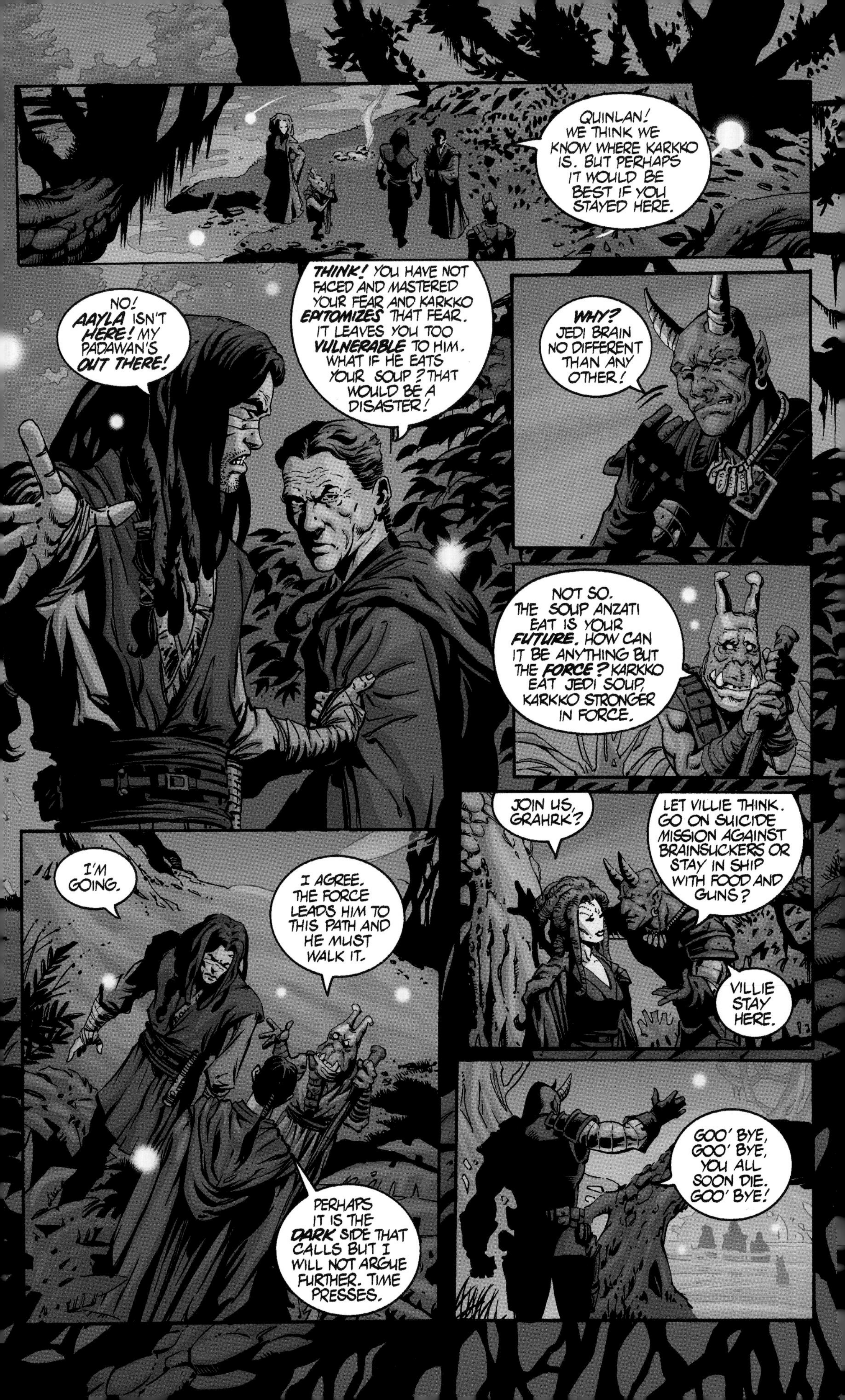
QUINLAN! WE THINK WE KNOW WHERE KARKKO IS. BUT PERHAPS IT WOULD BE BEST IF YOU STAYED HERE.
NO! AAYLA ISN'T HERE! MY PADAWAN'S OUT THERE!
THINK! YOU HAVE NOT FACED AND MASTERED YOUR FEAR AND KARKKO EPITOMIZES THAT FEAR. IT LEAVES YOU TOO VULNERABLE TO HIM. WHAT IF HE EATS YOUR SOUP? THAT WOULD BE A DISASTER!
WHY? JEDI BRAIN NO DIFFERENT THAN ANY OTHER!
NOT SO. THE SOUP ANZATI EAT IS YOUR FUTURE. HOW CAN IT BE ANYTHING BUT THE FORCE? KARKKO EAT JEDI SOUP, KARKKO STRONGER IN FORCE.
I'M GOING.
I AGREE. THE FORCE LEADS HIM TO THIS PATH AND HE MUST WALK IT.
PERHAPS IT IS THE DARK SIDE THAT CALLS BUT I WILL NOT ARGUE FURTHER. TIME PRESSES.
JOIN US, GRAHRK?
LET VILLIE THINK. GO ON SUICIDE MISSION AGAINST BRAINSUCKERS OR STAY IN SHIP WITH FOOD AND GUNS?
VILLIE STAY HERE.
GOO' BYE, GOO' BYE, YOU ALL SOON DIE. GOO' BYE!

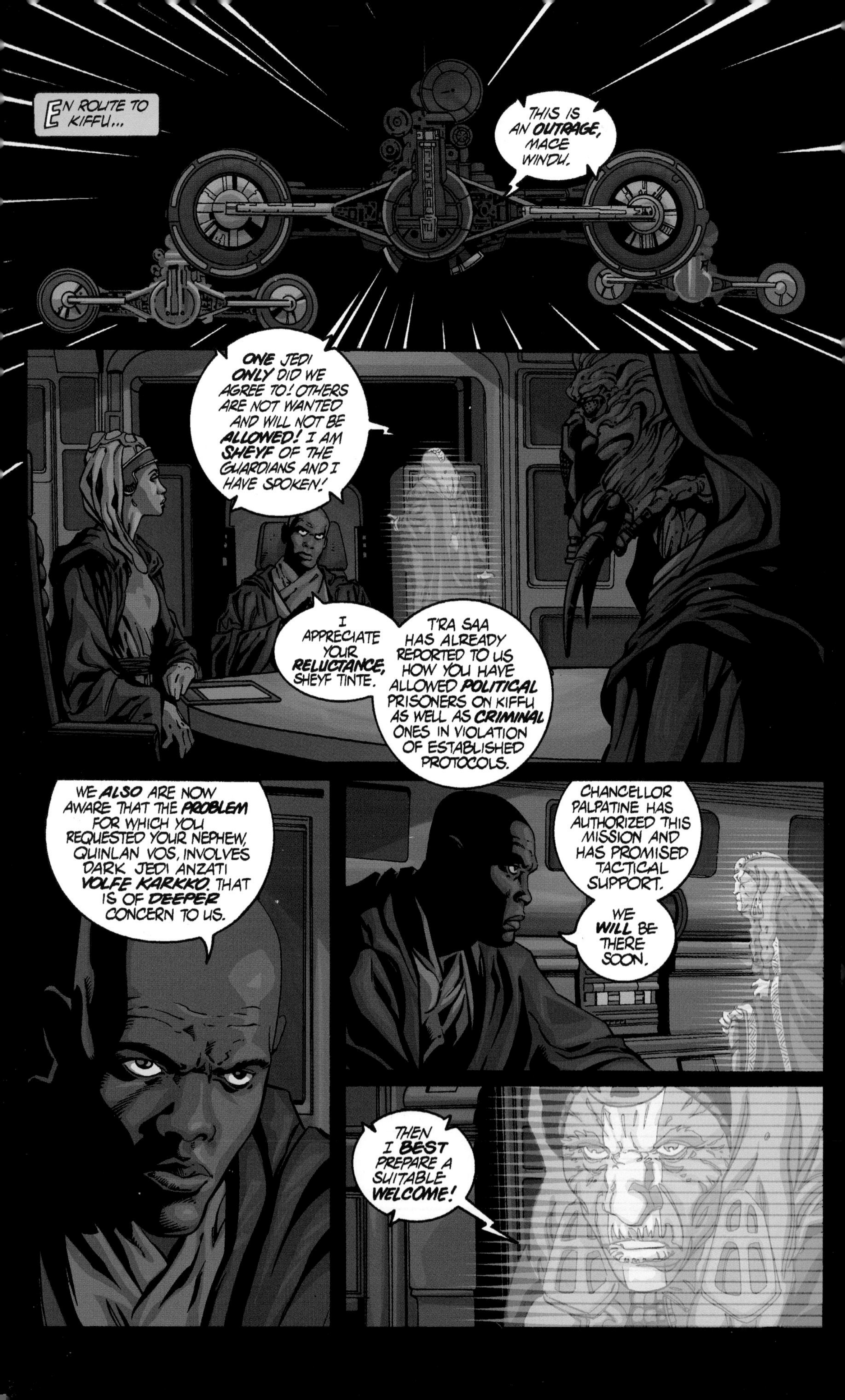
EN ROUTE TO KIFFU...
THIS IS AN OUTRAGE, MACE WINDU.
ONE JEDI ONLY DID WE AGREE TO! OTHERS ARE NOT WANTED AND WILL NOT BE ALLOWED! I AM SHEYF OF THE GUARDIANS AND I HAVE SPOKEN!
I APPRECIATE YOUR RELUCTANCE, SHEYF TINTE.
T'RA SAA HAS ALREADY REPORTED TO US HOW YOU HAVE ALLOWED POLITICAL PRISONERS ON KIFFU AS WELL AS CRIMINAL ONES IN VIOLATION OF ESTABLISHED PROTOCOLS.
WE ALSO ARE NOW AWARE THAT THE PROBLEM FOR WHICH YOU REQUESTED YOUR NEPHEW, QUINLAN VOS, INVOLVES DARK JEDI ANZATI VOLFE KARKKO. THAT IS OF DEEPER CONCERN TO US.
CHANCELLOR PALPATINE HAS AUTHORIZED THIS MISSION AND HAS PROMISED TACTICAL SUPPORT.
WE WILL BE THERE SOON.
THEN I BEST PREPARE A SUITABLE WELCOME!

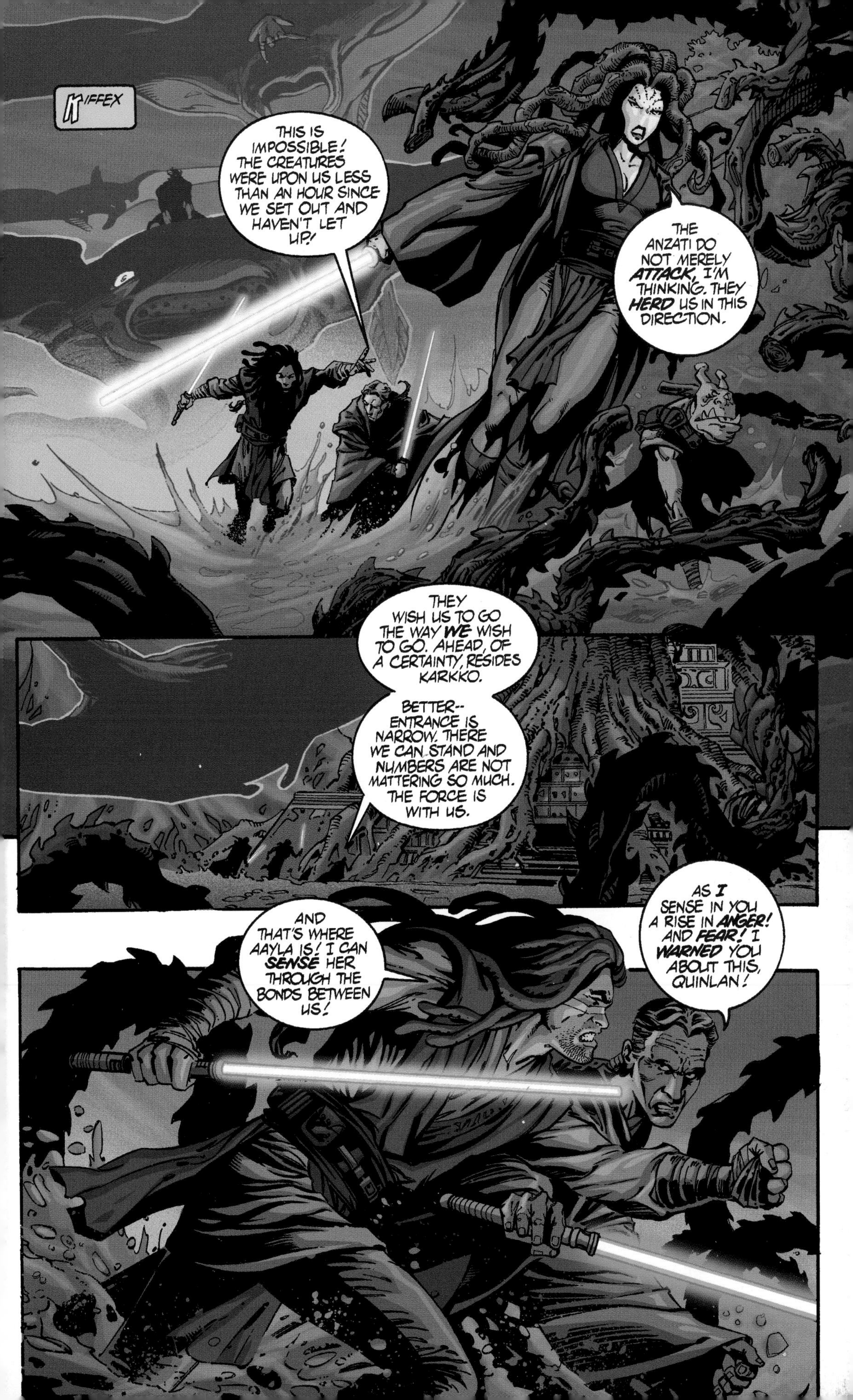
KIFFEX
THIS IS IMPOSSIBLE! THE CREATURES WERE UPON US LESS THAN AN HOUR SINCE WE SET OUT AND HAVEN'T LET UP!
THE ANZATI DO NOT MERELY ATTACK, I'M THINKING. THEY HERD US IN THIS DIRECTION.
THEY WISH US TO GO THE WAY WE WISH TO GO. AHEAD, OF A CERTAINTY, RESIDES KARKKO.
BETTER-- ENTRANCE IS NARROW. THERE WE CAN STAND AND NUMBERS ARE NOT MATTERING SO MUCH. THE FORCE IS WITH US.
AND THAT'S WHERE AAYLA IS! I CAN SENSE HER THROUGH THE BONDS BETWEEN US!
AS I SENSE IN YOU A RISE IN ANGER! AND FEAR! I WARNED YOU ABOUT THIS, QUINLAN!

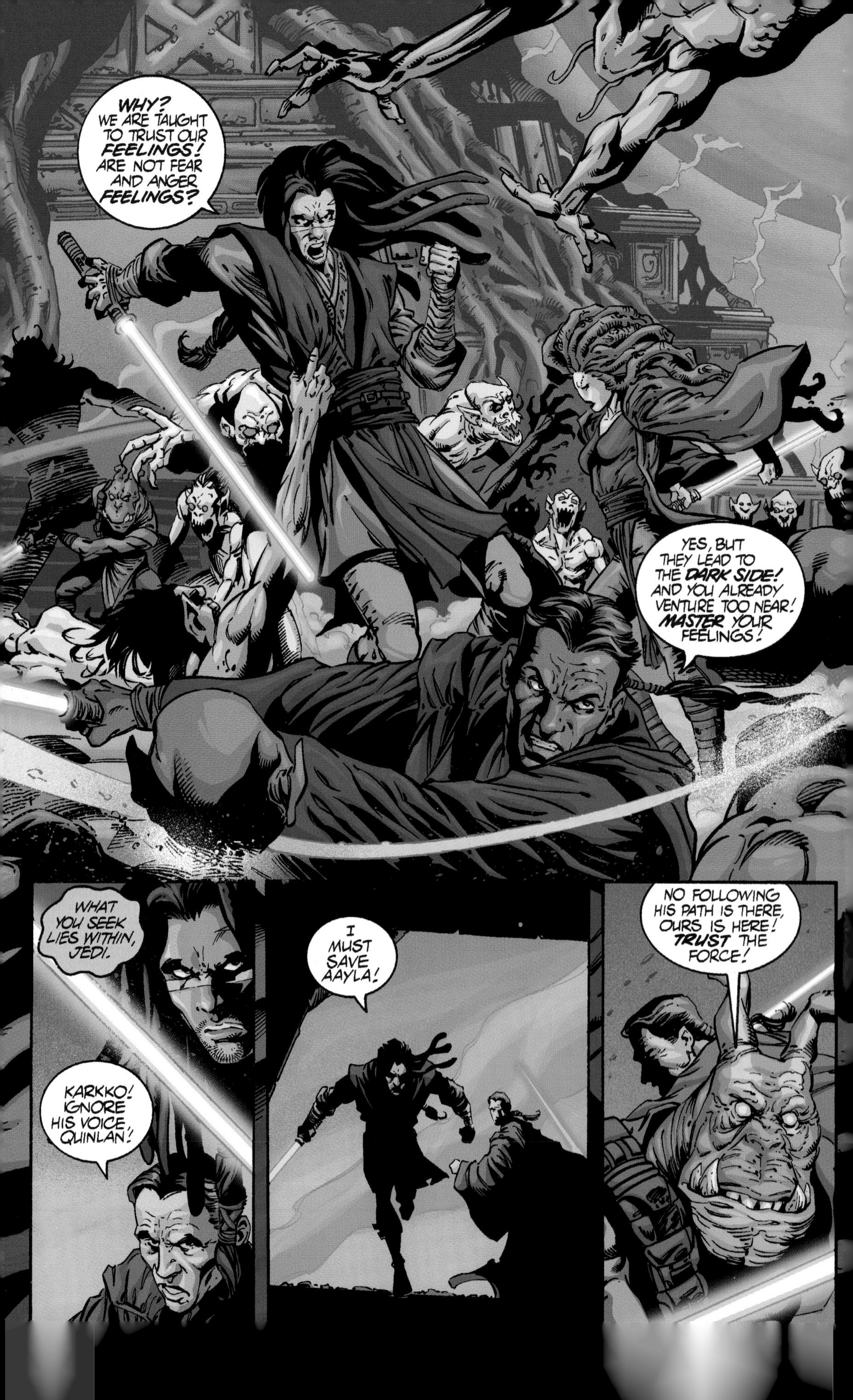
WHY? WE ARE TAUGHT TO TRUST OUR FEELINGS! ARE NOT FEAR AND ANGER FEELINGS?
YES, BUT THEY LEAD TO THE DARK SIDE! AND YOU ALREADY VENTURE TOO NEAR! MASTER YOUR FEELINGS!
WHAT YOU SEEK LIES WITHIN, JEDI.
KARKKO! IGNORE HIS VOICE, QUINLAN!
I MUST SAVE AAYLA!
NO FOLLOWING HIS PATH IS THERE, OURS IS HERE! TRUST THE FORCE!

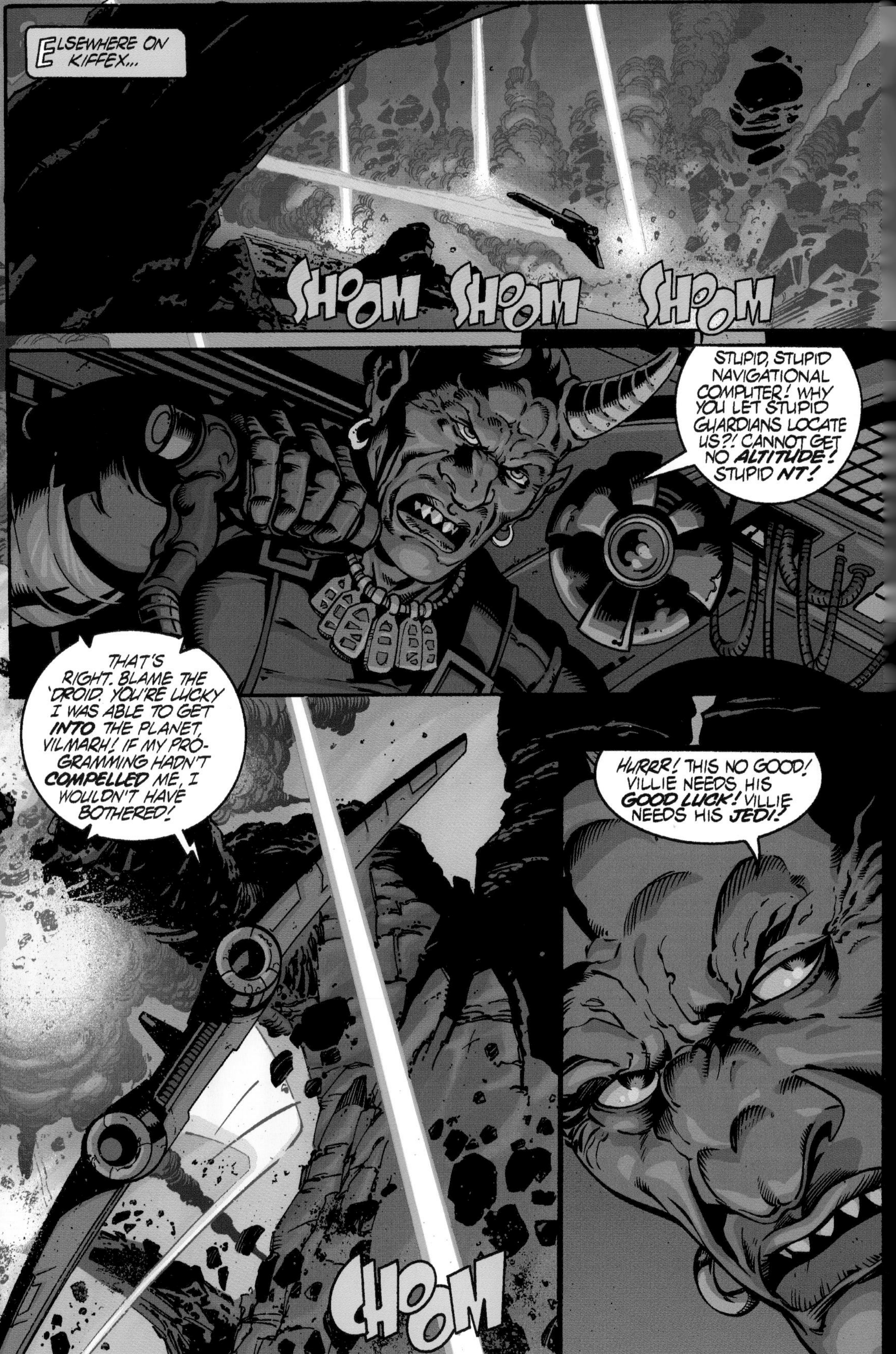
ELSEWHERE ON KIFFEX...
SHOOM SHOOM SHOOM
STUPID, STUPID NAVIGATIONAL COMPUTER! WHY YOU LET STUPID GUARDIANS LOCATE US?! CANNOT GET NO ALTITUDE! STUPID NT!
THAT'S RIGHT. BLAME THE 'DROID. YOU'RE LUCKY I WAS ABLE TO GET INTO THE PLANET, VILMARH! IF MY PRO-GRAMMING HADN'T COMPELLED ME, I WOULDN'T HAVE BOTHERED!
HURRR! THIS NO GOOD! VILLIE NEEDS HIS GOOD LUCK! VILLIE NEEDS HIS JEDI!
CHOOM

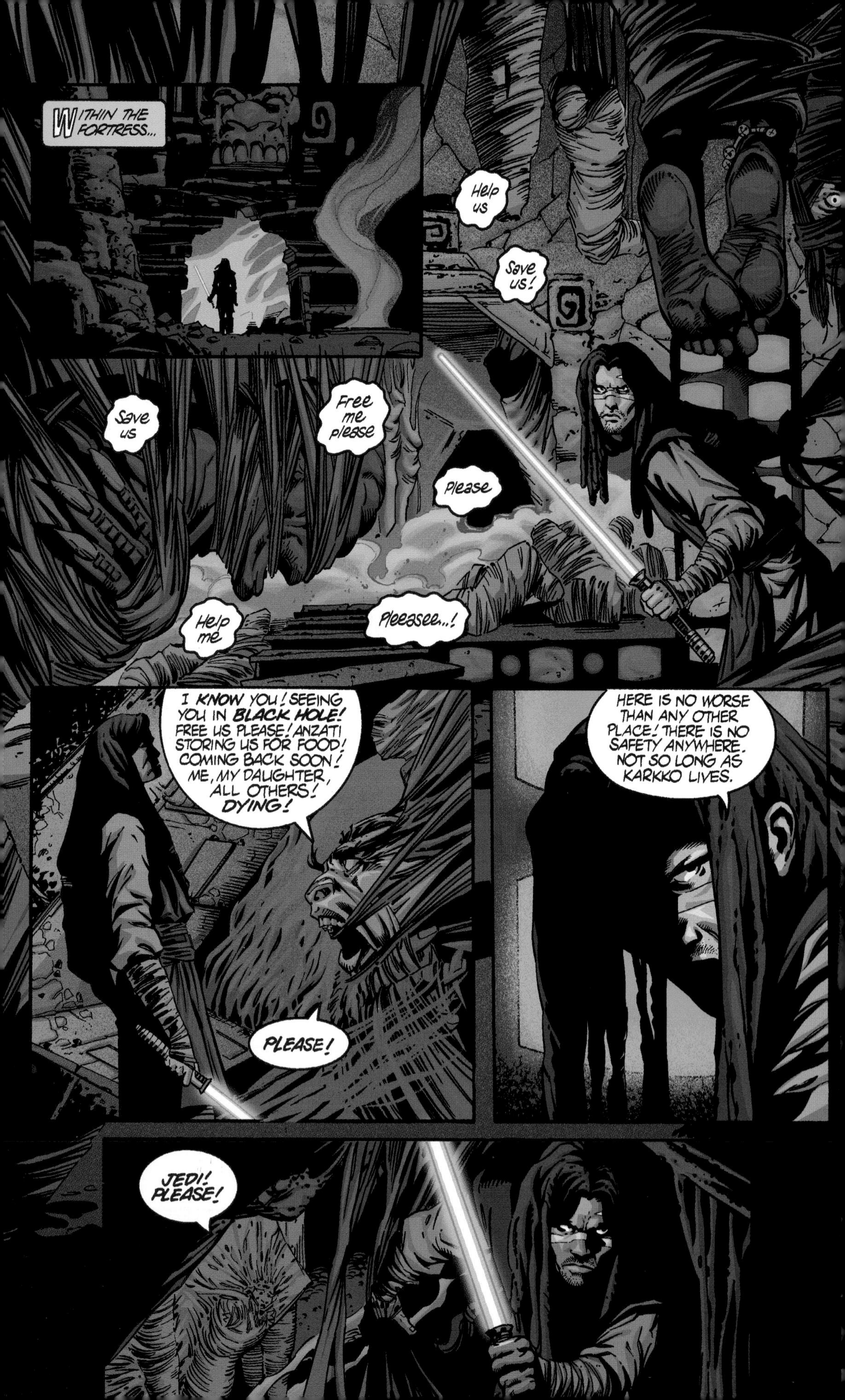
WITHIN THE FORTRESS...
Help us
Save us!
Save us
Free me please
Please
Help me
Pleeasee...!
I KNOW YOU! SEEING YOU IN BLACK HOLE! FREE US PLEASE! ANZATI STORING US FOR FOOD! COMING BACK SOON! ME, MY DAUGHTER, ALL OTHERS! DYING!
PLEASE!
HERE IS NO WORSE THAN ANY OTHER PLACE! THERE IS NO SAFETY ANYWHERE. NOT SO LONG AS KARKKO LIVES.
JEDI! PLEASE!

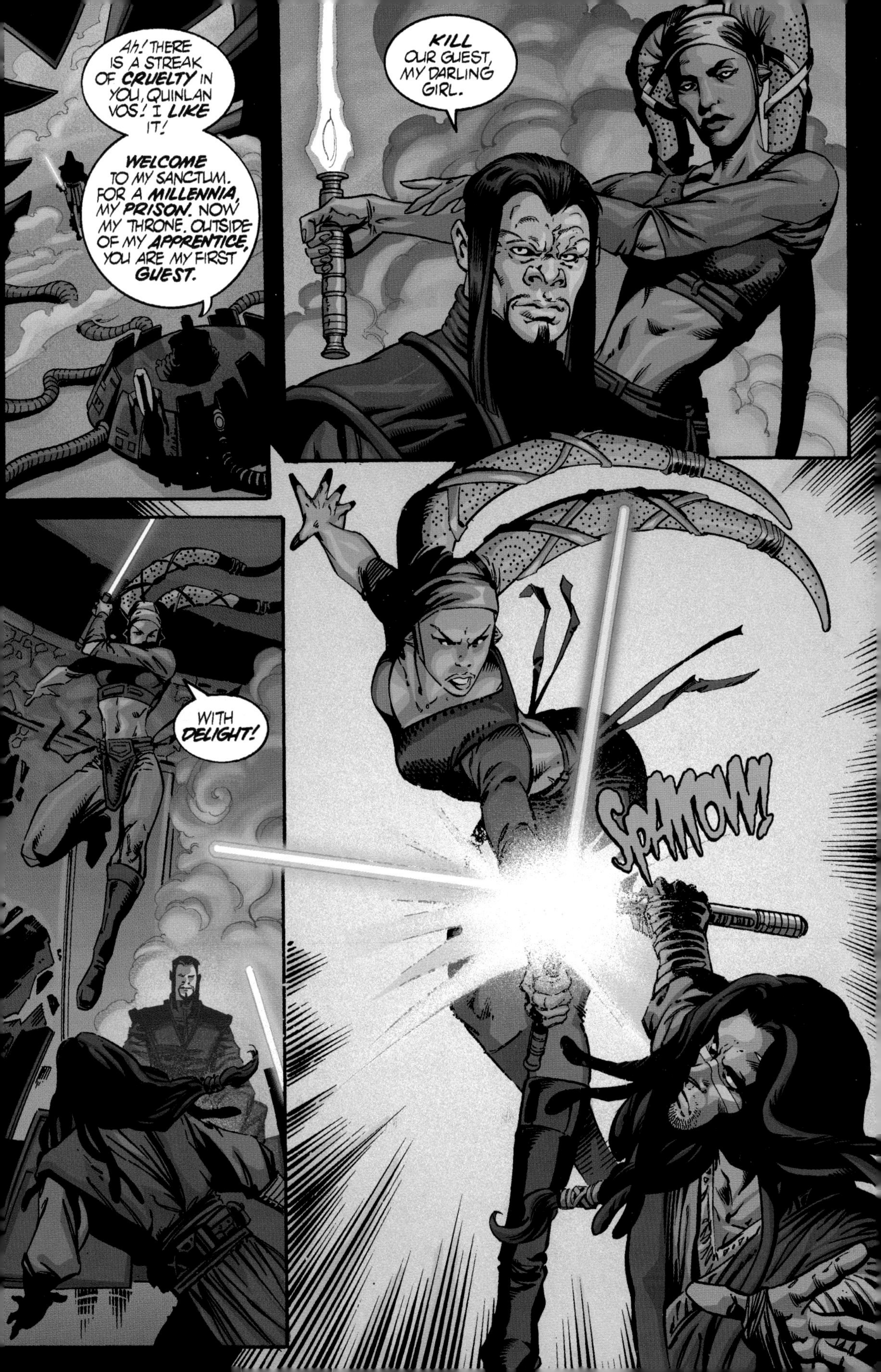

AH! THERE IS A STREAK OF CRUELTY IN YOU, QUINLAN VOS! I LIKE IT!
WELCOME TO MY SANCTUM. FOR A MILLENNIA, MY PRISON. NOW MY THRONE. OUTSIDE OF MY APPRENTICE, YOU ARE MY FIRST GUEST.
KILL OUR GUEST, MY DARLING GIRL.
WITH DELIGHT!
SPAMOM!

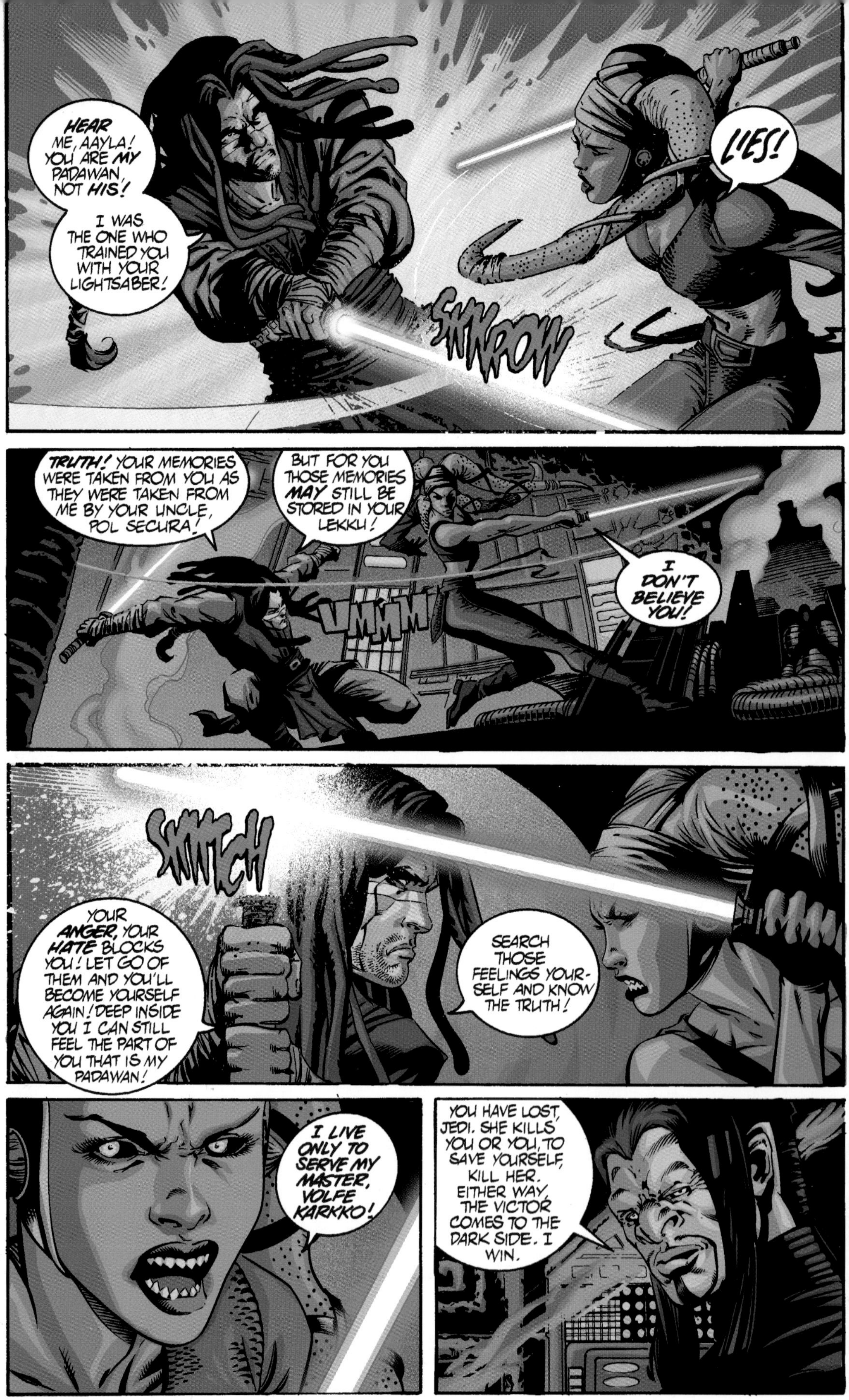
HEAR ME, AAYLA! YOU ARE MY PADAWAN, NOT HIS!
I WAS THE ONE WHO TRAINED YOU WITH YOUR LIGHTSABER!
LIES!
SHKPOW
TRUTH! YOUR MEMORIES WERE TAKEN FROM YOU AS THEY WERE TAKEN FROM ME BY YOUR UNCLE, POL SECURA!
BUT FOR YOU THOSE MEMORIES MAY STILL BE STORED IN YOUR LEKKU!
I DON'T BELIEVE YOU!
UMMM
SKTTCH
YOUR ANGER, YOUR HATE BLOCKS YOU! LET GO OF THEM AND YOU'LL BECOME YOURSELF AGAIN! DEEP INSIDE YOU I CAN STILL FEEL THE PART OF YOU THAT IS MY PADAWAN!
SEARCH THOSE FEELINGS YOURSELF AND KNOW THE TRUTH!
I LIVE ONLY TO SERVE MY MASTER, VOLFE KARKKO!
YOU HAVE LOST, JEDI. SHE KILLS YOU OR YOU, TO SAVE YOURSELF, KILL HER. EITHER WAY, THE VICTOR COMES TO THE DARK SIDE. I WIN.

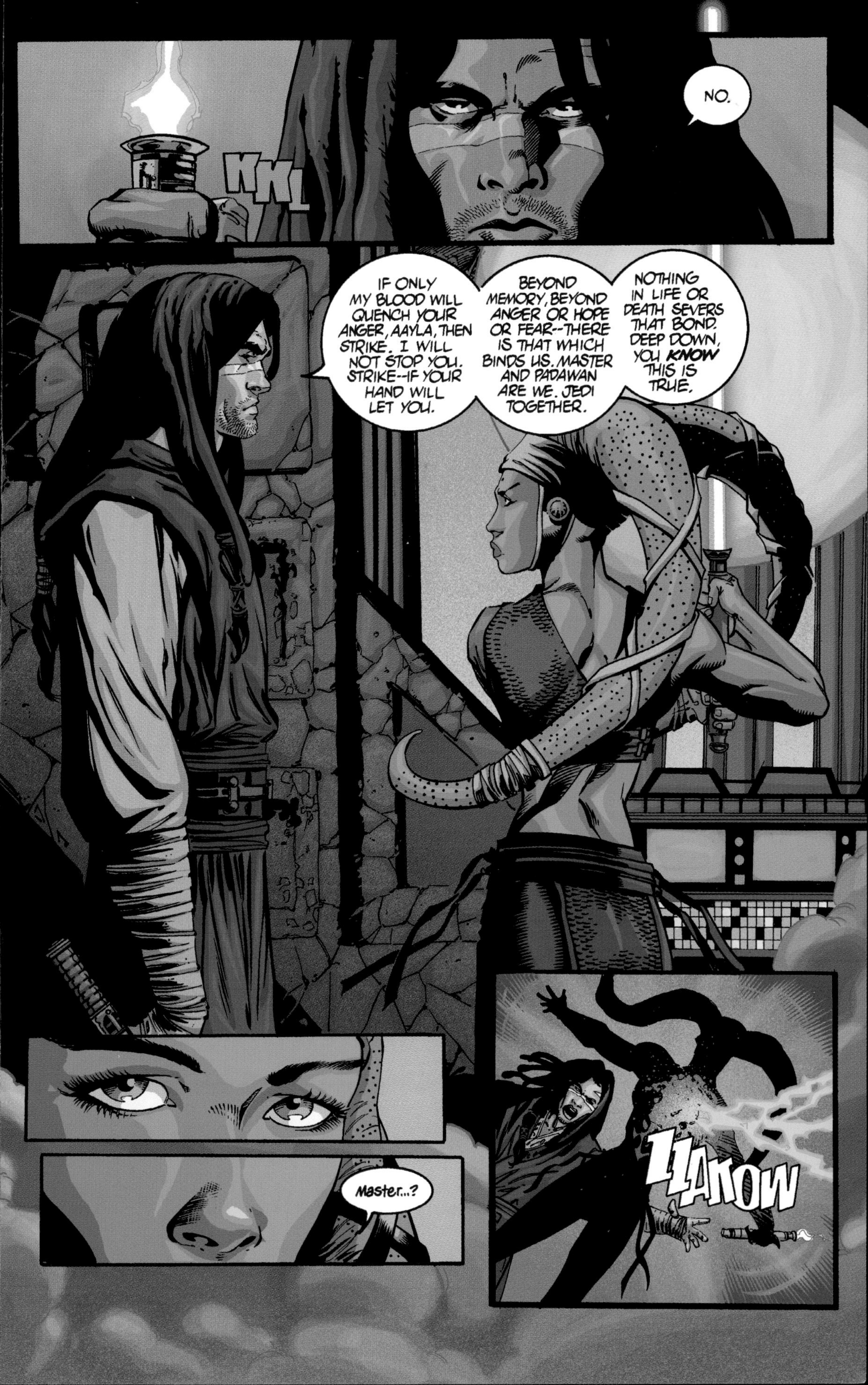
KKL
NO.
IF ONLY MY BLOOD WILL QUENCH YOUR ANGER, AAYLA, THEN STRIKE. I WILL NOT STOP YOU. STRIKE--IF YOUR HAND WILL LET YOU.
BEYOND MEMORY, BEYOND ANGER OR HOPE OR FEAR--THERE IS THAT WHICH BINDS US. MASTER AND PADAWAN ARE WE. JEDI TOGETHER.
NOTHING IN LIFE OR DEATH SEVERS THAT BOND. DEEP DOWN, YOU KNOW THIS IS TRUE.
Master...?
LLAKOW

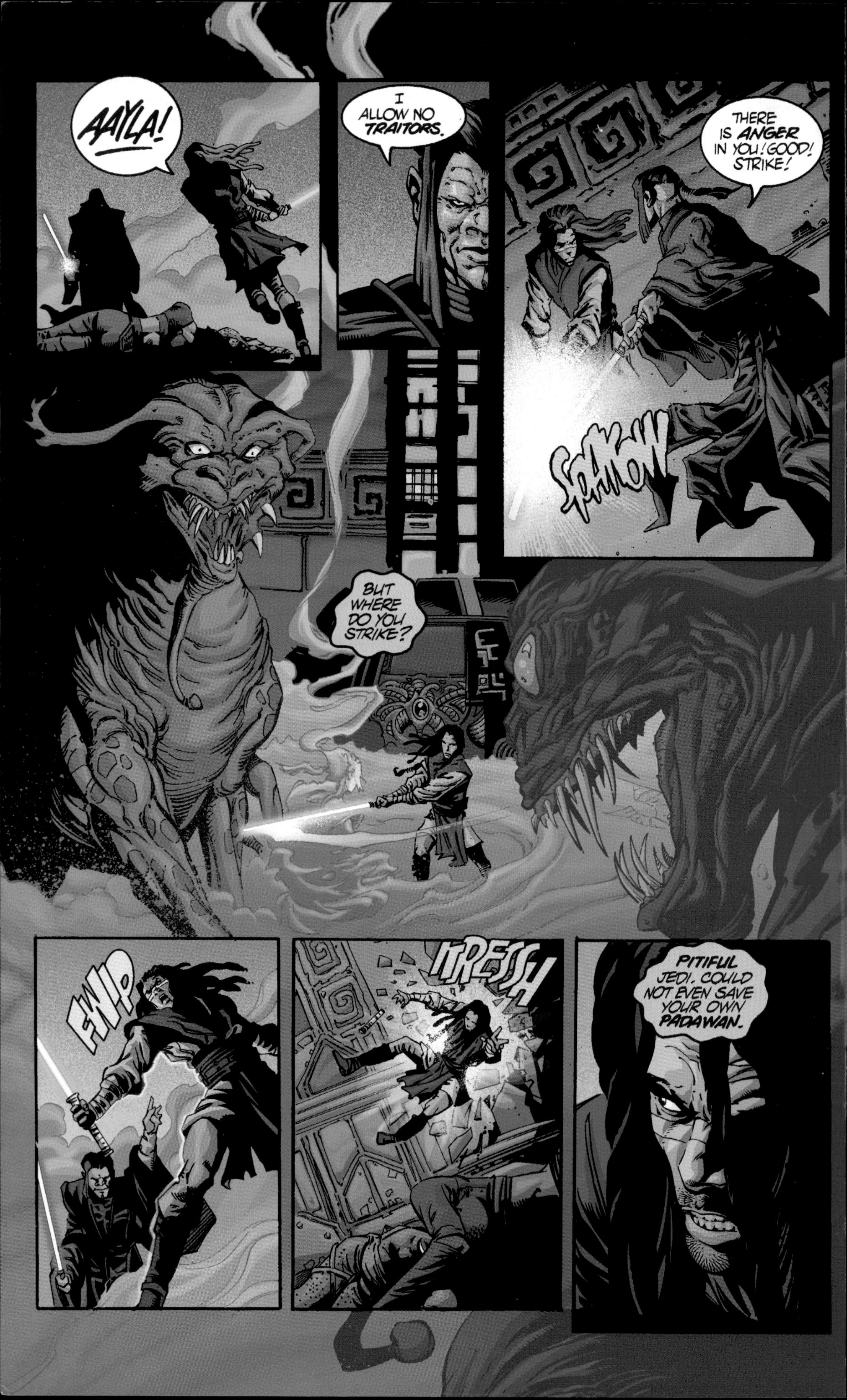
AAYLA!
I ALLOW NO TRAITORS.
THERE IS ANGER IN YOU! GOOD! STRIKE!
SPAKOW
BUT WHERE DO YOU STRIKE?
FWIP
KRESSH
PITIFUL JEDI. COULD NOT EVEN SAVE YOUR OWN PADAWAN.

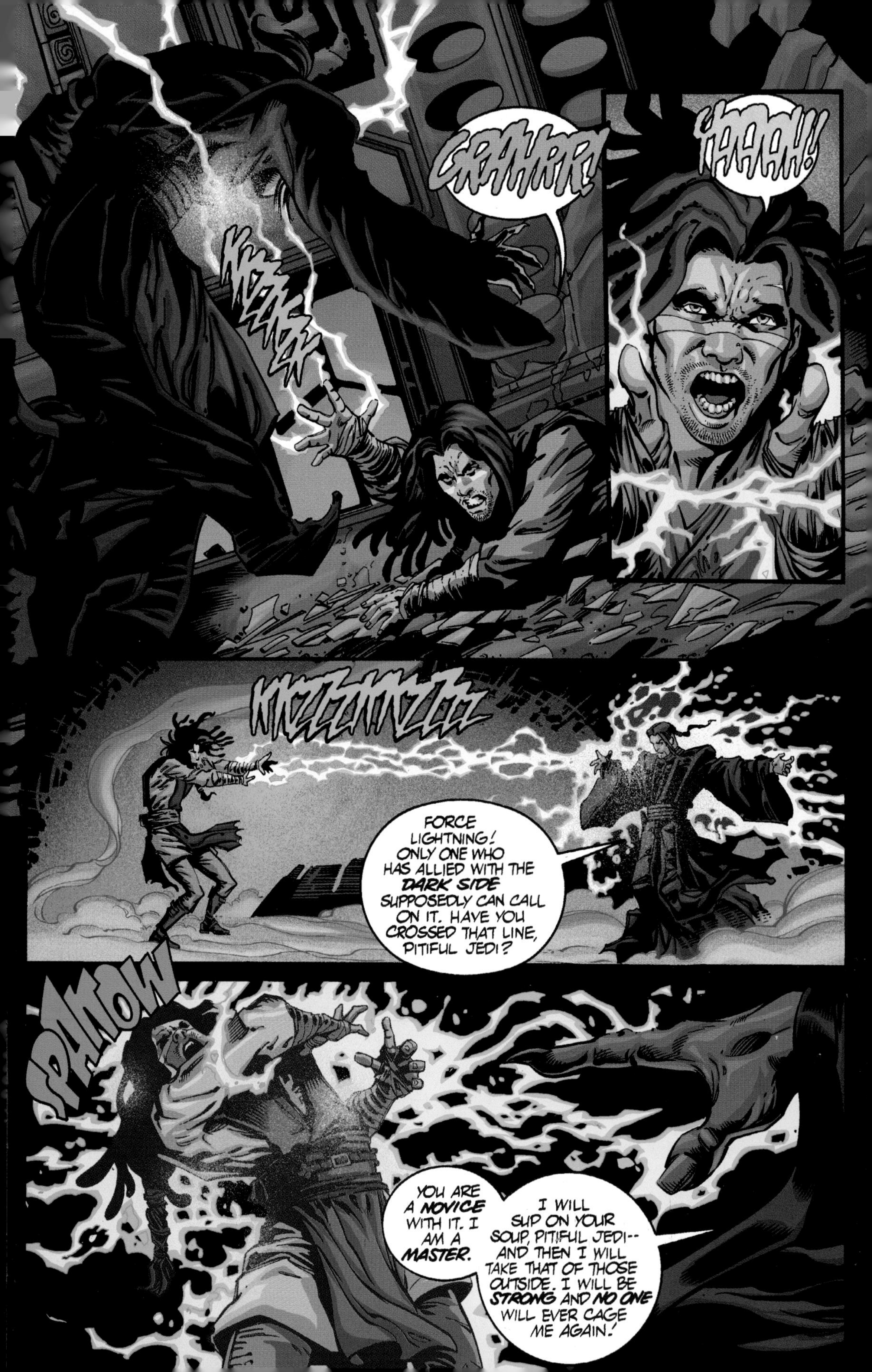
GRAHRR!
YAAAH!
FORCE LIGHTNING! ONLY ONE WHO HAS ALLIED WITH THE **DARK SIDE** SUPPOSEDLY CAN CALL ON IT. HAVE YOU CROSSED THAT LINE, PITIFUL JEDI?
SPAHOW
YOU ARE A **NOVICE** WITH IT. I AM A **MASTER**.
I WILL SUP ON YOUR SOUP, PITIFUL JEDI-- AND THEN I WILL TAKE THAT OF THOSE OUTSIDE. I WILL BE **STRONG** AND **NO ONE** WILL EVER CAGE ME AGAIN!

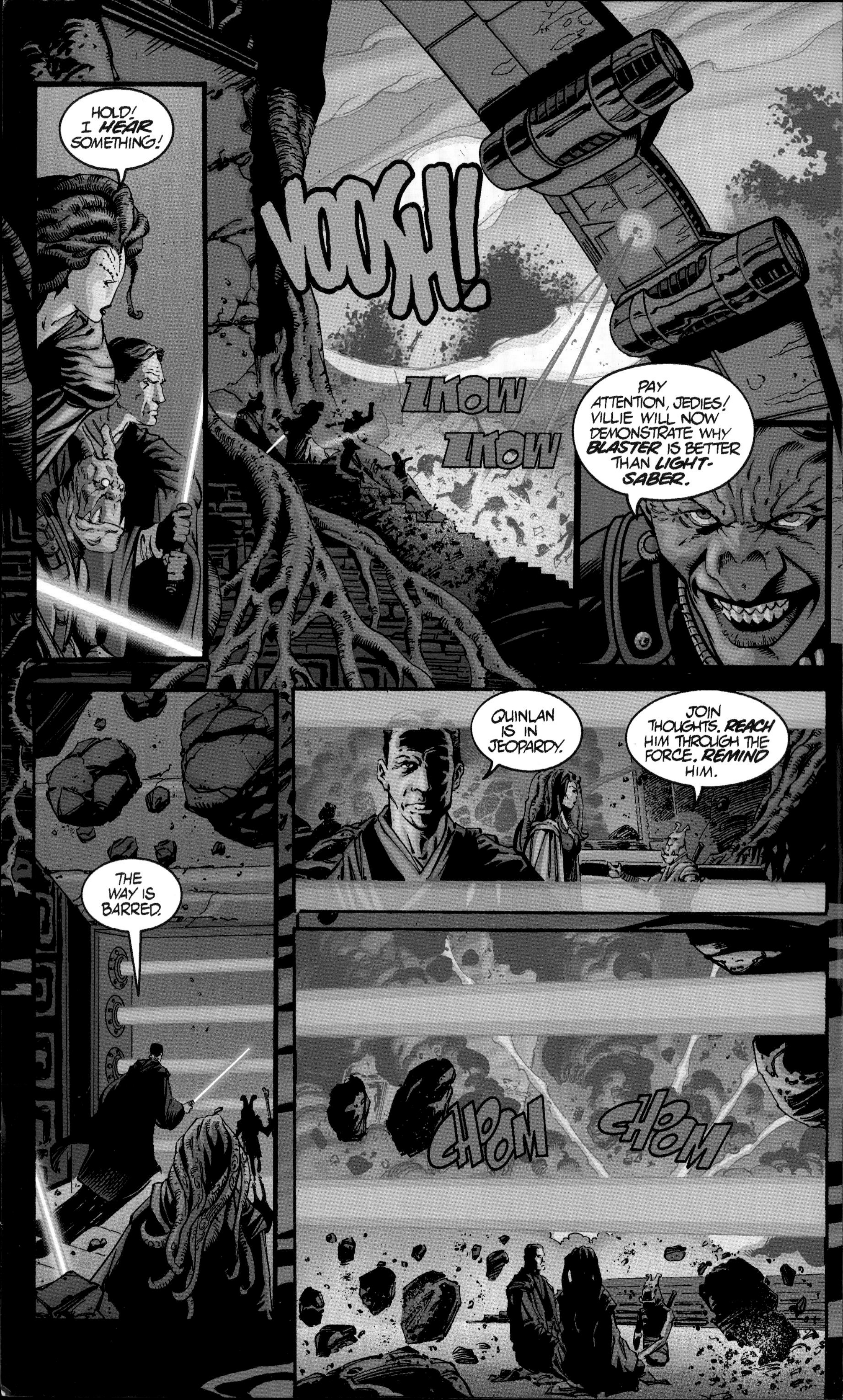
HOLD! I HEAR SOMETHING!
VOOSH!
ZKOW
ZKOW
PAY ATTENTION, JEDIES! VILLIE WILL NOW DEMONSTRATE WHY BLASTER IS BETTER THAN LIGHT-SABER.
THE WAY IS BARRED.
QUINLAN IS IN JEOPARDY.
JOIN THOUGHTS. REACH HIM THROUGH THE FORCE. REMIND HIM.
CHOOM
CHOOM

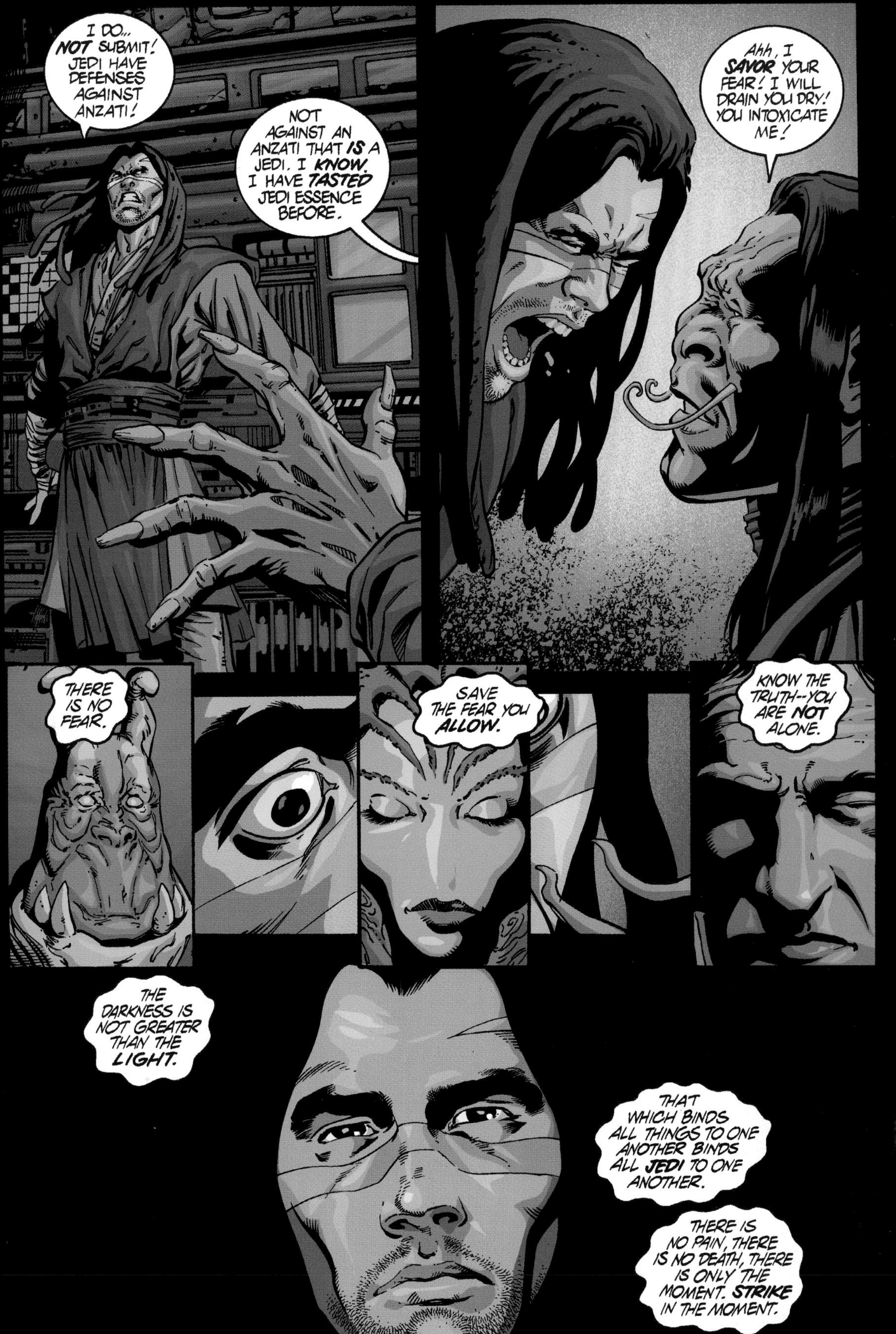
I DO... NOT SUBMIT! JEDI HAVE DEFENSES AGAINST ANZATI!
NOT AGAINST AN ANZATI THAT IS A JEDI. I KNOW. I HAVE TASTED JEDI ESSENCE BEFORE.
Ahh, I SAVOR YOUR FEAR! I WILL DRAIN YOU DRY! YOU INTOXICATE ME!
THERE IS NO FEAR.
SAVE THE FEAR YOU ALLOW.
KNOW THE TRUTH--YOU ARE NOT ALONE.
THE DARKNESS IS NOT GREATER THAN THE LIGHT.
THAT WHICH BINDS ALL THINGS TO ONE ANOTHER BINDS ALL JEDI TO ONE ANOTHER.
THERE IS NO PAIN, THERE IS NO DEATH, THERE IS ONLY THE MOMENT. STRIKE IN THE MOMENT.

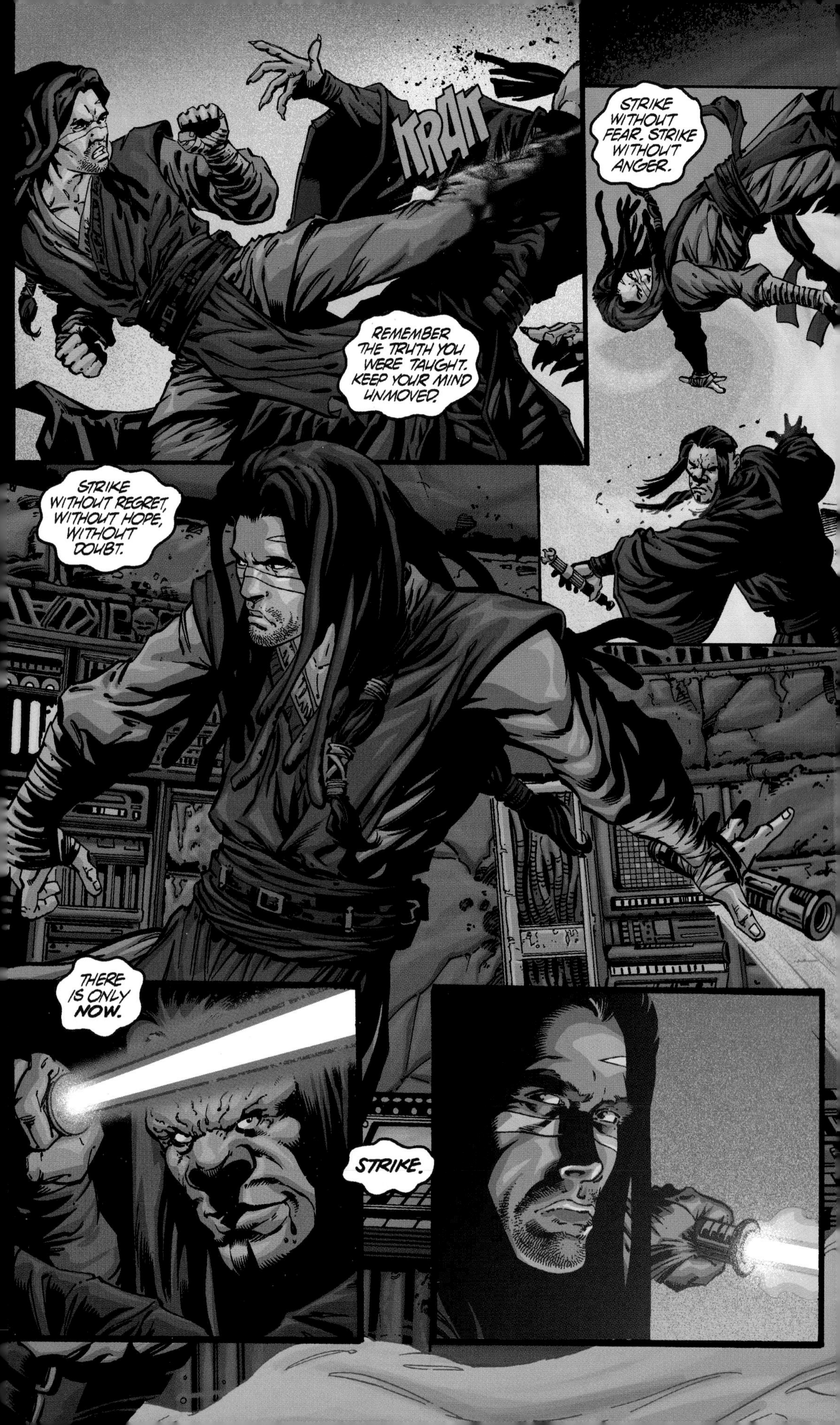
KRAK
REMEMBER THE TRUTH YOU WERE TAUGHT. KEEP YOUR MIND UNMOVED.
STRIKE WITHOUT FEAR. STRIKE WITHOUT ANGER.
STRIKE WITHOUT REGRET, WITHOUT HOPE, WITHOUT DOUBT.
THERE IS ONLY NOW.
STRIKE.

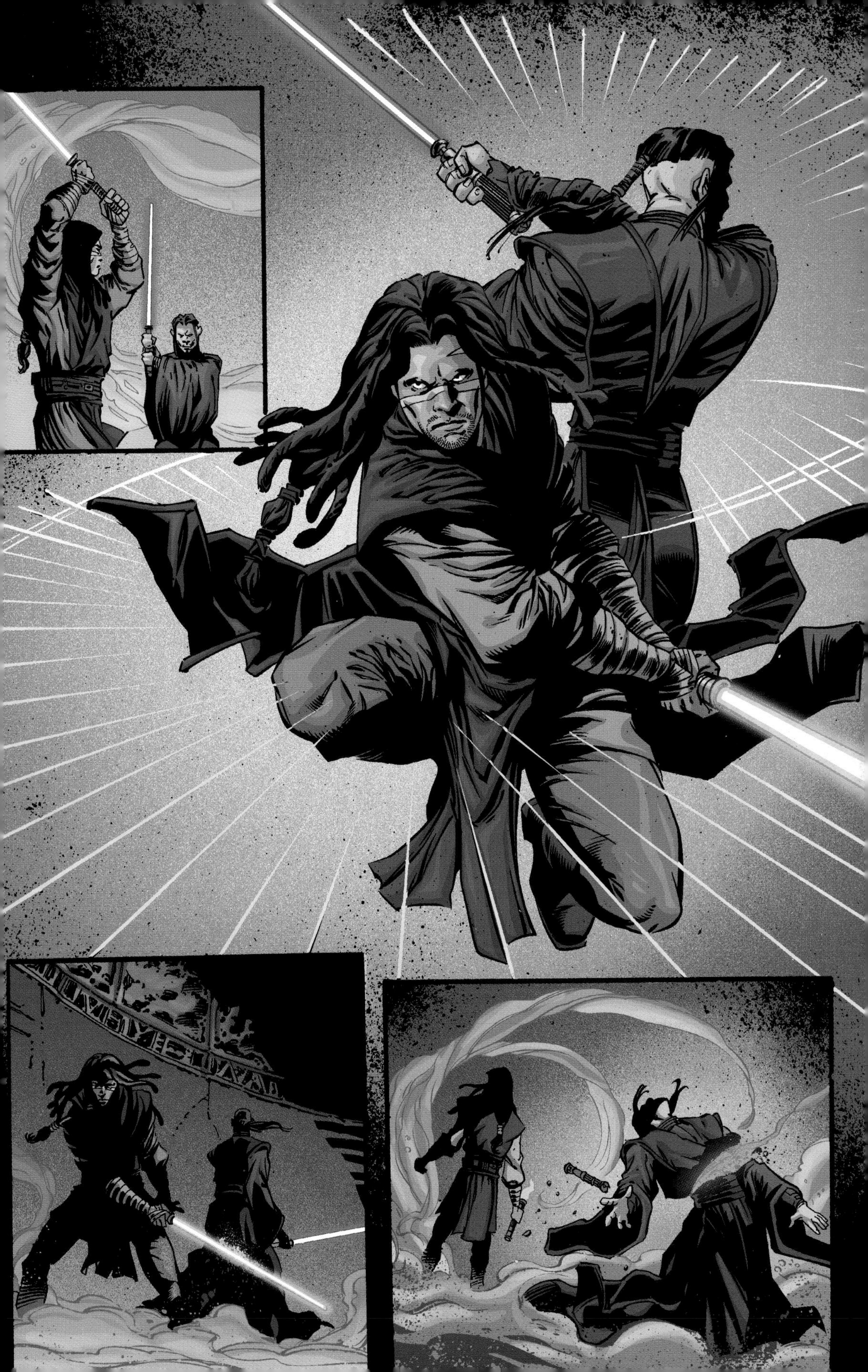

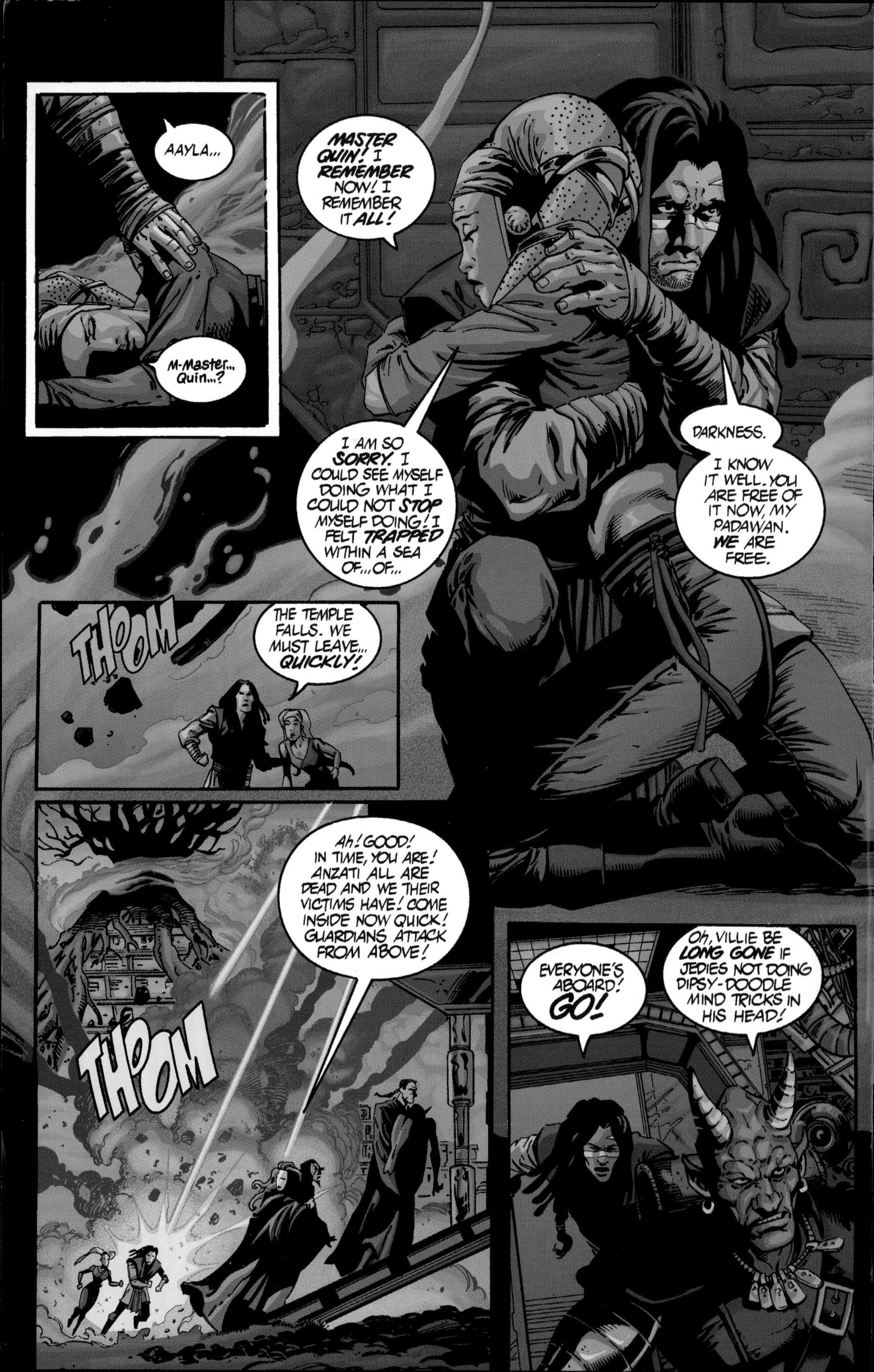
AAYLA...
M-MASTER... QUIN...?
MASTER QUIN! I REMEMBER NOW! I REMEMBER IT ALL!
I AM SO SORRY. I COULD SEE MYSELF DOING WHAT I COULD NOT STOP MYSELF DOING! I FELT TRAPPED WITHIN A SEA OF... OF...
DARKNESS.
I KNOW IT WELL. YOU ARE FREE OF IT NOW, MY PADAWAN. WE ARE FREE.
THOOM
THE TEMPLE FALLS. WE MUST LEAVE... QUICKLY!
THOOM
AH! GOOD! IN TIME, YOU ARE! ANZATI ALL ARE DEAD AND WE THEIR VICTIMS HAVE! COME INSIDE NOW QUICK! GUARDIANS ATTACK FROM ABOVE!
EVERYONE'S ABOARD! GO!
OH, VILLIE BE LONG GONE IF JEDIES NOT DOING DIPSY-DOODLE MIND TRICKS IN HIS HEAD!

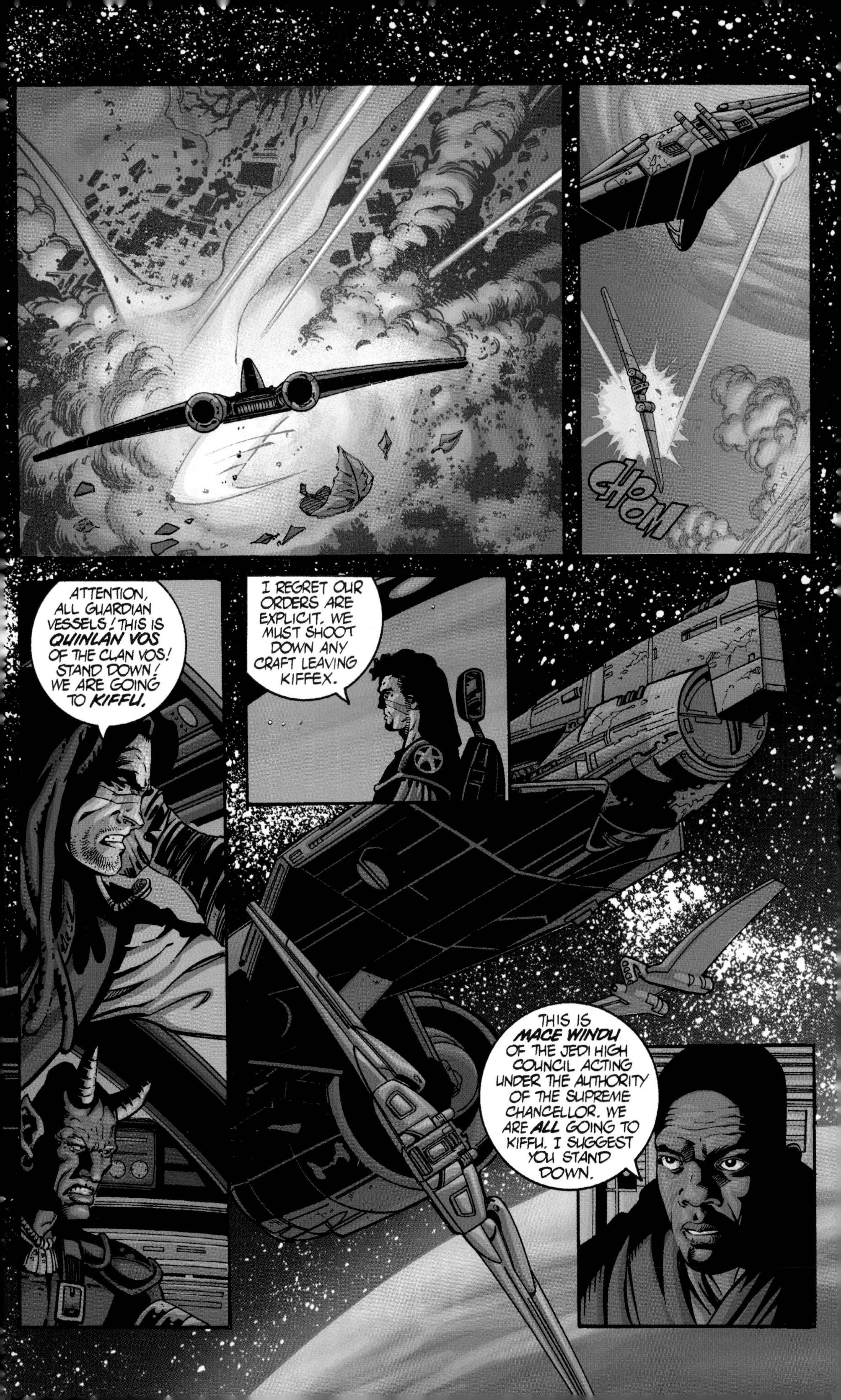
CHOOM
ATTENTION, ALL GUARDIAN VESSELS! THIS IS QUINLAN VOS OF THE CLAN VOS! STAND DOWN! WE ARE GOING TO KIFFU.
I REGRET OUR ORDERS ARE EXPLICIT. WE MUST SHOOT DOWN ANY CRAFT LEAVING KIFFEX.
THIS IS MACE WINDU OF THE JEDI HIGH COUNCIL ACTING UNDER THE AUTHORITY OF THE SUPREME CHANCELLOR. WE ARE ALL GOING TO KIFFU. I SUGGEST YOU STAND DOWN.

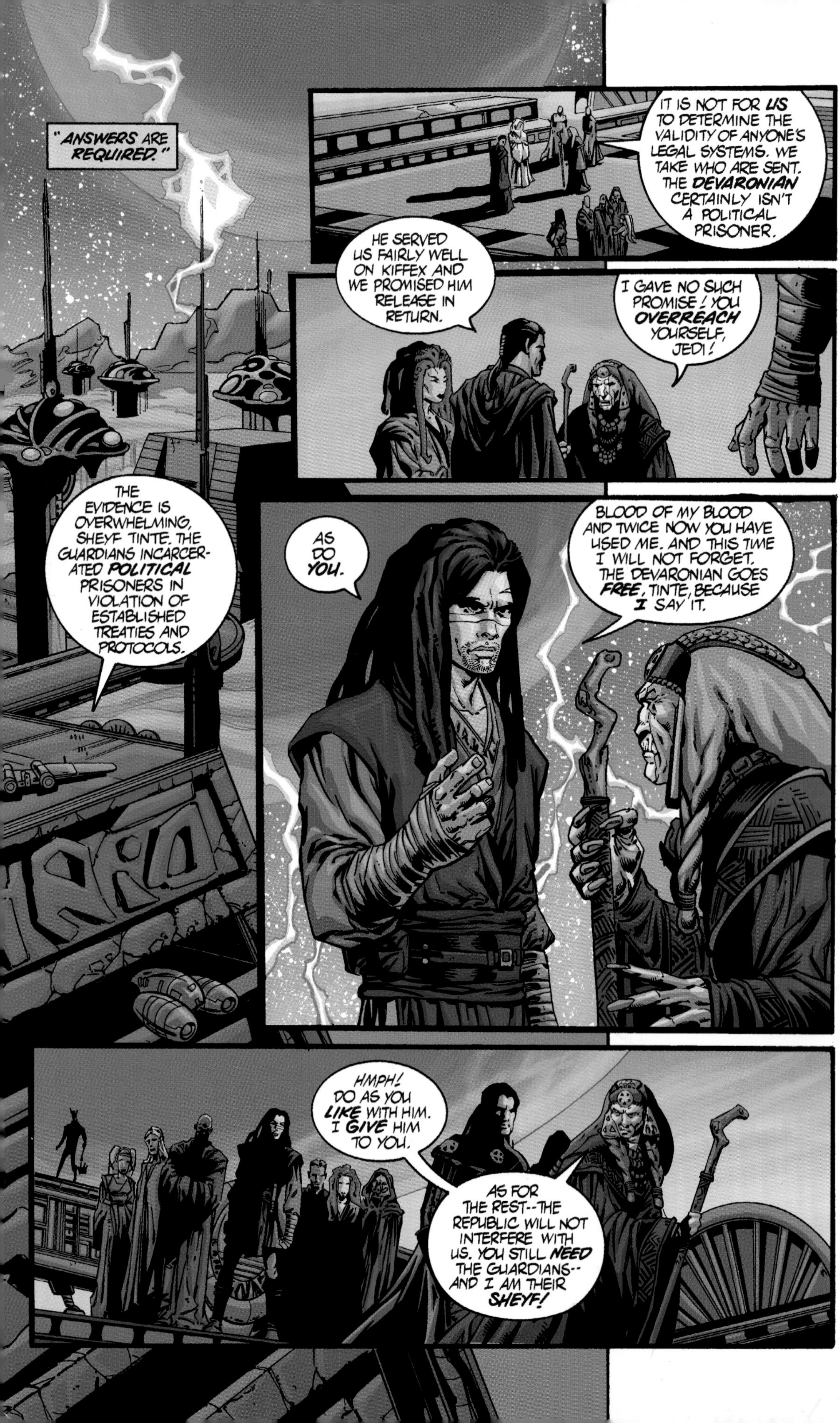
"ANSWERS ARE REQUIRED."
IT IS NOT FOR US TO DETERMINE THE VALIDITY OF ANYONE'S LEGAL SYSTEMS. WE TAKE WHO ARE SENT. THE DEVARONIAN CERTAINLY ISN'T A POLITICAL PRISONER.
HE SERVED US FAIRLY WELL ON KIFFEX AND WE PROMISED HIM RELEASE IN RETURN.
I GAVE NO SUCH PROMISE! YOU OVERREACH YOURSELF, JEDI!
THE EVIDENCE IS OVERWHELMING, SHEYF TINTE. THE GUARDIANS INCARCERATED POLITICAL PRISONERS IN VIOLATION OF ESTABLISHED TREATIES AND PROTOCOLS.
AS DO YOU.
BLOOD OF MY BLOOD AND TWICE NOW YOU HAVE USED ME. AND THIS TIME I WILL NOT FORGET. THE DEVARONIAN GOES FREE, TINTE, BECAUSE I SAY IT.
HMPH! DO AS YOU LIKE WITH HIM. I GIVE HIM TO YOU.
AS FOR THE REST--THE REPUBLIC WILL NOT INTERFERE WITH US. YOU STILL NEED THE GUARDIANS--AND I AM THEIR SHEYF!

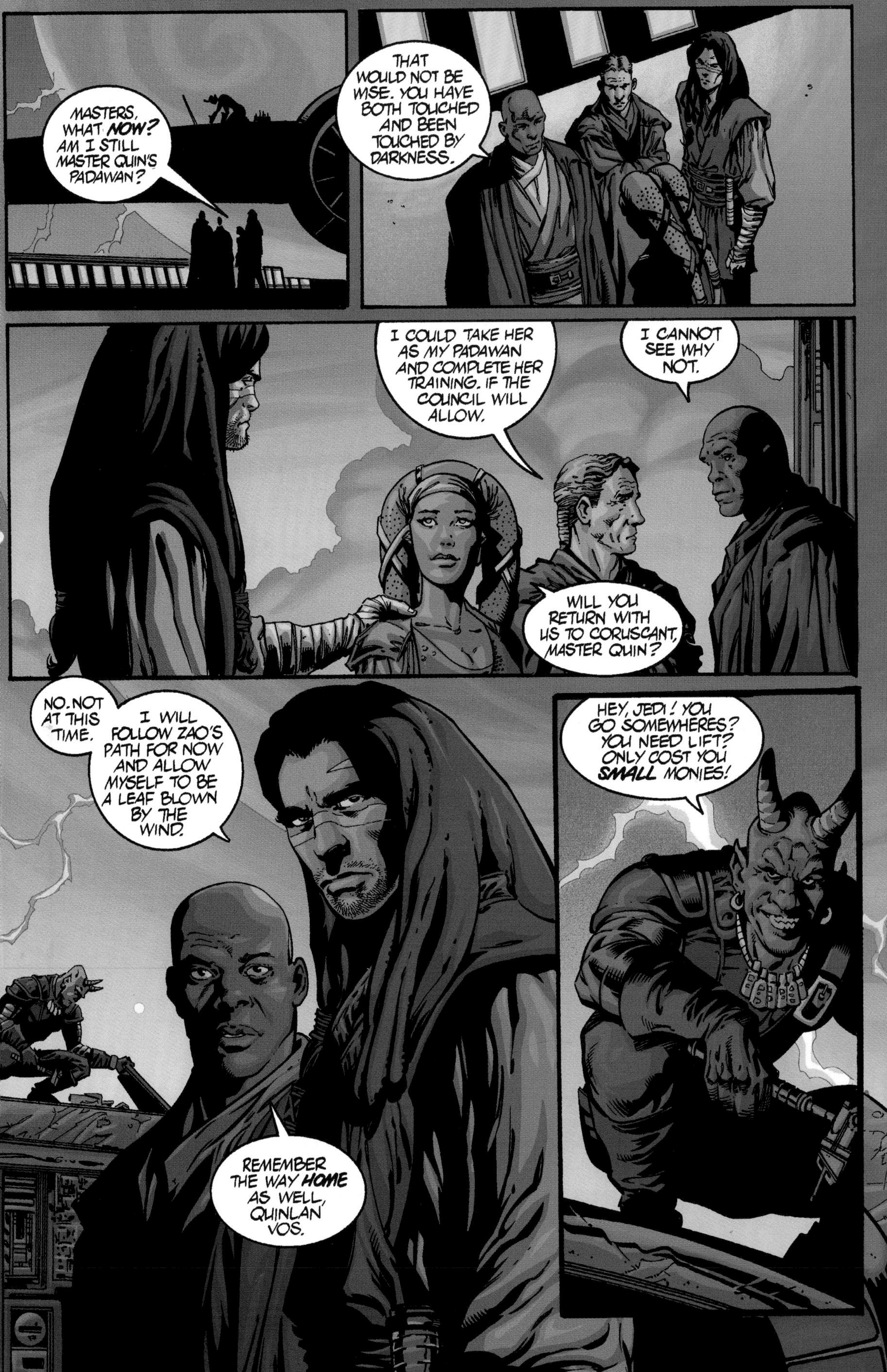
MASTERS, WHAT NOW? AM I STILL MASTER QUIN'S PADAWAN?
THAT WOULD NOT BE WISE. YOU HAVE BOTH TOUCHED AND BEEN TOUCHED BY DARKNESS.
I COULD TAKE HER AS MY PADAWAN AND COMPLETE HER TRAINING. IF THE COUNCIL WILL ALLOW.
I CANNOT SEE WHY NOT.
WILL YOU RETURN WITH US TO CORUSCANT, MASTER QUIN?
NO. NOT AT THIS TIME.
I WILL FOLLOW ZAO'S PATH FOR NOW AND ALLOW MYSELF TO BE A LEAF BLOWN BY THE WIND.
REMEMBER THE WAY HOME AS WELL, QUINLAN VOS.
HEY, JEDI! YOU GO SOMEWHERES? YOU NEED LIFT? ONLY COST YOU SMALL MONIES!

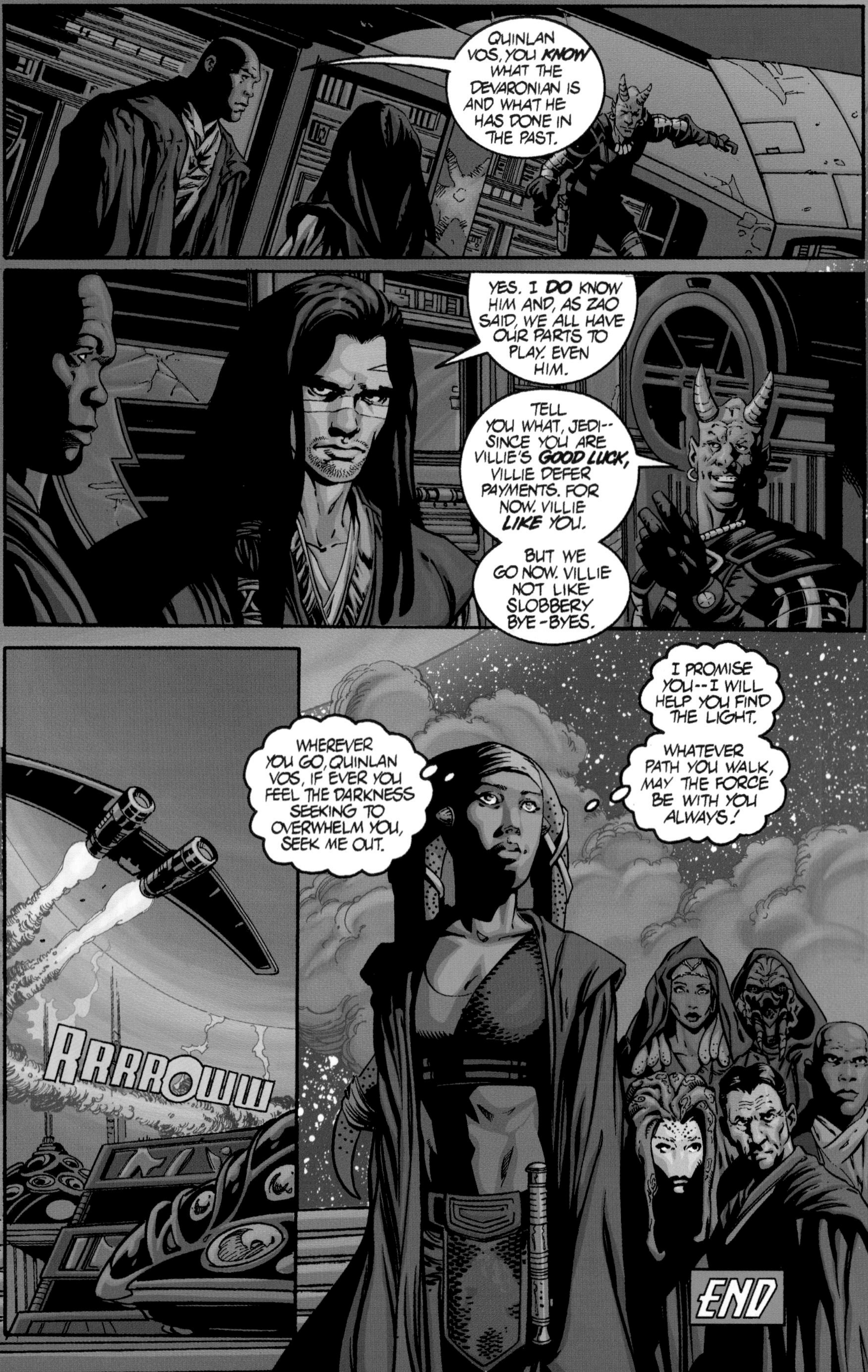
QUINLAN VOS, YOU KNOW WHAT THE DEVARONIAN IS AND WHAT HE HAS DONE IN THE PAST.
YES. I DO KNOW HIM AND, AS ZAO SAID, WE ALL HAVE OUR PARTS TO PLAY. EVEN HIM.
TELL YOU WHAT, JEDI-- SINCE YOU ARE VILLIE'S GOOD LUCK, VILLIE DEFER PAYMENTS. FOR NOW. VILLIE LIKE YOU.
BUT WE GO NOW. VILLIE NOT LIKE SLOBBERY BYE-BYES.
RRRROWW
WHEREVER YOU GO, QUINLAN VOS, IF EVER YOU FEEL THE DARKNESS SEEKING TO OVERWHELM YOU, SEEK ME OUT.
I PROMISE YOU--I WILL HELP YOU FIND THE LIGHT.
WHATEVER PATH YOU WALK, MAY THE FORCE BE WITH YOU ALWAYS!
END

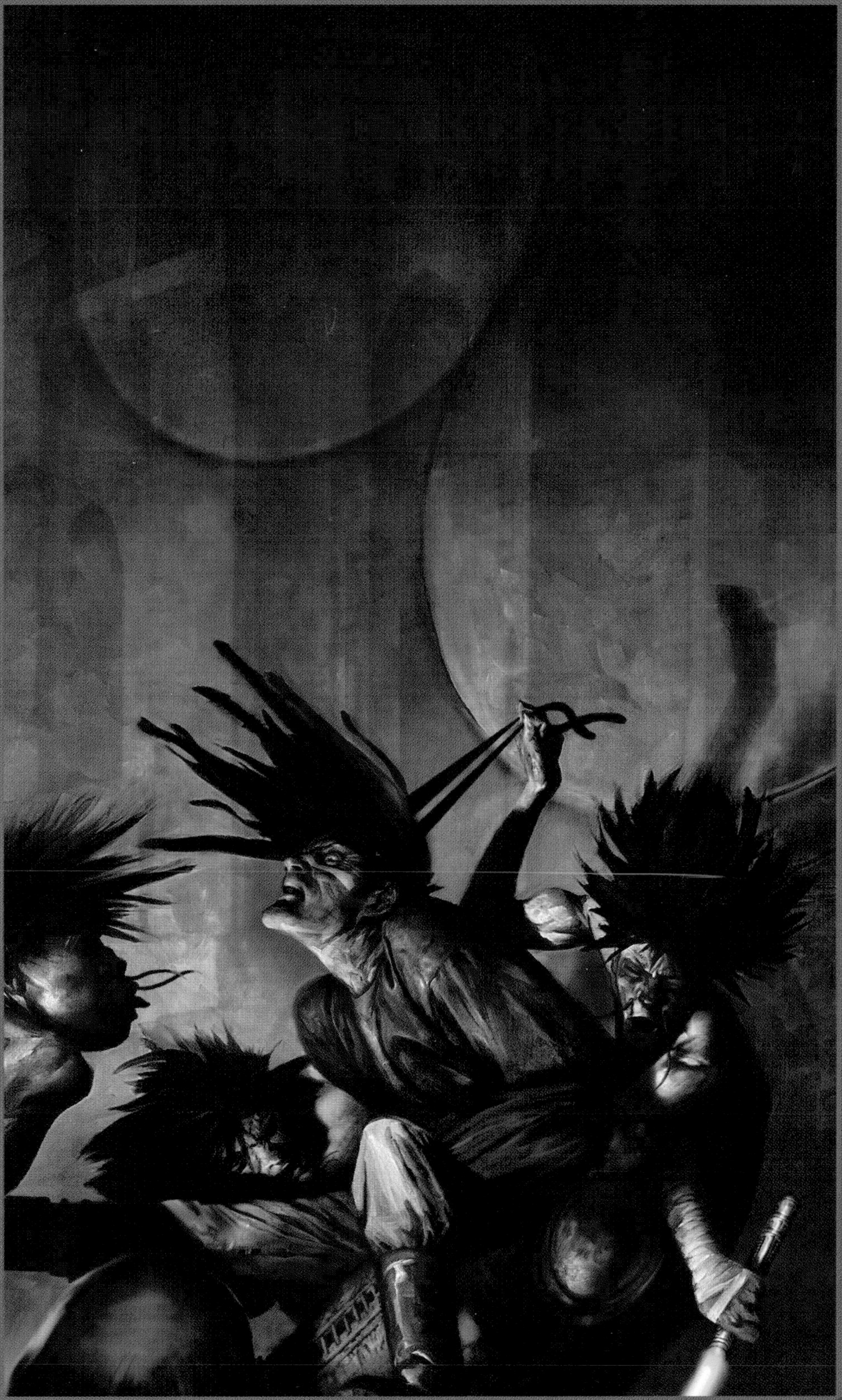

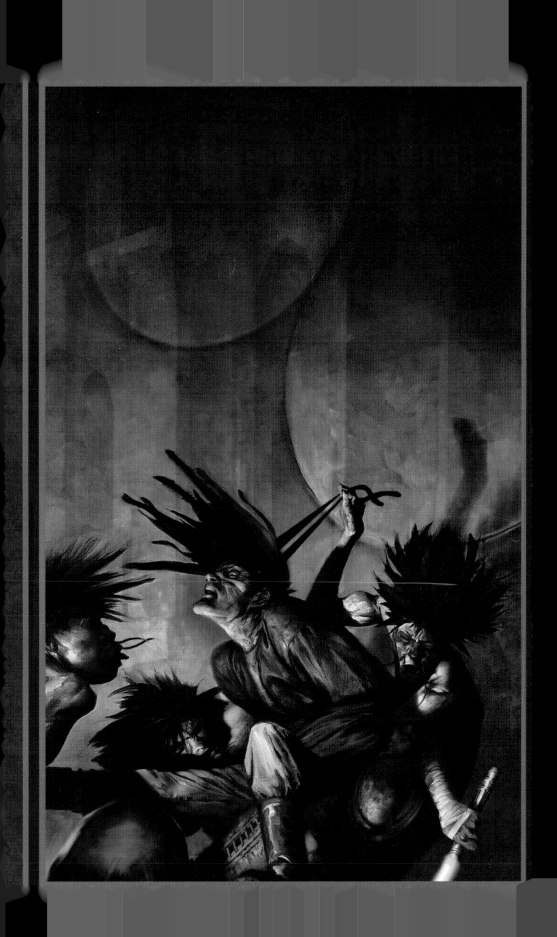

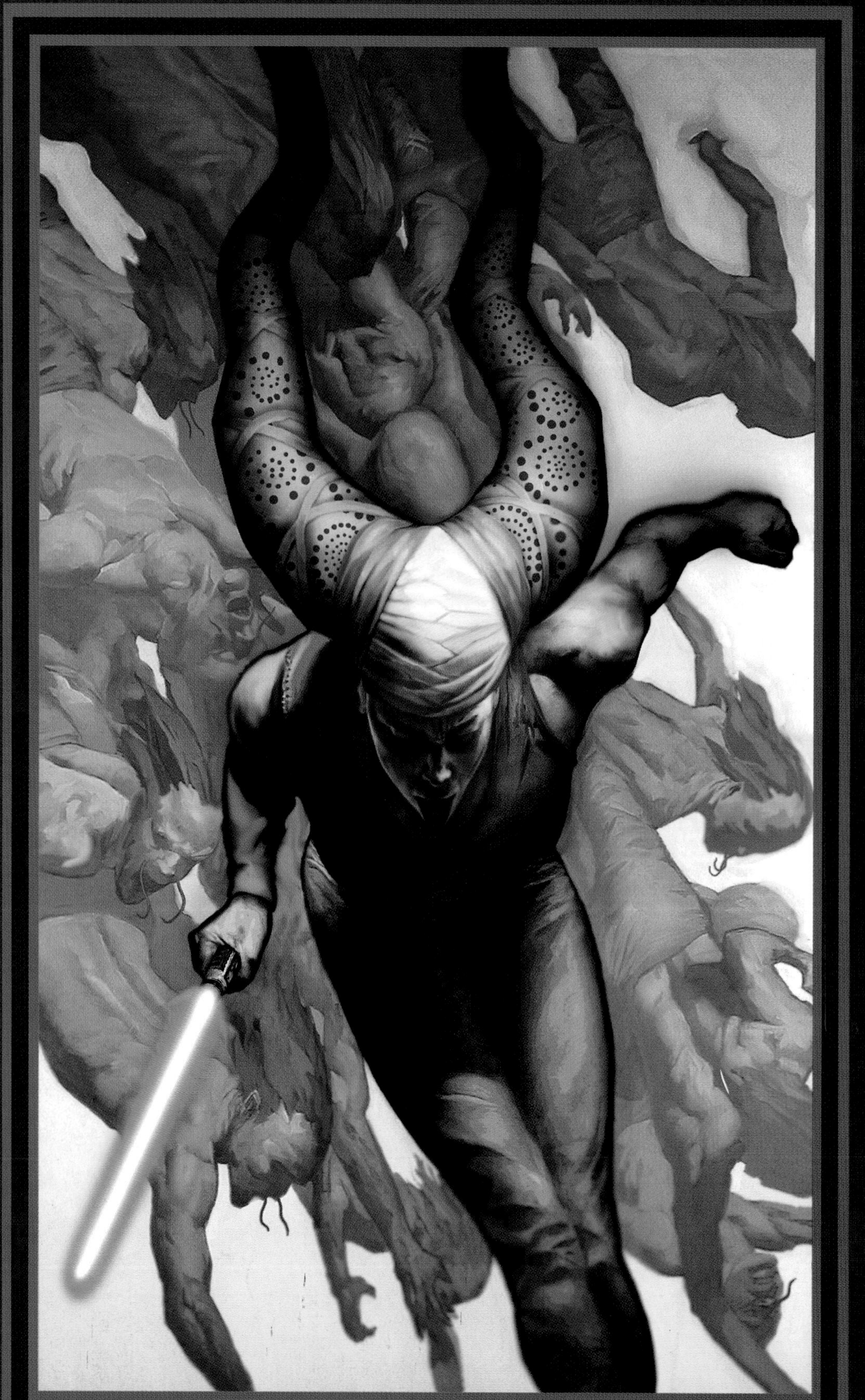

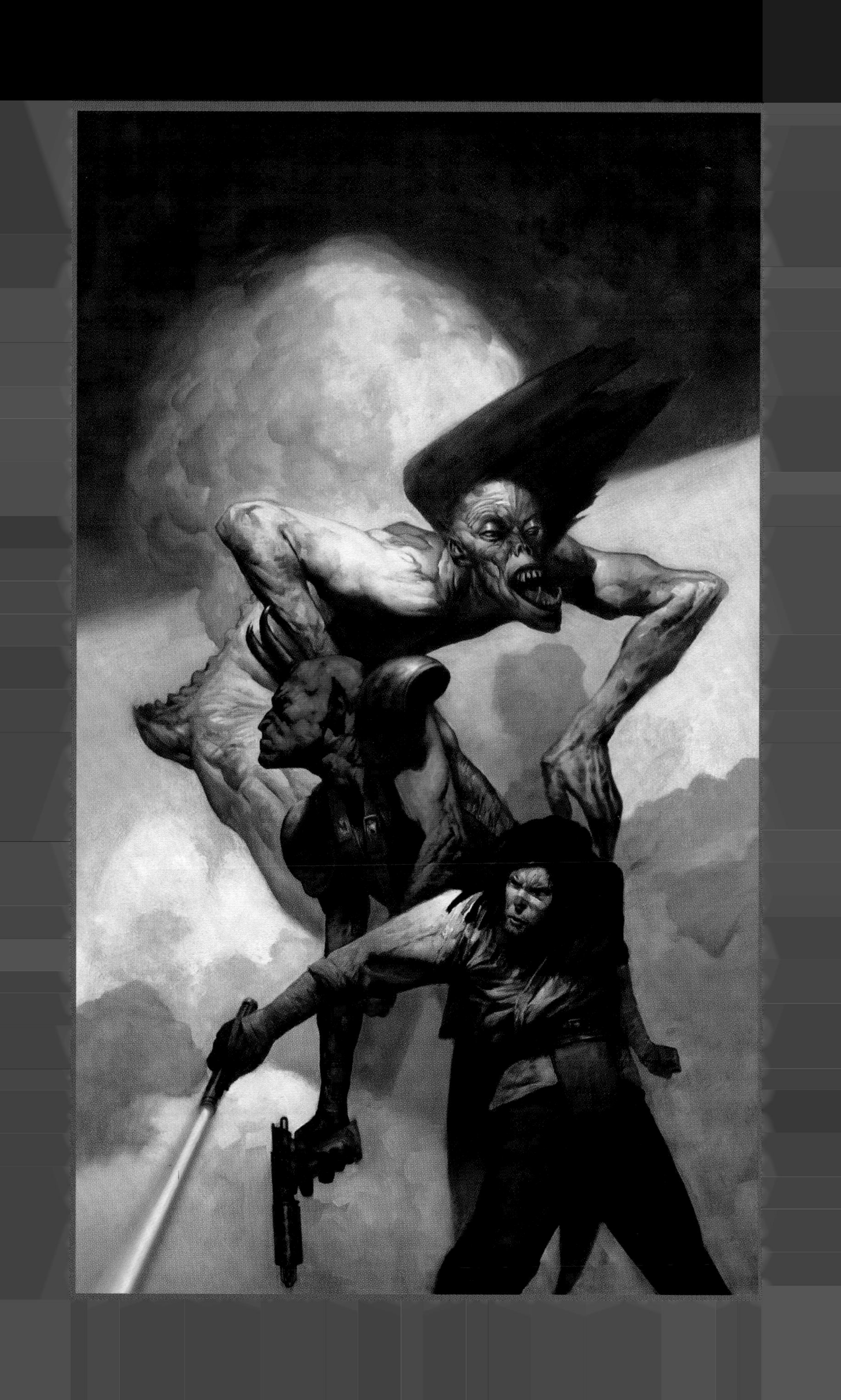

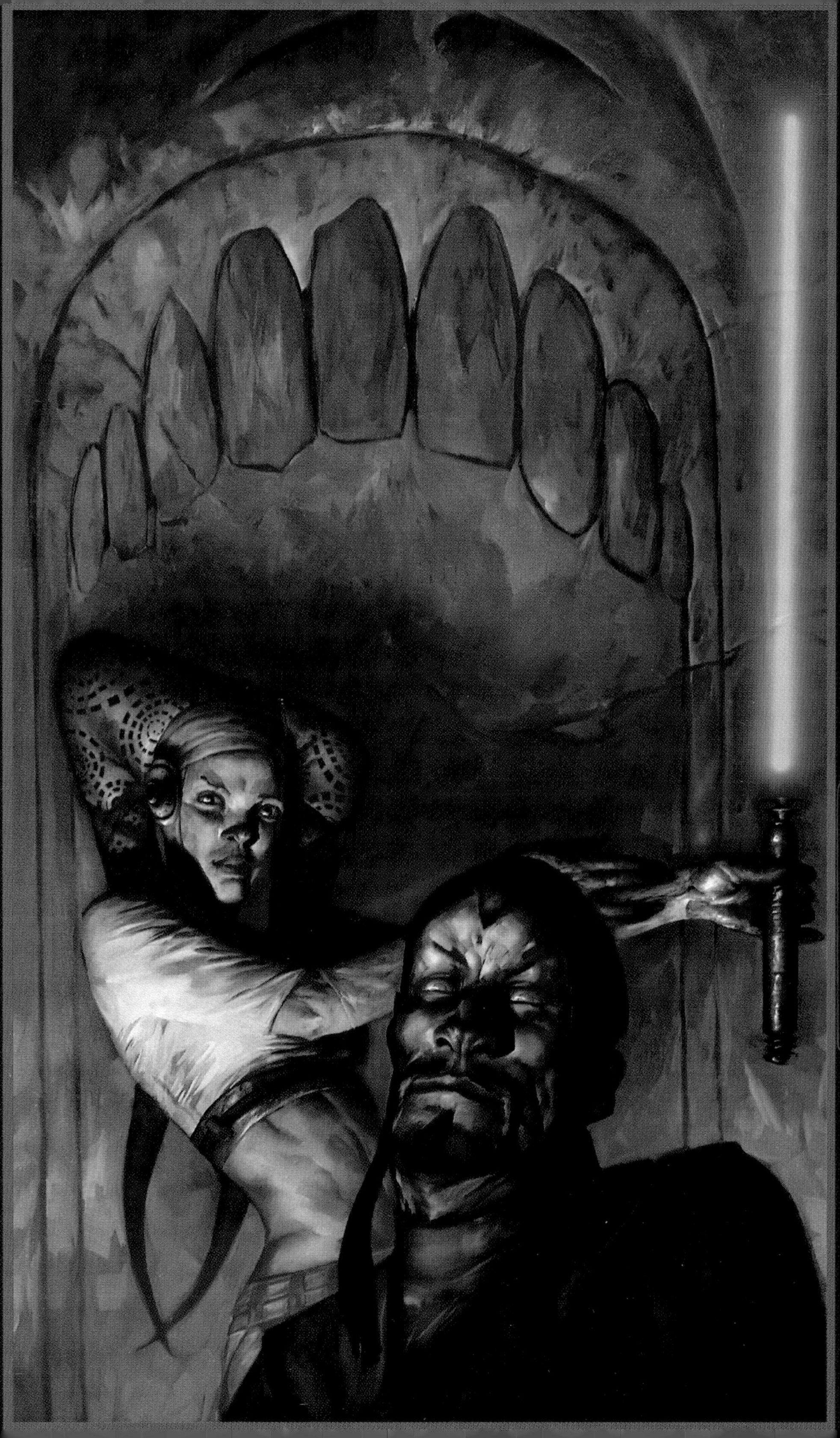